Snollygosters, Airheads & Wimps:
John Clay's Dictionary
of Presidential Words

John E. Clay

Foreword
Eugene J. McCarthy

John Clay
Carleton Clay of 1943

Snollygosters, Airheads & Wimps
by John E. Clay

Published by Lone Oak Press, Ltd.
Red Wing, Minnesota

Printed in the United States of America

First Edition
ISBN 1-883477-41-7 (Paperback)
ISBN 1-883477-42-5 (Cloth)
Library of Congress CIP: 99-068864

To Mary Dailey, *Mavourneen*

ACKNOWLEDGMENTS

I want to thank Carol Fujimoto, Laurie Walker, Laura Hamilton, Karen Casebolt and Carrie Ryan for their word processing, editing and other technical skills and patience that have been essential to the preparation of *Snollygosters, Airheads and Wimps*.

I also want to thank my wife, Mary Dailey, who has been my stringer in spotting words and quotations for inclusion, and has also exercised a good deal of forbearance with my preoccupation with the book over the last fifteen years.

I want to express my appreciation to the family of Frank H. Young for permission to reprint the wonderful cartoons of Presidents Theodore Roosevelt, William Howard Taft and Woodrow Wilson. Frank Young was an exceptionally talented cartoonist and artist and the founder of the American Academy of Art in Chicago.

My grateful acknowledgement to the following for permission to reprint cartoons: to the family of Jim Dobbins for a cartoon of George Bush; to Len Borozinski for a cartoon of Jesse Jackson, Michael Dukakis and Lloyd Bentsen; Doonesbury cartoon strips by Garry Trudeau, and cartoons by Pat Oliphant, Copyright, 1999, reprinted with permission from Universal Press Syndicate, all rights reserved; to Hank Parker for his cartoon of Bill Clinton; and to Brian Basset for his cartoons of Ronald Reagan.

My thanks to my good friend Richard Arnesen for his constant support, perspicacious eye and for the cover design. I very much appreciate the steadfast support and encouragement of my publisher, Ray Howe, whose tireless efforts have made this book possible.

KEY TO ABBREVIATIONS

Br	British
Fr	French
Ger	German
Ir	Irish
It	Italian
L	Latin
Sp	Spanish
Y	Yiddish
cf.	compare
esp.	especially
lit.	literally
OM	word has a meaning other than those in the definition.
Sl	slang

FOREWORD

In living with a language which is in a continuing process of change, as is the English of the United States, it is important to stop occasionally to note the changes, to evaluate them and to define or redefine some words. These changes are not always by new additions, but also include changes in definition and usage. Such reflections can also identify words which will probably disappear soon, as well as those that are more likely to survive and become useful, stable, elements of the language. John Clay, in this book of words, a product of long study and the collection and winnowing of words, has accomplished all of these objectives.

In *Snollygosters, Airheads and Wimps*, Clay has selected words and presented them within a fascinating context of presidential politics. This is not a *Devil's Dictionary*, of Ambrose Bierce, nor a dictionary of slang, in the manner of Henry Mencken. There are traces of both of these word masters and of William Safire, William Buckley and other current language practitioners, to whom credit is duly given. The book should prove a useful aid to readers of Buckley, as it includes words frequently used by him, such as oxymoron, a word which has become popular with David Broder of the *Washington Post*, Warren Hinckle of the *New York Times* and other columnists. One Buckley favorite, the word retromingent (urinating backwards) has been taken up by other writers, most notably Molly Ivins, who is given recognition for creative use of language in a number of inclusions in the book.

Among the historical phrases of note in the book, is "nattering nabobs of negativism", delivered by Spiro Agnew while he was Vice President, and performing, as one observer noted, as "Nixon's Nixon." William Safire, subsequently identified himself, with Agnew's permission, as the author of the phrase. This phrase has survived while Pat Buchanan's "pusillanimous pussyfooters" has not. The process may have set the example for other ghost writers, who, if a ghosted speech turns out well, are disposed to claim authorship, in the manner of surrogate mothers who claim children. The ultimate demonstration of this kind of claim was when Sen. Joe Biden thought that he had plagiarized language from Robert Kennedy, only to be contradicted by Adam Wolinsky, a Kennedy speechwriter, who claimed authorship.

Clay includes a good selection of neologisms, nonce words, literary allusions, classical references, foreign words, slang and acronyms. An example of the latter is BOMFOG, meaning "brotherhood of man, fatherhood of God", first applied by reporters to Nelson Rockefeller's often used campaign phrase. In addition to its usefulness as a source of definitions, and as a supplemental word study base (much superior to the *Readers Digest* word power exercises), *Snollygosters, Airheads and Wimps* can and should be read for entertainment, incidental knowledge and sheer pleasure.

Eugene J. McCarthy

Introduction

American English is continually enriched by a steady coinage of new words, new meanings for old words and the adoption of words from other languages. The fascination of Americans with words has been matched by the almost irresistible attraction which the public finds in the lives and PECCADILLOES of our presidents and vice presidents and those who campaign for those offices. This book is intended to appeal to people who are both logophiles and persons interested in presidential politics. The words included are in many cases unusual or new coinages used by presidents and vice presidents or included in stories about them or their families or those who campaign for these offices. Some are nonce words that will not last, e.g. BILLARY, BOMFOG, CORRECTOGRAM, FORNIGATE, BUSHSPEAK. Others, such as NATTERING NABOBS, MUSHROOM CAMPAIGNING, PSYCHOBABBLE, RAMBOISM, MICROMANAGE and BORK may become part of regular English usage.

I have included a number of new words (BEDROOM HAIR, PREBUTTAL, VIAGRA ELITE) and new uses for old words (CATTLE CALL, RED MEAT, ROOT CANAL) as well as words too good to pass up when used in the context of a presidential reference (BONEHEAD, HATCHET MAN, MÉNAGE-À-TROIS). President Bill Clinton has also inspired the use of many words (CLINTON HATER, CANOODLE, LOWLIFE, LIBIDO). I have resisted, however, any temptation to include nonce words like 'monicagate', 'zippergate' or, most recently, 'sallygate' (a reference to President Thomas Jefferson's putative mistress, Sally Hemings).

These "presidential" words are sometimes not very presidential. When President Nixon referred to George Schultz as a CANDY ASS, when President Reagan said he's had it up to his KEISTER and when George Bush said that he was in deep DOO-DOO, it had a certain shock value and these expressions definitely got our attention.

Our leaders are not spared when it comes to derogatory names - i.e. AIRHEAD, CHARLATAN, SCOLD, WIMP, JUDAS GOAT, ELMER GANTRY, MOUNTEBANK, PHILANDERER, WOMANIZER, URIAH HEEP, DWEEB, DORK.

Presidents and vice presidents have the ability to resurrect old words as President Harry S. Truman demonstrated with SNOLLYGOSTER and President Clinton did with BUMFUZZLE, and to create expressions that linger in our memory such as "NATTERING NABOBS of negativism."

The quotations used to illustrate the meanings of the words included have come from a variety of sources in the course of my general reading. I have not consciously sought out biographies of presidents and most of the references have come from newspapers and periodicals. Some of these words are much more commonly encountered in written form than in oral conversation, at least unless you hang out with the likes of William F. Buckley, Jr. or William Safire. I have illustrated the meanings of the words with long, and, in many cases, multiple quotations in order to give the full flavor of the words. I have also included quotations which are substantively interesting, amusing and witty which should help to fix the meanings of the words in the readers' minds.

I express my appreciation to all of the writers whose quotations I have included for their felicitous and colorful use of language and to all of the periodicals and newspapers from which quotations have been taken, particularly *The New Yorker*, the *Chicago Tribune* and *The New York Times*, for nurturing these writers.

John E. Clay
August, 2000

Writers Quoted

A

Abramson, Jill
Adelman, Ken
Adler, Bill
Alessio, Carolyn
Alter, Jonathan
Anderson, Donald F.
Anderson, Monroe
Apple, R. W., Jr.
Arndt, Michael
Atlas, Terry
Auletta, Ken
Axelrod, David
Ayers, H. Brandt
Ayres, Jr., B. Drummond

B

Bagby, Robert J.
Baker, Russell
Balmer, Randall
Barron, James
Bauer, Gary L.
Beatty, Jack
Beck, Joan
Bendavid, Naftali
Bennet, James
Berke, Richard L.
Bernstein, Dennis
Beschloss, Michael R.
Binder, David
Bines, Jonathan
Blaney III, Harry C.
Bliven, Naomi
Blumenthal, Sidney
Boller, Jr., Paul F.
Bonesteel, Michael
Boyd, Gerald M.
Boyd, L. M.
Bradsher, Keith
Brandon, Karen
Brinkley, Alan
Brinkley, Douglas
Brinkley, Joel
Broder, David
Broder, John M..
Brooks, David
Bruni, Frank
Buckley, Wm F., Jr.
Bumiller, Elisabeth
Burka, Paul
Butler, Stuart M.
Buursma, Bruce

C

Carlson, Margaret
Carlson, Peter
Caro, Robert
Carvajal, Doreen
Carville, James
Cawley, Janet
Chapman, Stephen
Charen, Mona
Chira, Susan
Christopher, Nicholas
Clarity, James F.
Clark, Kenneth R.
Clay, John E.
Clines, Francis X.
Clinton, Hillary Rodham
Clymer, Adam
Collin, Dorothy
Collins, Gail
Cook Jr., Charles E.
Cooke, Alistair
Curry, George E.

D

Daley, Steve
Daly, Meg
Dao, James
De Santis, Hugh
Debenport, Ellen
DeParle, Jason
DeVries, Peter
DeWitt, Karen
Dionne Jr., E.J.
Donald, David
Dorning, Michael
Dowd, Maureen

9

Drew, Elizabeth.
Dubose, Lou
Duscha, Julius

E

Egan, Timothy
Elgin, Robert S.
Elliot, Stuart
Ellis, Joseph J
Engelberg, Stephen
Entman, Robert M.
Estrich, Susan

F

Felsenthal, Carol
Firestone, David
Fiske, Edward B.
Fitzgerald, Frances
Flaherty, Roger
Foderaro, Lisa W.
Frady, Marshall
Friedman, Thomas L.
Fuller, Edmund

G

Gabler, Neal
Gailey, Phil
Gaines, William
Gallagher, James P.
Gelb, Leslie H.
Germond, Jack
Gerth, Jeff
Gillmore, Robert
Gold, Allan R.
Goldberg, Carey
Goodman, Ellen
Goodman, Walter
Grady, Sandy
Granger, Bill
Gray, Jerry
Greenberg, Paul
Greenhouse, Linda
Groer, Anne
Grossman, Ron
Grundberg, Andy

H

Hagood, Wesley O.

Hardy, Thomas
Harris, Sydney J
Henneberger, Melinda
Herbert, Bob
Hersh, Seymour
Hertzberg, Hendrik
Hoffman, Adonis E.
Holmes, Steven A.
Holzer, Harold
Honan, William H.
Horrock, Nicholas M.

I

Ifill, Gwen
Ivins, Molly

J

Janofsky, Michael
Jehl, Douglas
Johnson, Kirk
Johnston, David
Johnston, William B.
Jouzaitis, Carol
Judis, John B.

K

Kaiser, Charles
Kakutani, Michiko
Kaus, Mickey
Kean, Leslie
Kelly, Michael
Kemper, Bob
Kennedy, Eugene
Kilian, Michael
King, Wayne
Kinsley, Michael
Klein, Joe
Kogan, Rick
Kolbert, Elizabeth
Kondracke, Morton
Krauthammer, Charles
Kristof, Nicholas D.
Kristol, William
Kurtz, Howard

L

Labaton, Stephen
Lacey, Marc

10

Larsen, Leonard
Lavin, Cheryl
Lehmann-Haupt, C.
Lentz, Philip
Leo, John
Levy, Clifford J.
Lewis, Anthony
Lewis, Neil A.
Lincoln, Abraham
Locin, Mitchell
Longworth, R. C.
Lorber, Leah
Loury, Glenn C.
Lubet, Steven
Lyman, Rick

M

MacKinnon, Catharine A.
Maclean, John N.
Macy, John W.
Madigan, Charles M.
Manning, Robert A.
Maraniss, David
Margolis, Jon
Marks, Peter
McCarron, John
McCarthy, Eugene J.
McClain, Lenita
McGrory, Mary
McLellan, Diana
McNulty, Timothy J.
Mencken, H. L.
Michener, James A.
Mitchell, Alison
Mitgang, Herbert
Molotsky, Irvin

N

Nachman, Jerry
Nagourney, Adam
Neal, Steve
Neikirk, William
Noonan, Peggy

O

Oppel, Jr., Richard A
O'Rourke, P. J.
O'Shea, James

Oshinsky, David

P

Page, Clarence
Pear, Robert
Petersen, Clarence
Phillips, Kevin
Podhoretz, Norman
Povich, Elaine S.
Powers, Thomas
Preston, Jennifer
Purdum, Todd S.

Q

Quindlen, Anna
Quintanilla, Ray

R

Radcliffe, Donnie
Rainie, Harrison
Rasky, Susan
Raspberry, William
Rauch, Jonathan
Rich, Frank
Rimer, Sara
Rivers, Caryl
Roberts, Steven V.
Roeper, Richard
Roosevelt, Theodore
Rosenbaum, David E.
Rosenberg, Debra
Rosenthal, A. M.
Rosenthal, Andrew
Rowan, Carl T.
Rowley, Storer
Royko, Mike
Rubin, Trudy

S

Safire, William
Seelye, Katharine Q.
Senior, Jennifer
Shapiro, Walter
Shawcross, William
Sheehy, Gail
Shields, Mark
Shiflett, Dave
Sidey, Hugh

Sigal, Clancy
Slatta, Richard W.
Snow, Tony
Sorenson, Theodore C.
Stanley, Alessandra
Staples, Brent
Steinfels, Peter
Stevenson, Adlai E.
Stewart, James B.
Suro, Roberto
Sweet, Lynn

T

Tackett, Michael
Talbott, Strobe
Thomas, Benjamin P.
Thomas, Karen
Toner, Robin
Toobin, Jeffrey
Trillin, Calvin
Trudeau, Garry
Tyler, Patrick E.

V

Van Natta, Jr., Don
vanden Heuvel, William. J.
Verhovek, Sam Howe
von Hoffman, Nicholas
Vonnegut, Kurt

W

Walker, Martin
Wallis, David
Walsh, Kenneth T.
Ward, Geoffrey C.
Warren, James
Wayne, Leslie
Weaver, Jr., Warren
Weinraub, Bernard
Weisberg, Jacob
White, Theodore
Wicker, Tom
Wieghart, James G.
Wilentz, Sean
Will, George F.
Wills, Garry
Winerip, Michael
Wines, Michael
Witt, Linda
Wolfe, Alan
Wouk, Herman
Wright, Susan Webber

Y

Yoder, Edwin

Z

Zorn, Eric

CONTENTS

16

TTT

AAA

ACOLYTE

noun - an assistant or follower.

"If he stays on the ballot until November, [Ross] Perot will be provided with still another bath for his ego. Come Election Day, he will point to those melancholy, doom-struck votes as a measure of his corporate-cowboy appeal. When the votes are counted, he'll remind himself and his ACOLYTES of what might have been, and chances are he'll sniff at the mere mortal who wins the White House." Steve Daley, *Chicago Trib.*, 7/19/92, S 4, p. 4.

"Mr. Gramm has their [the Republican new right] hearts, but needs to persuade them that he can outpoint Mr. Dole and win the nomination. Mr. Dole looks like a winner, but needs to persuade them that he has their interests at heart. For Mr. Dole, this is no easy task. For one thing, he is majority leader in a Senate whose Republicans are, by and large, far less radical than the Gingrich ACOLYTES, and he cannot appease the right without risking the loss of his colleagues' support in legislative battles to come." Michael Wines, *NYTimes*, 5/25/95, p. A1.

"In November 1976, ignoring the minor setback of having just lost his second campaign for Congress, [Newt Gingrich] and his ACOLYTES began to plot a presidential run scheduled for 2000 or 2004. According to a close source, 'We were all discussing the timing, his age, working out the one-term and two-term presidencies in between. I think the plan is still going. I think he will be president.'" Gail Sheehy, *Vanity Fair*, 9/95, p. 217.

"Others, however, have noted the contrast between Jackie, the maternal sparring partner, and the adoring ACOLYTE [his second wife, Marianne Ginther] he acquired in the younger woman. His sister Candace explains: 'Jackie was his equal. With Marianne initially, he was the authority figure, the high power.'" Gail Sheehy, *Vanity Fair*, 9/95, p. 219.

"Even if George W. Bush tries to re-invent himself, claiming once again to be a 'COMPASSIONATE CONSERVATIVE,' the presence of [William] Weld (or someone like him) on the Democratic ticket would serve as a constant reminder of the Republicans' link to the religious right. John McCain - a Reagan ACOLYTE and Barry Goldwater's heir - was pilloried as a closet Democrat by the fundamentalists who dictated Republican Party policies." Steven Lubet, Chicago Trib., 3/14/00, S 1, p.13.

"In the interview, Gore portrayed Bush as a captive of his party's conservative wing and an ACOLYTE of conservative economists, favoring policies that would curb the economic expansion that Gore suggests is the product of Democratic leadership." Bob Kemper and Karen Brandon, *Chicago Trib.*, 5/5/00. S1, p. 8.

ADDLEPATED

adjective - confused, mixed-up, crazy, eccentric.

"The bosses were dupes of Democratism, just as clearly as ADDLEPATED, pinko, ultra-left-liberal fellow travelers in the old days had been dupes of Communism. Victory in the war against Clintonhood and Goredom will not be won by softness on dupes." Russell Baker, *NYTimes*, 8/22/92, p. 15.

À DEUX (FR)

adjective or *adverb* - involving two people; for two (usually in private).

"First Lady Nancy Reagan and fast - if not first - friend George Will, the columnist and TV sage, have been known to motor off for quiet country lunches A DEUX, she seeking his political counsel and he the recipient of more motherly advice." Michael Kilian, *Chicago Trib.*, 2/27/87, S 1, p. 20.

"...Kohl made a date with Clinton to chow down together at a Georgetown restaurant best known for its giant portions. The German ambassador to the U.S., Imo Stabreit, tried to put a patina of diplomacy on Monday's visit, telling reporters that Kohl and Clinton needed to get together again so soon after Brussels because they hadn't had a chance to talk A DEUX." Maureen Dowd, *Chicago Trib.*, 2/1/94, S 1, p. 11.

AD HOMINEM (L)

adjective or *adverb* - appealing to a person's prejudices rather than his intellect as by attacking one's opponent rather than debating the issues.

"...Theodore White wrote about as the cause of Nixon's downfall: 'The sly innuendo, the false accusation and the AD HOMINEM attack.' Nixon attacks the person of the arguer and neglects the arguments of the person.... Truth is not often served by the use of the brutal AD HOMINEM argument." Daniel H. Ryan, *Chicago Trib.*, 10/20/83, S 1, p. 18.

"A number of the students [at Galesburg's Knox College] said they were bothered by the two candidates' use of AD HOMINEM attacks, such as Mr. Quayle's description of Mr. Dukakis as 'Tax-Hike Mike,' and Mr. Bentsen's comment to Mr. Quayle 'You're no Jack Kennedy.'" R. W. Apple, Jr., *NYTimes*, 10/7/88, p. 10.

"Bob Dole followed through on his promise to confront President Clinton face to face on the issue of character in their second debate Wednesday, accusing the Clinton administration of ethical lapses that have eroded Americans' trust in government. Clinton sought to appear above the fray, saying he could respond 'tit for tat' to the charges but preferred to talk about policy issues that affect the country's future rather than engage in what he called 'AD HOMINEM' attacks. 'No attack has created a job or educated a child or helped a family to make ends meet,' Clinton said. 'No insult ever cleaned up a toxic waste dump or helped an elderly person.'" Thomas Hardy and Michael Dorning, *Chicago Trib.*, 10/17/96, p. 1.

AFOOT

adjective or *adverb* - being developed, under way.

"Mrs. Clinton added: 'One of the great lies that is currently AFOOT in the country is that the President's plan will limit choice. To the contrary, the President's plan enhances choice.'" Adam Clymer, *NYTimes*, 11/2/93, p. A1.

"On at least seven occasions, President Reagan met privately with some of Channell's prospects, and helped raise funds. A spokesman for the President said that Reagan thought he was raising money for advertising, not for guns, and that he did not realize criminal activity might be AFOOT." Nicholas M. Horrock, *Chicago Trib.*, 5/3/87, S 4, p. 1.

"The mere fact that Michael Dukakis, a man of actuarial vision and near narcoleptic passion, could have stayed so close for so long signals a major change AFOOT." William B. Johnston, *Chicago Trib.*, 1/26/89, S 1, p. 21.

AGEIST

adjective and *noun* - one who discriminates against a particular age group, such as the elderly.

"But the president has to make sure that he doesn't make some knee-jerk mistakes. He can't be AGEIST. Clinton should avoid the obvious temptation, amply indulged by George Bush in his selection of Thomas, to choose a young candidate in order to influence the courts for the next 40 years. Judge Wald is 64, which would put her in good company: justices appointed after age 60 include Harry Blackmun, Benjamin Cardozo and Oliver Wendell Holmes." Anna Quindlen, *Chicago Trib.*, 4/6/93, S 1, p. 17.

"Mr. Clinton, a devotee of group discussions, said later that he relished the event. And despite the seriousness of the topic [affirmative action programs] and the occasional moments of passion and argument, the audiences had several good laughs. Early on, Mr. Morgan said that the most prejudice was concentrated among 'the older people, the older generations,' whom he identified as '30's, 40's, 50's and up.' As the audience began to laugh, the President observed, 'Maybe we need a panel on AGEISM instead of racism.'" James Bennet, *NYTimes*, 12/4/97, p. A18.

AGENT PROVOCATEUR

noun - a person who associates with a suspect to incite the suspect to engage in incriminating action.

"The [Clinton] White House's protests and references to the new material pointed once more toward a defense that Mrs. Tripp acted as an AGENT PROVOCATEUR for the President's political opponents in her conversations with and tapings of Ms. Lewinsky." Francis X. Clines, *NYTimes*, 10/3/98, p. A9.

AIRHEAD (OM) (SL)

noun - a simpleton, fool, NINCOMPOOP.
adjective - AIRHEADED.

"Mr. Reagan's ignorance about the Soviet Union and his AIR-HEADED rhetoric on the issues of foreign policy and arms control have reached the limit of tolerance and have become an embarrassment to the U.S. and a danger to world peace. Mr. Reagan's performance in the debates suggests that he is indeed a cue-card President who must rely heavily on the advice of his staff and cabinet for a successful second term." Editorial (endorsing Reagan for President), *Chicago Trib.*, 10/28/84, S 5, p. 2.

"'I play golf with him [Republican vice presidential candidate Dan Quayle] a lot. He's a personal friend on a private basis outside the U.S. Senate. Most people on the Armed Services Committee think he's a perfectly competent member.... He's certainly not an AIRHEAD, or anything of that type' [said Senator Alan Dixon]." Campaign Notes, *Chicago Trib.*, 10/17/88, S 1, p. 5.

"Meanwhile, Bush got away with the biggest blunder by either candidate. The selection of J. Danforth Quayle, draft dodger and AIRHEAD, as his running mate." Mike Royko, *Chicago Trib.*, 11/10/88, S 1, p. 3.

"'Dutch,' Morris writes, calling Reagan by the youthful nickname he uses throughout the book, 'remained a mystery to me, and worse still - dare I entertain such heresy, in the hushed and reverent precincts of his office? - an apparent AIRHEAD.'" Hendrik Hertzberg (Review of Edmund Morris, Dutch: A Memoir of Ronald Reagan), *New Yorker*, 10/11/99, p. 99.

"Fourteen years ago, Edmund Morris, a Pulitzer prize-winning historian, began a quest to find Ronald Reagan's inner life. He traveled far and wide, basking in unprecedented access to his President, hunting for the golden fleece of biography, the inner life.... The more access Mr. Morris got, the more illusive Dutch became. Every time the biographer scratched away one veneer, he found an identical veneer underneath. Was Ronald Reagan an 'AIRHEAD,' to use Mr. Morris's words, or 'a colossus'? A colossal AIRHEAD? An airy colossus?" Maureen Dowd, *NYTimes*, 9/22/99, p. A27.

"`He [George W. Bush] was the best-known guy at Yale', Mr. Betts added. Some other classmates regard that as a huge exaggeration, but even those who frowned on Mr. Bush, seeing him as an AIRHEAD party boy, tended to think of him as affable and unusually helpful to his friends." Nicholas D. Kristof, *NYTimes*, 6/19/00, p. A14.

ALL HAT AND NO CATTLE

noun - A person who plays the part but has no substance; by extension from the person with the cowboy hat and boots but no cattle; a person who talks the talk but doesn't walk the walk; cf. EMPTY SUIT.

by Garry Trudeau

AMANUENSIS

noun - one employed as a secretary.

"Then there was the room in which [Franklin] Roosevelt had installed an ailing Louis Howe, his devoted AMANUENSIS, who had once slept at the foot of his bed, like Fala, dreaming of little but the master." Sidney Blumenthal, *New Yorker*, 3/8/93, p. 40.

"The important question remains: Is history really explained by personal details about Eleanor's ambivalent feelings toward her husband and about Missie LeHand's almost pathological devotion as an AMANUENSIS to the President and about [Franklin] Roosevelt's own MERCURIAL personality - one would almost call these items gossip." Christopher Lehmann-Haupt, Review of No Ordinary Time: Franklin and Eleanor Roosevelt: The Home Front in World War II by Doris Kearns Goodwin, *NYTimes*, 9/19/94, p. B2.

ANACHRONISM

noun - a person or thing chronologically out of place.

"Ever since World War II the planet has lived with the threat of nuclear war. Thirty years ago, the Limited Test Ban Treaty drove U.S., Soviet and British nuclear testing underground. But a total ban on nuclear tests has eluded the world's grasp. President Clinton is now in a position to help achieve that goal.... Nuclear testing is a dangerous ANACHRONISM, in a world of potential proliferators. It's time for Mr. Clinton to start thinking about tomorrow." Editorial, *NYTimes*, 6/24/93, p. A12.

"New Zealand may someday be prepared to modify its nuclear-free-zone legislation. But Mr. Clinton and his Secretary of State, Warren Christopher, should not make that a condition for ending an ANACHRONISTIC quarrel and bringing an old friend in from the cold." Editorial, *NYTimes*, 11/19/93, p. A14.

ANATHEMA (OM)

noun - a person loathed or greatly disliked.

"Despite their many differences, New York's Senate candidates, Rudolph Giuliani and Hillary Rodham Clinton, hold at least one belief in common. Both assert that there should be what Mrs. Clinton calls a 'zone of privacy' around the personal lives of elected officials and their families....Also no one knows how deeply the tradition of tolerance runs among voters who identify themselves as cultural and religious conservatives. Mrs. Clinton has been ANATHEMA to many of them. Mr. Giuliani [after referring to his frequent companion, Ms. Judith Nathan, as a 'very good friend'] could now face slippage in sectors of that coalition - for example, Catholics, Orthodox Jews, upstate independents - where he had expected an advantage." Editorial, *NYTimes*, 5/10/00, p. A29.

ANCIENT

noun - an old person.

"One of the younger ANCIENTS said Mr. Clinton's ordeal by Dole, Gingrich, Limbaugh, *Wall Street Journal*, Harry and Louise was a Girl Scout jamboree compared with what President Nixon had undergone." Russell Baker, *NYTimes*, 8/16/94, p. A15.

ANGST

noun - a feeling of generalized anxiety or insecurity.

"This may end up as the worst legacy of the Reagan years. Not that Ronald Reagan either initiated or is personally responsible for the worship of money. In fact, there is something refreshing about the unconcealed joy of wealthy Republicans, compared with the guilt-ridden ANGST that besets so many rich Democrats." Jon Margolis, *Chicago Trib.*, 10/1/84, S 1, p. 13.

"But while the White House may be correct that [the Congressional Report on the Iran-Contra affair] is not likely to set off new waves of criticism and ANGST, it is because the public view calcified many months ago that the affair had already diminished Mr. Reagan as a leader." Joel Brinkley, *NYTimes*, 11/19/87, p. 1.

"A USA Today-CNN-Gallup poll last week found that 84 percent of the people are dissatisfied with the state of the nation, and it showed Perot is the chief beneficiary of that national ANGST." Thomas Hardy, *Chicago Trib.*, 6/21/92, S 4, p. 4.

ANHEDONIA

noun - the lack of capacity to experience pleasure in normally pleasurable situations.

Note: Woody Allen originally planned to title his Oscar-winning movie "Annie Hall" with the title "ANHEDONIA." The marketing people insisted on changing the name since no one knew what ANHEDONIA meant.

"Both Pat and Al laugh easily. Moynihan addresses you as 'kind sir' without apparent affectation. D'Amato gets away with calling everyone 'babe.' Both the First Lady [Hillary Rodham Clinton] and the Mayor [Rudolph Giuliani] grimace.

"I'm not certain that either prospective Senate candidate is a particularly happy person. The ANHEDONIA shows. Perhaps it's the torture of ambition. Whoever wins, New York will suffer. And we'll look back at Pat and Al as another cheery chapter of New York's good old days." Jerry Nachman, *NYTimes*, 6/21/99, p. A19.

ANODYNE

adjective - soothing, innocuous, pain relieving.
noun - pain killer, something that calms or comforts.

"But while the White House may lump her various causes under the ANODYNE rubric of 'children's issues,' Mrs. Clinton is still pursuing a far broader agenda of causes - from foreign development to immunization in the inner cities to expanding financial credit for women - than almost any predecessor in the undefined role of First Lady." James Bennet, *NYTimes*, 1/20/97, p. A12.

ANTIC

adjective and *noun* - frolicsome, clownish.

"Like the Penguin who bedeviled Batman, Jerry Brown is underground in Gotham City, making political mischief for Bill Clinton. Mr. Brown has never been seen eating raw herring or riding in a motorized duck, but there are similarities. Deserted by his family, the Penguin ran an ANTIC campaign for mayor with the help of the disenfranchised. Despite pressure from his own annoyed family, Mr. Brown continues his RAG-TAG campaign. He has even left open the possibility of nominating himself for President rather than endorsing the Democratic ticket in exchange for a less-than-prime time speaking slot." Maureen Dowd and Frank Rich, *NYTimes*, 7/14/92, p. A9.

"As for Mr. Clinton himself, his aides agree that he has finally settled into the Presidency. The black rages that used to punctuate his workdays are 'less frequent,' in the words of one aide who bore the brunt of them, and he has more time to think, read and telephone informal advisers. Gone forever are the moments of ANTIC informality that marked his last campaign, as when he was once asked his favorite Elvis Presley movie and replied enthusiastically with a straight face, *'Viva, Las Vegas!'*" Todd S. Purdum, *NYTimes*, 11/6/96, p. A12.

"Mr. Ayres [a Republican pollster] said that Mrs. Dole was a serious prospect for Vice President but added: 'She is a higher risk choice now because you won't know how she would react in the heat of a campaign as a candidate'. The news conference [at which she announced she was withdrawing from the race for President], an unusual event itself for Mrs. Dole, veered between the tearful and the ANTIC. At one point, she turned to her husband, who was standing behind hear, and pecked him on the cheek. As she returned to the microphone, her husband fought back tears too." Katharine Q. Seelye, *NYTimes*, 10/21/99, p. A20.

ANTINOMIAN

noun - a person who is free of socially accepted standards of morality; one who prescribes his own moral code.

Note:The following poem by Eugene J. McCarthy, inspired by Oliver North's activities in the Iran-Contra matter, has appeared in *The New Republic* and his *Selected Poems* (Lone Oak Press).

Fawn Hall Among The ANTINOMIANS

"And I can type," she boldly said

35

With a toss of her carefully tousled locks,
"Smuggle papers and run the Xerox.
And I know how and what to shred.
For I am an ANTINOMIAN."

She never turned brave Ollie's head
For he honored his oaths, he said,
Unless directed by some authority
Which gave lying a higher priority,
Sustained, as he was by the Fifth and immunity
And basic ANTINOMIAN impunity.

Admirable, Admiral John Poindexter
Came with his lawyer, his pipe,
And his clerical wife.
Certain he knew what the President thought
He wrought a deniable, plausible plot
Never thinking that he'd be caught
In his ANTINOMIAN coup d'etat.

APOCALYPTIC

adjective - terrible, portending final doom or disaster.

"During the dizzying weekend after the Monica S. Lewinsky scandal broke, the Washington establishment was all but ready to dump President Clinton. Pundits spoke in grave tones of high crimes and misdemeanors. By midweek, public opinion polls were suggesting that the country beyond the Potomac was far less APOCALYPTIC. The long national nightmare was short." Alessandra Stanley, *NYTimes*, 2/2/98, p. A19.

APOTHEOSIS

noun - (1) elevation to the status of a god, (2) the perfect example or quintessence.

"The explanation of this rather unexpected access of fame and notoriety [for William Herndon] lay in the immediate APOTHEOSIS of the martyred Lincoln." David Donald, <u>Lincoln's Herndon</u>, Knopf, 1948, p. 167.

"If Ronald Reagan represents the APOTHEOSIS of cowboy values, symbolizing the enduring American myths of self-help, self-sufficiency and self-confidence, George Bush embodies the patrician ideal of responsibility begotten by privilege...." R. W. Apple, Jr., *NYTimes*, 1/20/89, p. 1.

"In a time of gilt and glitz and perpetual revelation, she [Jacqueline Bouvier Kennedy Onassis] was associated with that thing so difficult to describe yet so simple to recognize, the APOTHEOSIS of dignity." Anna Quindlen, *Chicago Trib.*, 5/23/94, S 1, p. 13.

"The flirtation [with running for President on the Reform Party ticket] of the Trumpster, as he calls himself, is the APOTHEOSIS of our Gilded Age.

Our politics is warped by money, celebrity, polling and crass behavior, and our culture is defined by stock market high-rolling, boomer NARCISSISM, niche marketing mania, rankings and a quiz show called 'Who Wants to Be a Millionaire?' 'I love Regis,' Mr. [Donald] Trump says. Why shouldn't billionaires play 'Who Wants to Be a President?' 'I've already got my own airplane,' he says. 'We could save money on Air Force One.'" Maureen Dowd, *NYTimes*, 11/17/99, p. A29.

"It's hard to find a major candidate in either party who will risk offending anyone by uttering an unscripted remark, countering an ideological orthodoxy or choosing a wardrobe that might not sit well with a pollster or focus group. Seventy-five years after the Scopes trial, even evolution is too hot an issue for most of them to handle. The APOTHEOSIS of this cautious VACUOUSNESS - the ultimate unVentura - was Elizabeth Dole, who mercifully dropped out of the Republican race this week. In running what she called a campaign of 'substance,' she took no-holds-barred stands in favor of 'promoting integrity in government' and against illegal drugs." Frank Rich, *NYTimes*, 10/23/99, p. A27.

APPARATCHIK

noun - a bureaucrat or government or party (especially Russian) official.

"But the two men [Viktor S. Chernomyrdin, the stolid former Russian Prime Minister, and Al Gore, the stolid American Vice President], lifelong party APPARATCHIKS and loyal lieutenants to more CHARISMATIC leaders, do not traffic in breakthroughs. Their specialty is dialogue; their advanced degrees are in 'process.'
"The Gore-Chernomyrdin discussions may in the end yield nothing. Nevertheless, both men stand to gain from these high-profile sessions. Should their talks bear fruit, each would be seen as a peacemaker, an effective negotiator and a credible leader." John M. Broder, *NYTimes*, 5/5/99, p. A11.

ARGLE-BARGLE (BR)

noun - argument.

"In order to restore common sense and integrity to our political system, I'd like to see all candidates pledge to abstain from pledging to abstain from negative campaigning. Of all the sanctimonious ARGLE-BARGLE traditionally heard during election season, the idea that for candidates to criticize their opponents' record or behavior corrodes our civic life and undermines democracy is most annoying ....Further, the attack ad often reveals as much about the attacker as it does about the person being attacked. For instance the general wisdom in South Carolina is that Arizona Sen. John McCain's ad during the primary campaign that said Bush distorts the truth 'like Clinton' was a disreputably low blow that showed the ugly side of McCain's nature and turned voters away from him." Eric Zorn, *Chicago Trib.*, 2/22/00, S 2, p. 1.

ARGOT

noun - the vocabulary, idioms and slang used by a class or group of people.

"The ARGOT of health-care reform is often stupefying, but if President Clinton and his opponents maintain today's oratorical pace, managed care and preferred provider organizations and health care alliances may become fascinating, if not understandable." Michael Wines, *NYTimes*, 10/28/93, p. A10.

ARM CANDY (SL)

noun - female escort, companion, lover, armpiece.

Note: Garry Trudeau uses this term in his Doonesbury cartoon strip to refer to Donald Trump's girl friend(s).

ARMAGEDDON

noun - the place where the final battle will be fought between good and evil; any decisive battle or confrontation.

"The approaching Pennsylvania primary may not be ARMAGEDDON for Gary Hart, but a Democrat who loses four major industrial states in less than four weeks will be in the soup, any way you look at it." Germond/Witcover, *Chicago Trib.*, 4/7/84, S 1, p. 11.

"I had fallen asleep after George Stephanopoulos had ominously warned Sam and Cokie that White House allies were considering the 'explosive' strategy of opening up every sexual closet in the city - Congressmen, reporters, *pundits*. 'The President said he would never resign and I think some around him are willing to take everybody down with him,' he said. A sexual ARMAGEDDON, a bedroom doomsday strategy. If Bill Clinton has to have his dirty linen aired before the House Judiciary Committee, the Clintonites will insure that there is no clean linen anywhere." Maureen Dowd, *NYTimes*, 2/11/98, p. A31.

ASPERITY

noun - severity, roughness, harshness.

"He [Bill Clinton] also firmly defended having Vernon E. Jordan as his transition chairman while Mr. Jordan sits on the board of a tobacco company. Mr. Clinton noted with ASPERITY that he, not aides like Mr. Jordan, would be making the decisions in the new Administration." Michael Kelly, *NYTimes*, 11/13/92, p. A1.

AUTO-DA-FÉ

noun - the public execution or burning of a heretic at the stake by secular authorities (after excommunication by a religious body, i.e. the Spanish Inquisition); lit., in the Portuguese, "act of the faith."

"'Altho we are free by the law, we are not so in practice. Public opinion erects itself into an Inquisition, and exercises its office with as much fanaticism as fans the flames of an AUTO DA FÉ,' wrote [Thomas] Jefferson, referring to the Spanish Inquisition's public practice of burning those considered to be heretics." *Chicago Trib.*, 10/30/86, S 1, p. 3.

"Our sexual AUTO-DA-FÉ, in which every revelation about a politician's private life becomes ammunition in the sulfurous partisan wars, is enough to make the benign neglect of yesteryear look like a democratic kind of discretion." Maureen Dowd, *NYTimes*, 1/17/99, p. 17.

"Some had feared an awkward moment, when the 'M' word might come up during the meetings between the pope and president [Clinton], but mercifully, no one mentioned Monica or the Republican AUTO-DA-FÉ against the president unfolding in Washington." Editorial, *Chicago Trib.*, 1/28/99, S 1, p. 18.

"The Arizona senator [John McCain] wasn't running a campaign so much as an AUTO-DA-FE, with himself as the martyr in the flames. He called Big Tobacco 'jerks.' He ranted that the people running Bob Jones University were 'idiots.' He blasted the televangelists of the right as 'evil.' He dubbed his own party establishment the 'Death Star.' He mocked his colleagues in Congress by christening Washington the 'city of Satan.'" Maureen Dowd, *NYTimes*, 3/8/00, p. A27.

AVUNCULAR

adjective - (1) acting or speaking with the kindness of an uncle; (2) patronizing, condescending.

"Most people assume that Reagan, despite his Hollywood training, is just what he appears to be: warm, manly, AVUNCULAR. The task of his campaign is to make people ask whether there's a real person behind Hart's carefully crafted image." Stephen Chapman, *Chicago Trib.*, 3/8/84, S 1, p. 18.

"Everybody flunked. We just didn't know it until now, when we are no longer under the voodoo-economics spell of an AVUNCULAR, folksy, not terribly bright guy [Ronald Reagan] who only said the nation's finances were in a helluva mess when he thought the microphone was turned off." Anna Quindlen, *NYTimes*, 10/11/90, p. A15.

"Indeed, the image of Lyndon Johnson portrayed throughout the exhibit - of an AVUNCULAR, high-spirited but sincere and caring man who tried to make the presidency more human and humane, in the tradition of Andrew Jackson - is at radical odds with the portrait of venality and chicanery meticulously traced by Robert A. Caro in his best-selling biography of Johnson's political rise, Means of Ascent (Knopf)." Andy Grundberg, *NYTimes*, 6/1/90, p. B3.

Born To Command

King Andrew The First - Artist Unknown
(President Andrew Jackson)-

BBB

BAKSHEESH

noun - a tip or bribe for service.
Note:BAKSHEESH was a favorite S.J. Perelman word.

"Thanks to the glare of election year news coverage, both parties [in their presidential campaigns] have been exposed taking fancy money from foreign corporations. Is it cynical to suspect that their interest in American democracy may not be as intense as their interest in the BAKSHEESH dispensed by Congress and Presidents?" Russell Baker, *NYTimes*, 10/26/96, p. 19.

BANAL

adjective - trite, lacking originality; *noun* - BANALITY.

"What a disappointment. The themeless pudding called this year's State of the Union address was a series of BANALITIES intended to ingratiate the President with his political opposition; instead, this worst of Reagan's speeches invited the grinning contempt it received." William Safire, *Chicago Trib.*, 2/1/83. S 1, p. 17.

"...Reagan's America is the kind of book that we have come to expect from Garry Wills - literate, dispassionate, ICONOCLASTIC, relentlessly analytical and never bound by the BANALITIES and certitudes that have appeared in print before." Michael R. Beschloss, *Chicago Trib.*, 1/11/87, S 14, p. 7.

"It was discouraging enough to hear the President [Bush] expressing BANALITIES ('I am in the mode of being deeply concerned and would like to be a part of finding a national answer') on one of the deadliest problems Americans face; or reaching for political advantage ('I'd like to find a way to be supportive of the police who are out there on the line all the time') when he has been unwilling even to endorse a ban on 'cop-killer' bullets." Tom Wicker, *NYTimes*, 2/24/89, p. 27.

"[Edmund] Morris is 'distressed by the relentless BANALITY, not to say incoherence, of the President's replies in interviews.' He is confounded by Reagan's monumental incuriosity." Hendrik Hertzberg, *New Yorker*, 10/11/99, p.98.

BASKET CASE

noun - a worn out or incapacitated person.

"Mr. Gingrich, an ethical BASKET CASE who has proved to be even more reckless with the reins of government than Mr. Clinton (and who would like to be President himself), said: 'I don't understand how people can rush to a solution before they finish the investigation...' Mr. Gingrich and his blatant partisanship come hard on the heels of the terminally prurient Kenneth Starr. Bill Clinton has always been blessed with the best of enemies." Bob Herbert, *NYTimes*, 9/24/98, p. A29.

BATHOS

noun - triteness, BANALITY, sentimentalism.

"Political sophisticates were not impressed by the [Checkers] speech. Some scoffed, arguing that Nixon had not yet fully exonerated himself. Many criticized him for BATHOS. He had indulged in 'a private soap opera,' The New York Post said, in which, 'the corn overshadowed the drama.' Others acknowledged the emotional appeal of the performance but were still not persuaded. *NYTimes* took UMBRAGE with 'the lack of recognition by Senator Nixon that he had made any sort of mistake in accepting these funds in the first place.'" Sean Wilentz, *NYTimes*, 8/24/98, p. A19.

BEDROOM HAIR (Sl)

noun - disheveled, unkempt hair.

"Since her marriage last weekend to John F. Kennedy Jr., Carolyn Bessette has been breathlessly described as the beautiful and brainy new Queen of Camelot.... Former associates still talk about Ms. Bessette-Kennedy's sense of style. One remembers the day she turned up at the office wearing a tight black leather Calvin Klein jacket as a blouse, set off by the thick blond mane she often wore fashionably unkempt in the 'BEDROOM HAIR' style much in vogue on the runways." Elisabeth Bumiller, *NYTimes*, 9/29/96, p. 26.

BEJESUS

noun - a mild oath ("by Jesus") used for emphasis.

"Mr. Inman's appointment may satisfy those who remain uneasy with Mr. Clinton's grasp of military affairs, but it also troubles some of those who saw an advantage to the Democratic President's post-cold-war approach to international conflict and shrinking the military. Representative Patricia Schroeder, a Colorado Democrat who serves on the House Armed Services Committee, said that watching Mr. Inman's performance in the Rose Garden 'scared the BEJESUS out of me. I don't know who he is,' she said. 'He hasn't been around and in the milieu. His whole life has been focused on, in and out of the military-industrial complex during the cold war. Is this back to business as usual?'" Gwen Ifill, *NYTimes*, 12/18/93, p. 7.

BENIGHTED

adjective - unenlightened, morally deficient.

"Coming as they do amid massive worldwide movements of people, [the grounding outside New York harbor of a boatload of Chinese refugees and the court-ordered admission to the U.S. of HIV-infected Haitians] can make it seem that half the world is in flight and headed in our direction. That is an exaggeration, of course, and one that should not stampede Congress or the Clinton administration into reckless, BENIGHTED attempts to slam shut 'the golden door.'" Editorial, *Chicago Trib.*, 6/21/93, S 1, p. 14.

"Every time I hear some philosopher of the water cooler explain that Abraham Lincoln was 'a racist,' I am touched by the display of eagerness of modern Americans to boast that their own enlightenment puts to shame the great figures of the past. What makes it comical is the assumption that the present is a pinnacle of some sort. Poor BENIGHTED Lincoln hadn't the good luck to be of the present age, so how could he avoid being 'a racist,' even though in some respects he was not half as unenlightened as a lot of the old-timers?" Russell Baker, *International Herald Tribune*, 10/15/93, p. 20.

BÊTE NOIRE (FR)

noun - a person or object of fear, a worricow, a bugbear, a BUGABOO.

"Speakers [at the 1984 Republican Convention] have quoted the Bible, Ronald Reagan, Gary Hart, Harry Truman and have fully 'Hooverized' President Jimmy Carter as the all-purpose, thoroughly condemned and apparently never-to-be forgotten BÉTE NOIRE of the Reagan campaign." Francis X. Clines, *NYTimes*, 8/22/84, p. 10.

Pat Oliphant

"It should not be forgotten that it was Herbert Hoover, BÉTE NOIRE of the Democratic Left, who created the Reconstruction Finance Corp. and set in motion the initiatives that produced unemployment compensation and Social Security." Michael Kilian, *Chicago Trib.*, 8/20/84, S 1, p. 15.

"The departure of the California 'old guard' marks a victory for the so-called pragmatists, represented by White House chief of staff James Baker, a BÉTE NOIRE for conservatives suspicious of his close ties to Vice President George Bush." John N. Maclean and Storer Rowley, *Chicago Trib.*, 1/6/85, S 1, p. 3.

BIBLIOPHILIA

noun - a love of books.

"In addition to his BIBLIOPHILIA, the President-elect [Bill Clinton] loves to sing, calls himself a movie addict and once in his youth considered becoming a professional jazz musician. Mrs. Clinton, who jokes with friends about her inability to carry a tune, prefers classical music to pop." William H. Honan, *NYTimes*, 12/10/92, p. B1.

BICOASTAL (SL)

noun - a person equally at home on the east and west coasts.

"So for the television fan, the lines are drawn. It is the soap opera of the BICOASTALS [Mia Farrow-Woody Allen] versus the soap opera of middle America [Bush-Quayle], the late-night jazz club (clarinet and saxophone) versus Sunday morning in church, the separate dwellings versus the double bed." Walter Goodman, *NYTimes*, 8/22/92, p. 12.

"Like a brightly lit ocean liner on a dark sea, the White House floated above the scandal for five hours, as 240 guests clinked glasses and basked in

43

the glow of being rich, of being powerful, of being there. It was eerie. Just getting the most coveted ticket in Washington - to dine with those two powerful heads of state - lent the evening an illusion of invulnerability: that all is right in the world because all is right at this moment. There was the President, charming and being charmed by the BICOASTAL masters of the Universe: Steven Spielberg, Barry Diller, Jack Welch, Warren Buffett, Tom Hanks, Ralph Lauren, John F. Kennedy, Jr., Tina Brown, Anna Wintour, Barbara Walters, Peter Jennings." Margaret Carlson, *Time*, 2/16/98, p. 47.

BILDUNGSROMAN (GER)

noun - a novel about the moral development of the principal character.

"I had heard that Mr. Nichols and some of the cast members were trying to play down the idea that 'Primary Colors' is about the Clintons, even though 'Primary Colors' is about the Clintons.... It's like saying that 'All the President's Men' was simply a buddy movie about two guys who started out in Adams-Morgan. Do they think they'll be able to sell 'Primary Colors' as a BILDUNGSROMAN about a young black man in America?" Maureen Dowd, *NYTimes*, 8/27/97, p. A15.

"'All Too Human,' the awkward title of the new memoir by President Clinton's former advisor, George Stephanopoulos, seems meant as a commentary on the author's famously flawed former boss and on the author himself. The book depicts Mr. Clinton as a man of contradictions, a politician whose very 'shamelessness is a key to his political success,' a man whose 'capacity for denial is tied to the optimism that is his greatest political strength.' At the same time, it creates a sort of BILDUNGSROMAN portrait of the author as a young man whose idealism is tempered by 'raw ambition,' a onetime altar boy turned political operative, whose messianic fervor on behalf of the candidate he helped get elected gradually gives way to disillusion and doubt." Michiko Kakutani, *NYTimes*, 3/12/99, p. B45.

BILLARY (SL)

adjective - referring jointly to both President Clinton and first lady Hillary Rodham Clinton.

"There also have been several joint 'BILLARY' sightings around town. One night it was dinner at Restaurant Nora, a delightful establishment whose owners scribbled words of encouragement and advice on Clinton's menu; once it was Red Sage, which serves terrific, albeit expensive, Southwestern cuisine." Anne Groer, *Chicago Trib.*, 7/4/93, S 12, p. 7.

BILLINGSGATE

noun - coarse, abusive and vulgar language. From a London fish market notorious for bad language.

"Mr. Bush, in deplorable contrast, has repeatedly used the veto and Horton incidents not just to question an opponent's performance in office (as 'Where was George?' did), or even his judgment, but to impugn his patriotism and charge him with being a partisan and a patron of murderers and rapists. That went well beyond expectable campaign BILLINGSGATE into the personal character of Michael Dukakis." Tom Wicker, *NYTimes*, 11/8/88, p. 27.

BIMBO (SL)

noun - a sexually promiscuous woman, a doxy.

"How flagrant must PHILANDERING be to be reported to the public? Should a long-term relationship with another woman (like Franklin D. Roosevelt's) get a pass but not a series of BIMBOS? Should the private lives of only presidential candidates be checked out or those of every elected, policy-making official down to dog-catcher?" Joan Beck, *Chicago Trib.*, 5/11/87, S 1, p. 13.

"In a way, it doesn't seem fair. Is what [Gary] Hart did so terrible? Not really. [John] Kennedy was using BIMBOS even while in the White House. His press pals knew but didn't tattle." Mike Royko, *Chicago Trib.*, 7/20/88, S 1, p. 3.

"Warren G. Harding went through as many Washington grandes dames and floozies as he did whisky bottles and cigars. Franklin Roosevelt's secretaries busied themselves with far more than shorthand. JFK had a virtual conga line of BIMBOS traipsing up the White House back stairs, judging by recent revelations." Michael Kilian, *Chicago Trib.*, 2/5/92, S 7, p. 14.

"The current betting in Bill Clinton's camp is that Sen. Albert Gore of Tennessee will be his running mate. Since Gore ran for president in 1988, the guess is that he doesn't have any smoking BIMBOS in his past." O'Malley & Collin Inc., *Chicago Trib.*, 7/8/92, S 1, p. 16.

by Garry Trudeau

"But there was another explanation for Dole's seemingly irrational press policy, and it remained a closely held campaign secret. Dole had learned in early September that Charles Babcock, an investigative reporter for *Wash. Post*, was pursuing a charge that in the late nineteen-sixties, when Dole was married to his first wife, he had an affair. Babcock, it seemed, had interviewed the woman, who had confirmed the story. All at once, Dole - not Clinton - was fretting about 'BIMBO eruptions.'" Ken Auletta, *New Yorker*, 11/18/96, p. 48.

"But the President [Kennedy] did not simply have affairs according to Hersh. Several Secret Service men assigned to guard the President told Hersh

47

he had a taste for BIMBOS, girls brought in off the street by friends acting as procurers; that he liked cavorting naked with such women in the White House pool, that friends often joined him, and sometimes his brothers Bobby and Teddy as well." Thomas Powers in review of The Dark Side of Camelot by Seymour Hersh, *NYTimes Book Review*, 11/30/97, p. 15.

"In telling pollsters that they continued to think that President Clinton was doing a good job even though they did not admire him as a person, they rated economic performance and welfare reform as more important to them than BIMBO eruptions." Alan Wolfe, *NYTimes*, 6/28/99, p. A21.

BLACKGUARD

noun - an unscrupulous person.

"They [the CLINTON HATERS] keep waiting for America, indeed for the world, to wake up and cast the BLACKGUARD out of office, to see through his poses and slick rationales for just about everything, recognize him as a SNAKE OIL salesman." Charles M. Madigan, *Chicago Trib.*, 6/13/99, S 2, pp. 1 & 4.

BLATHER

noun - nonsensical talk.

"Since funeral orations are not delivered under oath, we have all come to expect that the death of a national political figure will bring forth a tidal wave of pious BLATHER. Still, the outpouring of revisionism on the subject of Richard Nixon over the last week is enough to leave one slightly breathless with amazement. The problem is not just the willingness to overlook the criminality revealed by the Watergate scandal, chastely euphemized as Nixon's 'mistakes' in President Clinton's eulogy. Just as bad is the shameless magnification of everything else he did as president, combined with the perverse insistence on making a virtue out of his every character defect." Stephen Chapman, *Chicago Trib.*, 5/1/94, S 4, p. 3.

BLATHERSKITE

noun - a talkative, foolish person, given to nonsensical, empty talk; one who talks BLATHER.

"[Ross] Perot, whose preferred rhetorical mode is the murky expostulation, is what used to be called a BLATHERSKITE. There is an inverse relationship between the confidence he has in his opinions and the care he has taken in forming them." George F. Will, *Newsweek*, 6/29/92, p. 72.

BLINDSIDE

verb - to suddenly and unexpectedly surprise; to attack from a person's blind side.

"Another Administration official said Mr. Clinton deeply resented Mr. Netanyahu's decision to open a second entrance to a tunnel that passes close to

Islamic holy places in Jerusalem, a decision that triggered the new round of violence. The official said the President felt he had been 'BLINDSIDED.'" R.W. Apple Jr., *NYTimes*, 10/2/96, p. A6.

BLOOPER

noun - a blunder.

"The elements of berserker comedy that so distinguished Reagan's presidency were there right from the start. During the 1980 campaign - shortly after he announced that cars don't cause pollution, trees do - scholars in the press corps took to classifying Reagan's departures from reality. We're not talking BLOOPERS here - like the time he toasted Bolivia - in Brazil; greeted his own Secretary of Housing as 'Mr. Mayor'; called President Samuel Doe of Liberia 'Chairman Moe'; and announced at a 1983 GOP fund-raiser, 'We are trying to get unemployment to go up, and I think we're going to succeed.'" Molly Ivins, <u>Molly Ivins Can't Say That, Can She?</u>, Random House, 1991, p. 104.

BLOVIATE

verb - to orate verbosely and windily.

"It was only after the Civil War that candidates made a customary thing of going about the country 'BLOVIATING,' to use Warren Harding's expression for waving one's mouth around in front of the multitudes." Nicholas von Hoffman, *NYTimes*, 10/12/88, p. 27.

"Listening to Republicans BLOVIATE for hours on end has a curious effect on the brain. When they announce, 'And the door prize is breakfast with Ollie North!' you scarcely wince. The usual split between the two flavors of Republican women was once more in evidence. Half the women look like Nancy Reagan; the other half tend to wear polyester pantsuits." Molly Ivins, <u>Molly Ivins Can't Say That, Can She?</u>, Random House, 1991, p. 192.

"Was it coined by H.L. Mencken? Warren G. Harding? Gore Vidal? Lewis Carroll? To the many vocal readers who have searched in vain for a dictionary that might give the definition and derivation of the term 'BLOVIATE' since it appeared here, in a November column about the NATTERING NABOBS of Washington, I say: Forget the O.E.D. and consult the essential 'Safire's New Political Dictionary,' in which the history of this 'made up' word is traced back as far as 1850. Its creator? Unknown. Its meaning? 'To orate pompously.'" Frank Rich, *NYTimes*, 1/6/99, p. A27.

"... his [Larry Flint's] very presence exposes the DISINGENUOUSNESS of everybody else, conservative and liberal, Republican and Democrat, press and public, who inhabits the epic Bosch canvas that is Monicagate. In the land of the pious hypocrite, the honest pornographer is king... It is almost too delicious to watch Mr. Flynt throw his higher-minded colleagues in the news business into conniptions. Washington's BLOVIATOR-in-chief, David Broder, brooded on PBS about how 'the mainstream press' is now having its

49

agenda set by 'the bottom-feeders in our business.'" Frank Rich, *NYTimes*, 1/16/99, p. A31.

BLOWHARD

noun - a braggart.

"Repeated killings in Port-au-Prince, and the prospect that President Aristide would not step down as promised for new elections, and that the presence of U.S. troops might have to be extended, suggested that democracy may not be quite the word for what had been restored to Haiti. But Clinton had stood firm and presidential against congressional BLOWHARDS who insisted that the United States should only intervene when 'our vital interests are at stake.'" Martin Walker, The President We Deserve, Crown Publishers, 1996, p. 284.

BLUENOSE

noun - advocate of a strict moral code; a puritanical person, a WOWSER. *adjective* - BLUENOSED.

"Judging by history, the correlation between Puritan sexual behavior and wise political leadership is zero. Lloyd George, Franklin Roosevelt and John F. Kennedy all made great contributions to democracy, to name just a few of the numberless politicians who might never had held high office if put to the test of BLUE-NOSED moralism." Anthony Lewis, *NYTimes*, 5/5/87, p. 31.

"Poor George [Bush]. He may be a bumbler, a do-nothing, a BLUENOSE, but he's still the president and he's being kicked around like a mangy dog. July has been a nightmare for President Bush. His popularity is at an all-time low, he is trailing Democrat Bill Clinton 2 to 1 in national polls, and now his fellow Republicans are ganging up on him." Ellen Debenport, *Chicago Trib.*, 8/2/92, S 4, p. 3.

"Polls showed that even Mr. Perot's supporters disagreed with him, and some sympathizers privately warn that this is just the first surfacing of an officious, BLUENOSED Puritanism that may ruin his chances." Kevin Phillips, *NYTimes*, 6/4/92, p. A15.

"'He Cheats on His Wife' blares the cover of *Spy's* July-August issue, ample inducement to any but the most BLUENOSED Republicans to read the results of an investigation that concludes that Bush has had extramarital relations with several women." James Warren, *Chicago Trib.*, 6/21/92, S 5, p. 2.

BOGSAT

adjective and *noun* - an acronym for "bunch of guys sitting around a table," usually referring to action taken in a rather unorganized, unscientific manner.

"All of us official 'headhunters' agreed with Dan Fenn, special assistant to President John F. Kennedy for personnel, that each President was reduced to choosing his team by a process he calls 'BOGSAT' - 'a bunch of guys sitting around a table.' 'BOGSAT' is, more often than not, an innocent form of cronyism - getting trusted friends together who themselves are not interested in public office but are willing to suggest able people they know." John W. Macy, *NYTimes*, 2/9/84, p. 29.

"OPEC can be defeated now by BOGSAT - a 'Bunch of Guys Sitting Around a Table' in the White House, with a tough-minded directive from Mr. Reagan to make the world safe for free trade." William Safire, *NYTimes*, 1/3/85, p. 19.

BOLLIX

verb - to bungle or mess up.

"Whether he's calling Mario Cuomo 'Mary,' saying unemployment claims have 'ooched up,' or worrying that 'we'll be up to our neck in owls,' Bush's end-of-campaign enthusiasm reverberates through the audience. He gets his sentences BOLLIXED up, but the campaign crowds get the drift and cheer him on." Timothy J. McNulty, *Chicago Trib.*, 10/30/92, S 1, p. 16.

BOLL WEEVIL (OM)

noun - a conservative, southern Democrat.

"However, there's a chance that some freshman members of Congress regardless of party next year will be more change-oriented than their predecessors and willing to go along with the president, whether he is Bush or Bill Clinton. Reagan got a taste of that when conservative Democrats, or BOLL WEEVILS as they were called, banded together with the Republicans to pass the Reagan tax cuts in the 1980s." Elaine S. Povich, *Chicago Trib.*, 8/31/92, S 1, p. 7.

BOMFOG (SL)

noun - an acronym meaning "brotherhood of man, fatherhood of God."

"...the political reporters covering Nelson Rockefeller used to turn his UBIQUITOUS 'brotherhood of man and fatherhood of God' phrase into the acronym BOMFOG." Calvin Trillin, *New Yorker*, 9/26/83, p. 76.

"Cutting through the White House's Roosevelt Room BOMFOG and the will-you-love-me-next-December skepticism in Jerusalem...." William Safire, *NYTimes*, 12/15/83, p. 25.

BONEHEADED

adjective - stupid.

"By a voice vote, the Senate approved a Foreign Operations spending bill of nearly $13 billion for 1998 today - without providing for the United Nations and IMF payments. The House had passed similar legislation 333-76 shortly after midnight. The White House called the votes 'BONEHEADED.'" Jerry Gray, *NYTimes*, 11/4/97, p. 1.

"'This is a particularly ill-timed move by Congress at a moment when we are attempting to work with the United Nations to build an international support for an appropriate response to provocations by Saddam Hussein,' said Michael McCurry, the White House spokesman. 'It is utterly BONEHEADED for Congress to fail to meet the commitments that the United States has at the U.N. in terms of our arrears.'" Jerry Gray, *NYTimes,* 11/4/97, p. 1.

"So what *is* it with Hillary? The President's head is on the block, and the First Lady has never looked more radiant. As her husband gets dragged through the mud by BONE-HEADED Republicans, she glows. She looks as if she's traveling with her own pink baby spotlight." Maureen Dowd, *NYTimes,* 12/9/98, p. A31.

BONHOMIE

noun - geniality, friendliness.

"Another potential development at the Republican convention is that we'll all come to like George Bush, who is as easy to like as he is hard to respect. Once people get used to his fatuous BONHOMIE, it's actually rather endearing. He is given to saying silly things - his theory of caribou procreation will long be treasured - but BANALITY is not a sin." Molly Ivins, <u>Molly Ivins Can't Say That, Can She?</u>, Random House, 1991, p. 189.

"Midland [Texas], impatient with ideas and introspection, was a world of clear rights and wrongs, long on absolutes and devoid of ethical gray shades. It may be the source of some of Mr. [George W.] Bush's greatest political strengths, the unpretentiousness and mellow BONHOMIE that warm up voters, and also of his weaknesses, including an image of an intellectual lightweight that is underscored whenever he mixes up the likes of Slovenia and Slovakia." Nicholas D. Kristof, *NYTimes,* 5/21/00, p. 20.

BONKERS

adjective - crazy, meshugge.

"An unidentified Bush campaign official told Knight-Ridder reporters that Dole's 'inability to control his dark side is a major minus for him. The American people don't want a president to go BONKERS every time he takes a little heat.'" News Story, *Chicago Trib.,* 2/5/88, S 1, p. 6.

BOOTLESS

adjective - useless.

"That Bush's numbers had been lousy before Desert Storm and were rapidly returning thither seemed to impress no one but me. As late as last fall, when Bill Clinton announced his candidacy, the Say-Theyers thought it was all BOOTLESS. Nameless pygmies like Clinton and Tsongas, for pity's sake, to challenge the peerless prexy. None of the big guys wanted to play. Bradley of New Jersey, Gephardt of Missouri, Gore of Tennessee - all had assessed and judged it a no-hoper." Molly Ivins, <u>Nothin' but Good Times Ahead</u>, Vintage Books, 1993, p. 182.

BORK (Sʟ)

verb - to vigorously contest a presidential nominee, especially by using the nominee's own writings against him.

Note:From the vigorous and successful opposition to President Reagan's nomination of Judge Robert Bork to the United States Supreme Court.

The term "Bork" has been used both in an affirmative and in a negative sense, affirmatively as an effective political tactic and negatively as a political attack which is unfair.

The author was the organizer of a large group of Chicago lawyers who lobbied against the Bork nomination and testified before the Senate Judiciary Committee in opposition to the nomination.

Brian Basset

"In the next few weeks, however, Mort Halperin - like Zoe Baird and Lani Guinier - may well become a familiar name. Conservative Republicans have decided that Halperin is an opportune target, a chance to challenge the president [Clinton] and discredit his defense policy as the attack on Guinier wounded his civil rights program. 'We hope,' said one Republican congressional aide, 'to BORK him,' taking Halperin's extensive writings on foreign policy and, as in the confirmation hearings for Supreme Court nominee Robert Bork, use it to block his nomination." Nicholas M. Horrock, *Chicago Trib.*, 11/5/93, S 1, p. 12.

"There remain two diametrically opposite story lines,. One is Bork-the-victim. He was 'the victim of a misinformation campaign waged by liberal extremists who sought to further their own agenda,' in the words of Senator Orrin G. Hatch, the Utah Republican who as a member of the Judiciary Committee he now heads was one of Mr. Bork's chief defenders. 'They knew they couldn't defeat him on his qualifications, so they distorted his writing and his views.'... According to the other story line, the stop-Bork campaign was public education at its best, a 'civics lesson.' in the phrase of Senator Biden and others, that informed Americans of the content and consequences of the nominee's views. 'It was a legitimate effort to defeat a nominee on the basis of his views, views that were extreme.' Mr. Biden said, 'It was the most extensive civics lesson on the Constitution the American public has ever been exposed to.'" Linda Greenhouse, *NYTimes*, 10/5/97, p. 3.

BOSH

noun - empty talk, trash, humbug.

"[Henry Cabot] Lodge's keynote speech, of course, was BOSH, but it was BOSH delivered with an air - BOSH somehow dignified by the manner of its emission." H. L. Mencken, The Vintage Mencken, Vintage Books, 1956, p. 81.

"Hale produced sentence after sentence [by Woodrow Wilson] that has no apparent meaning at all - stuff quite as bad as the worst BOSH of Warren Gamaliel Harding. When Wilson got upon his legs in those days he seems to have gone into a sort of trance, with all the peculiar illusions and delusions that belong to a pedagogue gone mashugga." H. L. Mencken, A Mencken Chrestomathy, Vintage Books, 1982, p. 250.

BOWDLERIZE

verb - to expurgate vulgar or salacious material; to abridge by excising indecent material.

Note:after Thomas Bowdler who produced *The Family Shakespeare* in 1818. Bowdler removed from the plays whatever he believed was "unfit to be read by a gentleman in the company of ladies."

"'Wouldn't you at least like to see and hear from her?' asked the prosecutor, Representative Ed Bryant, his gentle Tennessee drawl inviting as he urged the Senate court to not be shy and to call Monica S. Lewinsky as the key witness in the case against President Clinton. With the request for the much interrogated former intern at last put before the court, the House Republican prosecutors faced a Senate very anxious about its own dignity. Instantly, repeatedly, the prosecutors promised it would be a BOWDLERIZED, expurgated Ms. Lewinsky summoned to testify, hardly the furtively tape-recorded, uninhibited storyteller already making some senators cringe in anticipation." Francis X. Clines, *NYTimes*, 1/27/99, p. A20.

BOWWOW (SL)

noun - a flop, a real dog.

"Q - How much of a chance does the Reagan tax plan have of getting through Congress?

"A - There are only 535 lawmakers but more than 15,000 registered lobbyists in Washington. Drop a piece of salami into a tank full of piranha and you'll have a good idea of what's going to happen to Reagan's tax-simplification plan.

"Q - Why is he coming out with this plan now?

"A - His last two movies, 'Return to Bitburg' and 'Hellcats of the Contras,' were box office BOWWOWS. In show biz, you've got to take work where you can find it." Michael Kilian, *Chicago Trib.*, 5/31/85, S 1, p. 22.

BOYO (IR)

noun - an Irish lad.

"I did receive an invitation to a party [Senator Ted Kennedy is] throwing for some author friend of his (though I think not the author of the recent Gentleman's Quarterly article that described him as 'a Senator Bedfellow figure, an aging Irish BOYO clutching a bottle and a blond')." Michael Kilian, *Chicago Trib.*, 5/23/90, S 7, p. 15.

BOZO

noun - a foolish, incompetent man.

Note: In the presidential election of 1992, President George H. W. Bush, running for reelection, referred to Clinton and Gore as BOZOS. This was generally considered by the pundits to be highly inappropriate language for a presidential campaign.

"Whether or not [John] McCain is Truman, the historian [David McCulloch] thinks that [George W.] Bush is Dewey. 'Their campaign strategy is similar,' he says. 'Don't rock the boat. We've got it wrapped up. Don't do anything dumb or controversial. Stick with platitudes and you'll come in with the tide.' He has no patience for Donald Trump and Steve Forbes and the rest of the rich and famous and vain who would be President. 'They're all clowns and BOZOS and show-offs with awful, embarrassing egos,' he says." Maureen Dowd, *NYTimes*, 12/19/99, p. 13.

BRAGGADOCIO

noun - empty or pretentious boasting, cockiness.

Note: neologism of Edmund Spenser in "Faerie Queene," to personify boasting.

"He [Lyndon Johnson] was given the public nickname 'Bull.' 'When you saw him, that's what you called him,' says Horace Richards. '"Hiya, Bull, Howya doing, Bull?" Bull Johnson was his name, as far as we were concerned.' 'That was what we called him to his face,' Edward Puls, another classmate, says. 'That was what he was generally called. Because of this constant BRAGGADOCIO. Because he was so full of bullshit, manure, that people just didn't believe him. Because he was a man who just could not tell the truth.'" Robert A. Caro, <u>The Years of Lyndon Johnson: The Path to Power,</u> Knopf, 1982, p. 160.

"Mr. White said that Mr. Perot 'talks the talk,' the Texas BRAGGADOCIO you can hear in beer joints and pool halls, which glosses over specifics and contrary opinions." *NYTimes*, 6/8/92, p. A8.

"The cue for Mr. [Dan] Quayle's re-emergence is his book, *"Standing Firm,"* a surprisingly readable mixture of bitchiness, blame-deflecting and BRAGGADOCIO in which it turns out that everyone except George Bush and Dan Quayle is responsible for everything that went wrong in their Administration and re-election campaign." Frank Rich, *NYTimes*, 5/12/94, p. A15.

BRAVURA

noun and *adjective* - a brilliant performance.

"Mrs. Clinton has often been on the Hill in recent months, lobbying and briefing lawmakers on the Administration's emerging health care proposal. But her BRAVURA in back-to-back appearances today before two House committees carried a sense of wonder." Maureen Dowd, *NYTimes*, 9/29/93, p. A11.

"[Hillary Rodham Clinton] staged a BRAVURA performance before Rostenkowski's tax-writing panel, outlining President Clinton's health-care reform package. And she was careful not to miss an opportunity to pay homage to Rostenkowski." Steve Daley, *Chicago Trib.*, 9/29/93, S 1, p. 4.

"Don't know if you were privileged to hear Gingrich on Saturday blaming the entire [budget agreement] impasse on President Clinton, but it was a BRAVURA performance. He sounded exactly like Oliver Hardy saying to Stan Laurel, 'Here's another fine mess you've gotten us into.' Unable to restrain himself, Gingrich also took several cheap shots at Clinton for having gone off to play golf after announcing that he wouldn't sign a continuing budget resolution draped with extraneous matter, including a Medicare premium increase." Molly Ivins, <u>You Got to Dance With Them What Brung You</u>, Random House, 1998, p. 146.

"Monica S. Lewinsky was stung enough to object to the prosecutor's use of the word 'salacious' in her deposition for President Clinton's impeachment trial. But otherwise she showed the BRAVURA demeanor that comes of being one of the most practiced criminal investigation witnesses in the annals of Presidential history." Francis X. Clines. *NYTimes*, 2/6/99, p. 1.

BRIO (It)

noun - vivacity, spirit, vigor.

"Mr. Dukakis is known as a cautious, thrifty, fastidious man; much is make of his predilection for bargain-basement suits, of his lukewarm smile, of the lack of BRIO in the way he makes a speech or works a crowd." R.W. Apple, Jr., *NYTimes*, 7/21/88, p. 11.

BROBDINGNAGIAN

adjective - huge, gigantic, gargantuan.

Note:From <u>Gulliver's Travels</u> by Jonathan Swift.

"Vice President Dan Quayle has changed since the 1988 campaign: He now appears less flustered, more at ease, light-years better in front of television cameras and even downright spontaneous at times. But he still has one BROBDINGNAGIAN barrier to being taken seriously. He continues to make GAFFES, and the media, to say nothing of the late-night comedians, continue to have a field day with them." Janet Cawley, *Chicago Trib.*, 9/20/92, S 1, p. 9.

BROMIDE (OM)

noun - a dull, trite, unoriginal statement.

"...the other night when Ronald Reagan exhumed a 1916 BROMIDE by the Rev. William J.S. Boetcker and passed it off as the wisdom of Abraham Lincoln, television instantly pumped the fraud into millions of American skulls." Russell Baker, *NYTimes*, 8/25/92, p. A15.

"For the long term, Mr. Perot's program seems to be more BROMIDES than concrete proposals. For example he calls for such things as the establishment of 'an independent Federal agency' to oversee cost containment efforts and the 'reaching of a consensus on a set of principles for reform.'" Steven A. Holmes, *NYTimes*, 10/17/92, p. 7.

"I seem to be the only person in the land, however, who was appalled by [Vice President] Quayle's suggestion that the sitcom is in the Washington saddle. Everybody else who is upset about the speech has focused on Quayle's BROMIDIC endorsement of love, marriage and family." Russell Baker, *NYTimes*, 5/23/92, p. 15.

"...since the election, Mrs. Clinton has demonstrated that she will not bury her sharper views with an avalanche of First-Ladylike BROMIDES. In a speech in Australia in late November, Mrs. Clinton criticized the free market, 'which by definition knows the price of everything but the value of nothing,' and reported that in the United States, women were still striving 'to claim their share of personal, political, economic, and civic power.'" James Bennet, *NYTimes*, 1/20/97, p. A12.

BROUHAHA

noun - excited public interest, a noisy stir or wrangle, hubbub.

"Of course, Ferraro's forceful performance does not mean Walter F. Mondale has escaped unscathed from the BROUHAHA over the finances of his choice for vice president." Germond/Witcover, *Chicago Trib.*, 8/25/84, S 1, p. 11.

"She [Marilyn Quayle] dealt with them [questions about Quayle's candidacy] by making the media the culprits. Cameramen knocked over her children, she said. It wasn't the people who were bothered by Quayle's candidacy, she said, it was the media. The whole BROUHAHA was created by the media, she said." Cheryl Lavin, *Chicago Trib.*, 1/15/89, S 5, p. 8.

"As a result of the BROUHAHA over Sununu's trips, President Bush's legal staff prepared to tighten rules on Sununu's use of government aircraft." News story, *Chicago Trib.*, 4/28/91, S 1, p. 3.

"Clinton does not seem to have been hurt by the Gennifer Flowers BROUHAHA or by the phony allegations of draft dodging or by this new flap over having a real estate investment with an S&L MAVEN. All of which caused Dave Barry of Miami to observe in jest, 'I don't think sticking up that grocery store is going to hurt him either, nor that thing with Madonna, nor'..." Molly Ivins, Nothin' But Good Times Ahead, Vintage Books, 1993, p. 67.

BROWNNOSE (SL)

verb - to ingratiate oneself or act in a servile manner, to kiss the KEISTER.

Note:Webster's 9th New Collegiate Dictionary states that BROWNNOSE carries "the implication that servility is equivalent to kissing the hinder parts of the person from whom advancement is sought."

"In an amusing speech just before the President's, the comedian Al Franken screened a home movie of a touch football game, as if it were an incriminating porno loop, to document the shameless BROWN-NOSING that took place between President [Clinton] and reporters at the off-the-record Renaissance Weekend in Hilton Head, S.C., over New Year's." Frank Rich, *NYTimes*, 4/28/94, p. A15.

"It was clear to insiders [George W.] Bush was going for president well before his second gubernatorial campaign, and it also became clear that at least some Austin bureau chiefs had decided to hitch their stars to Bush's wagon... The result was a genuinely embarrassing amount of ass-kissing by some political reporters. [Footnote: This tendency to BROWN-NOSE is so pronounced, The Texas Observer once opined that if the press corps' noses got any closer to Dubya's behind, reporters would be in violation of the state sodomy laws.] And some Texas newspapers feel it is their duty to support the homeboy in a national race. So Bush's second gubernatorial campaign was a CAKEWALK..." Molly Ivins and Lou Dubose, Shrub, The Short But Happy Political Life of George W. Bush, Random House, 2000, p. 55.

BUBBA

noun - a good old boy, a southern redneck or rustic.

"'The Bush people in Texas are just apoplectic,' said John C. White, the Washington lobbyist and former Democratic Party chief who hails from Texas. 'We've got a billion-dollar BUBBA [Ross Perot] here to deal with, and no one has figured out how to handle this. A lot of the time in Texas, we confuse money with intelligence. And that gets us in a lot of trouble.'" *NYTimes*, 6/8/92, p. A8.

"As a result, I wrote then, he [President Clinton] was the 'first Democrat since Robert F. Kennedy in 1968 to bring the BUBBAS, the Brothers and the Bunkers together.' (That's southern whites, urban blacks and northern Archie Bunker ethnics, if you're not quite following my wit.)" Clarence Page, *Chicago Trib.*, 1/4/95, S 1, p. 13.

"Mr. Clinton, who just emerged from a re-election campaign where the same questions were raised about his leadership and where some Republicans disparaged him as 'BUBBA,' might have had a sense of 'I've been there' this weekend in Manila as he saw the Chinese leadership stall on the substantive issues that divide the two nations." Patrick E. Tyler, *NYTimes*, 11/25/96, p. A4.

"'He [George W. Bush] understands BUBBA because there is more BUBBA in him,' Karl Rove, the long time political advisor to the Bushes, told a reporter in 1992, when Mr. Bush's friends were still carefree enough to say colorful things about him. 'He is clearly the wild son - even today. Part of it is rooted in Midland, where he grew up in an ordinary neighborhood, where houses are close together and risk was a way of life.'" Nicholas D. Kristof, *NYTimes*, 5/21/00, p. 20.

BUCKRAKER (SL)

noun - a former high government official, either elected or appointed, who "cashes in" on his government experience and connections with a high paying job as a business consultant or lobbyist.

"In the hoary White House gathering (to support China trade) of a political power elite, Lee Hamilton stood out for two obvious reasons, namely his brush cut and not having cashed in. The political personages represented a handy-dandy who's who of American government in recent decades: Gerald Ford, Jimmy Carter, Henry Kissinger, James Baker. But as one scanned the politicos, who were joined by an A-list of Nobel laureates and business leaders, one was reminded of the well-worn path toward riches taken by many after high-level government service in the capital. With a few notable exceptions, so many in the room have become wealthy. Ford, Kissinger, Haig and Strauss are those who have raked in large sums as consultants, members of corporate boards and beneficiaries of stock options given by friendly firms for which they do some modest labor...We hearken back to the White House meeting on the China trade vote. I wondered if it gave him [Lee Hamilton] pride to be in that group of men (and a few women) who, ideologies and post-government service BUCKRAKING notwithstanding, labored for a greater good." James Warren, *Chicago Trib.*, 5/21/00, S 2, p. 2.

BUGABOO

noun - bugbear, worricow, BETE NOIRE.

"He [Woodrow Wilson] went into the Peace Conference willing to yield everything to English interests, and he came home with a treaty that was so extravagantly English that it fell an easy prey to the anti-English minority, ever alert to the makings of a BUGABOO to scare the plain people. What lies under all this subservience is simple enough. The American, for all his BRAGGADOCIO, is quite conscious of his intrinsic inferiority to the Englishman, on all cultural counts." H. L. Mencken, <u>The American Scene</u>, Ed. by Huntington Cairns, Vintage Books, 1982, p. 104-105.

"Mr. Kemp, by contrast [to Bob Dole], made his mark in Republican politics as one of the early champions of supply-side economics. He has advocated sweeping tax cuts as a way to solve many, if not most, of the nation's problems, and has pointed to the Kennedy tax cuts as an inspiration. He has long maintained that deficits don't really matter and that the fears they generate are a mere 'BUGABOO.'" Elizabeth Kolbert, *NYTimes*, 9/29/96, p. 1.

"[Kemp] blamed high interest rates not on the Government's fiscal policies but on its monetary policies and argued [in 1981], as he often did, that the answer to the problem was a return to the gold standard. He called the ballooning deficit the 'new BUGABOO.'" Elizabeth Kolbert, *NYTimes*, 9/29/96, p. 18.

"Here's a fellow [Senator Orrin G. Hatch] that put together countless legislative enactments with none other than the BUGABOO of all conservatives, Ted Kennedy." David E. Rosenbaum, *NYTimes*, 10/3/99, p. 25.

BULLY PULPIT

noun - a good stage to get public attention.
Note:The expression "Bully Pulpit" was first used by President Theodore Roosevelt in reference to the office of the president of the United States.

"The closeness of the vote [on Clinton's economic plan], despite a much-improved communications effort to sell the Clinton program, indicated just how weakened the White House BULLY PULPIT had become through the damaging missteps in the five months since the inauguration." Carol Jouzaitis, *Chicago Trib.*, 6/27/93, S 1, p. 3.

"I [President Clinton] have to tell you that one of the things that I underestimated when I became President was the actual power of the words coming from the BULLY PULPIT of the White House to move the country." President Clinton's speech on AIDS on December 1, 1993, *NYTimes*, 12/2/93, p. A12.

"In his years as speaker, Mr. O'Neill transformed the office from a political and parliamentary post to a BULLY PULPIT that he used in his many battles against President Ronald Reagan.... Mr. O'Neill called Reagan 'the least knowledgeable of any president I've every met, on any subject. He works by three-by-five cards.'" AP, *Chicago Trib.*, 1/6/94, S 1 p. 6.

"When he was chided for not using the presidency as a 'BULLY PULPIT' like [Theodore] Roosevelt, Taft pleaded guilty and blamed his judicial training." Donald F. Anderson, William Howard Taft, Cornell University Press, 1973, p. 216.

BUMFUZZLE (BUMFOOZLE)

verb - to confuse, rattle or bewilder.

Note: This word came to the attention of the public when President Bill Clinton used it to accuse Republican leaders in congress of confusing the public. Clinton said they had "totally BUMFUZZLED" American voters. BUMFUZZLED is a good old southern word and according to the Dictionary of American Regional English is especially common in Texas, Arkansas and Louisiana. Clinton has brought this word to a national audience just as President Truman did with SNOLLYGOSTERS. Friends of mine from the South have said that they were familiar with BUMFUZZLE, but most people in the North had not heard of the word until its use by Clinton.

BUNCOMBE (OR BUNKUM)

noun - empty, insincere, deceitful speechmaking, intended to impress one's constituents; nonsense, rot, bunk.

Note:Derived from an incident in 1845 when a representative from Buncombe County, North Carolina, when urged to desist from speaking, declared that he was bound to make a speech for BUNCOMBE.

"The city proletariat, transiently flustered by him [William Jennings Bryan] in 1896, quickly penetrated his BUNCOMBE and would have no more of him; the cockney gallery jeered him at every Democratic national convention for twenty-five years." H. L. Mencken, The American Scene, Ed. by Huntington Cairns, Vintage Books, 1982, p. 227-28.

"What the informed voter needs in an election year, along with opinion polls and economic indicators, is a reliable way to measure the BUNKUM coefficient - that is, the degree of fakery in any public position taken by a political figure. If there were such a scale it would now be registered on overload. By themselves, Walter Mondale and Sen. Gary Hart would be making the needle quiver violently on the BUNKUM gauge.... This year almost everybody seems to be flunking the BUNKOMETER test. The exception, let us hope, will be the voters." Editorial, *Chicago Trib.*, 4/2/84, S 1, p. 18.

BUSHSPEAK (SL)

noun - the fractured English which George Bush frequently produces; speech containing non sequiturs, dangling participles, grammatical errors, etc. cf. IVYSPEAK.

"If Mr. Bush is elected, many things about him could become instantly chic, including his fractured syntax. (He boasted the other day that he controls the contents of his speeches - 'inarticulate as though I may be.') Students of the Republican campaign eagerly trade examples of 'BUSHSPEAK.' Consider the Vice President's recent comment about the electorate: 'It's no exaggeration to say the undecideds could go one way or another.' On one memorable day on the campaign trail Mr. Bush talked about how he and President Reagan had found the country 'in array' when they took over from Jimmy Carter; how the Poles had expanded their freedom 'under the very guise of the Soviet Union,' and how he wanted to give the death penalty 'to the narked-up terrorist kind of guys' who kill police officers." Bernard Weinraub, *NYTimes*, 11/4/88, p. 10.

"But could he [President George Bush] not express himself at least in, like, maybe, you know, sixth or seventh grade English, rather than speaking as if he were Dan Quayle trying to explain the Holocaust? Here is more BUSHSPEAK, concerning Middle East policy: 'Now we want to see that there's some follow on there. So the policy is set, I campaigned on what the policy is.... So the principles are there and I think we're, you know, we've got to, now, flesh that out and figure out what we do specifically.'" Tom Wicker, *NYTimes*, 2/24/89, p. 27.

"I knew it [the 'thousand points of light' phrase] couldn't have originated with President Bush, because he would have been more likely to say: 'I want to tell you about this points of lights thing. We have about one thousand of them. They represent this goodness thing.'" [Mike Royko making fun of BUSHSPEAK], Mike Royko, *Chicago Trib.*, 3/10/89, S 1, p. 3.

"The best case for BUSHSPEAK as an expression of the democratic impulse was made by Jacob Weisberg of *The New Republic* who compared Bush to 'a big, clumsy, golden retriever, drooling and knocking over furniture in his eagerness' to please everyone." Michael Kinsley, Introduction to Jonathan Bines, <u>Bushisms</u>, Workman Publishing Company, 1992.

BUSHWA (SL)

noun - bunk, bull, bullshit.
Note:See BRAGGADOCIO. One of President Lyndon Johnson's college classmates is quoted as saying "Bull" was Johnson's MONIKER "because he was so full of bullshit, manure, that people just did not believe him."

"As Christopher Hitchens pointed out in *The Nation*, the Reagan Turkey [his memoir, *An American Life*] contains any number of statements and implications about Reagan's life and his presidency that have been disproved in the public press over and over again. While Reagan may by now have actually convinced himself, for example, that he was among the returning G.I.s who fought the Second World War, Hitchens wonders about the culpability of editors and ghostwriters who consciously pass off a lot of this old BUSHWA as historical fact. Actually, he doesn't wonder much at all: he calls them 'accomplices to a fraud.'" Calvin Trillin, <u>Too Soon to Tell</u>, Warner Books, 1995, p. 57.

"That the government would even think of doing anything to enforce labor law-worker safety, hours, overtime, comp time and not firing workers during unionization drives! You can see why the [United States Chamber of Commerce] wants to get Dubya Bush in office p.d.q., before any more of this commie BUSHWA gets handed down. Chamber officials told the Times the rules are unclear, asserting that companies did not know how many violations - 2 or 20 or 200 - might bar them from government contracts.

"That's a problem, of course. How many times should a corporation be allowed to violate the law before the government refuses to do business with it?" Molly Ivins, *Sarasota Herald Trib.*, 8/99, p. 3F.

CCC

CACOPHONY

noun - harsh or discordant sounds.

"As Mr. Clinton rose to speak on this balmy Washington afternoon on Memorial Day, he was greeted with a CACOPHONY of enthusiastic applause peppered by catcalls of 'draft dodger!' 'Liar!' and 'Shut up, coward!'" Thomas L. Friedman, *NYTimes*, 6/1/93, p. A1.

"The primal source of Jefferson's modern-day appeal is that he provides the sacred space - not really common ground but more a midair location floating above all the political battle lines - where all Americans can come together and, at least for that moment, become a chorus instead of a CACOPHONY." Joseph J. Ellis, <u>American Sphinx</u>, Knopf, 1997, p. 10.

CAHOOTS

noun - a collusion or partnership.

"In America, let's see how much of this scandal even makes it into Murdoch publications like *The New York Post* and *The Weekly Standard*, let alone if any prominent conservatives, whether HarperCollins authors like Robert Bork and Peggy Noonan or not, speak up in protest. Will those who've accused the 'mainstream media' of being in CAHOOTS with a Democratic Administration remain silent while their own media patron TOADIES to the most powerful totalitarian Government in the world." Frank Rich, *NYTimes*, 3/4/98, p. A21.

CAKEWALK

noun - an intricate prancing dance; by extension, an easy endeavor.

Note: Originally the term for an American entertainment of intricate, prancing dance steps with a cake as a prize.

"[Janet] Reno's CAKEWALK through the constitutional advise-and-consent process closed the book on a Clinton Cabinet-selection process that got under way not long after his election last November." AP, *Chicago Trib.*, 3/12/92, S 1, p. 12.

"In an effort to persuade her, U.S. Rep. Charles Rangel, a veteran Manhattan Democrat, dangled the assurance that Mrs. Clinton's candidacy would be unopposed in a Democratic primary. And should she run in 2000, Moynihan himself predicted, 'She'd win.' Not so fast, cautioned former Democratic Mayor Ed Koch. 'I think she would win, but she should understand it's not a CAKE-WALK, that Giuliani and the Republicans will use every loathsome opportunity to throw mud at her,' said Koch, echoing the concerns of many of Mrs. Clinton's friends and supporters." Lisa Anderson, *Chicago Trib.*, 2/17/99, S 1, p. 16.

"Unlike [Elizabeth] Dole, [George W. Bush] has held elective office and performed well enough to be re-elected handily. Still, the Texans with whom I have talked in two recent visits to the Lone Star State sound mystified that their 'G.W.' has CAKEWALKED so effortlessly to the front of the parade of GOP hopefuls." Clarence Page, *Chicago Trib.*, 3/14/99, S 1, p. 21.

CANARD

noun - a falsehood.

"Remember the biased 'mainscream media' that would stop at nothing to protect the Clinton White House? Funny how you don't hear about *that* anymore. If there's one certain casualty of Monicagate so far, it's the notion that the likes of *Newsweek*, *Wash. Post*, *NYTimes* and the big three networks will suppress news out of loyalty to a supposed liberal comrade. This was always a CANARD. To take just one example, it was Jeff Gerth of *The Times* who broke the Whitewater story six years ago this week." Frank Rich, *NYTimes*, 3/4/98, p. A21.

"'We have all these new people coming into America, rushing through the immigration process,' Senator Dole said. 'We find out that maybe 10 percent are criminals. They want to get them ready for Election Day.' Senator Dole was referring there, in his cryptic way, to a CANARD circulated by Congressional Republicans and Governor Wilson: that an Immigration and Naturalization Service program to cut the backlog of citizenship applications by more efficient handling was designated to create citizens who would vote for President Clinton, and that in the process the I.N.S. let a large number of criminals become citizens." Anthony Lewis, *NYTimes*, 11/1/96, p. A15.

CANDY ASS (SL)

noun - a strait-laced person; a person unduly concerned with ethical matters.

"In 1971, President Nixon became obsessed with the idea that Jewish officials in the Bureau of Labor Statistics were out to hurt him politically. He demanded a list of names, promptly supplied by the White House personnel chief, Frederic V. Malek. Later Mr. Nixon ordered George Shultz, then Secretary of the Treasury, to audit the tax returns of Mr. Nixon's 'enemies.' Mr. Shultz flatly refused. These quite different responses to two equally distasteful directives offer a lesson about the perils of bending principle to loyalty. Mr. Shultz, whom Mr. Nixon called a 'CANDY ASS' for his refusal to play ball, is today Secretary of State. Mr. Malek, whose 1971 survey of Jews in the statistics bureau was disclosed by *Washington Post* over the weekend, has now been removed from a senior post in Vice President Bush's Presidential campaign." Editorial, *NYTimes*, 9/13/88, p. 26.

"Nixon often mistook civility for weakness, as one sees in his taped references to loyal followers as 'CANDY ASSES.' He admired people with a touch of the thug - and Connally certainly qualified, shocking even his own ruthless leader, Lyndon Johnson, with his cold-heartedness." Garry Wills, *New York Review of Books*, 8/13/92, p. 26.

CANOODLE

verb - to pet, caress or fondle, to engage in silly lovemaking; *noun* - CANOODLER

Note:CANOODLE was a favorite word of Peter DeVries, one of America's wittiest writers.

"On the talk-show circuit, Republicans continued to question Mr. Clinton's conduct and credibility. Senator Orrin G. Hatch of Utah, who chairs the Judiciary Committee, said that if Mr. Clinton engaged in a sexual relationship with Ms. Lewinsky and then lied about it to the nation, 'it's an EGREGIOUS breach of ethics. So if that happened to have happened, then, you know, we've got a big problem on our hands,' said Mr. Hatch, who in his spare time composes gospel hymns. 'We have perhaps the first Presidential CANOODLER in history.'" *NYTimes*, 2/2/98, p. A19.

CARAPACE

noun - a protective outer covering (as a turtle's shell).

"Conveying to Saddam Hussein the message that Moscow was standing with Washington and the rest of the world was meaningful in itself, of course; the chances [of Bush and Gorbachev] persuading him to pull out of Kuwait depend to a considerable degree on penetrating the Iraqi dictator's tough psychological CARAPACE and making him feel increasingly shunned, cornered, friendless." R. W. Apple, Jr., *NYTimes*, 9/11/90, p A1.

CATBIRD SEAT

noun - favorable position or advantage.

"The Democratic presidential candidates held perhaps their last debate Wednesday, with Walter Mondale in the political CATBIRD SEAT and Jesse Jackson in the strategic hot seat." Jon Margolis, *Chicago Trib.*, 5/3/84, S 1, p. 5.

"The Mondale forces would like to make sure they win at least one of the June 5 [1984] contests to prevent a Hart sweep, and so they are investing a heavy effort in New Jersey. But with such favorable delegate numbers,

Johnson was asked, isn't Mondale in the CATBIRD SEAT? 'We hope so,' he said. 'We've been there before, though.'" John W. Kole, *Milwaukee Journ.*, 5/13/84, Part 1, p. 4.

CATERWAUL

verb - to make an angry noise or harsh cry.

"I take the most exquisite satisfaction in the yowls of bad sportsmanship coming from the Bushies. Did you ever in your life hear such a CATERWAULING? Ever hear so much sour, boorish moaning? I especially like the ones who threaten to move to Australia. I feel sure they're the same people who like to impugn the patriotism of Democrats." Molly Ivins, <u>Nothin' But Good Times Ahead,</u> Vintage Books, 1993, p. 177.

CATTLE CALL (OR SHOW)

noun - an audition for actors or candidates.

"Karen Hughes, his [Governor George W. Bush's] press secretary, said that the Governor was not aware when he accepted the invitation that this event had been advertised as an early CATTLE CALL for would-be Presidents and that he had come here because 'he feels an obligation to help the party raise money.'" Richard L. Berke, *NYTimes*, 8/25/97, p. A12.

"When the Midwest Republican Leadership Conference last gathered in Indianapolis, in 1979, a reporter at the event noted that the joint appearances of Presidential competitors had become 'CATTLE SHOWS.' These days, CATTLE SHOWS are an established, albeit interminable, rite of American politics. But never in memory have the shows begun so early. The usual starting point for events like this is after the midterm elections, although in 1993, some traditionalists were aghast that New Hampshire Republicans dared stage a dinner with would-be Presidents in late October." Richard L. Berke, *NYTimes*, 8/24/97, p. 1.

"It was steak dinner in a private room of the '21' club in June 1991, and the top Democrat executives on Wall Street were gathered at a round table to hold one of a series of meetings with Presidential aspirants in what an organizer called 'an elegant CATTLE SHOW.' They were questioning a man with a meager salary but a silver tongue, and this was another show in which Gov. Bill Clinton charmed his way to a blue ribbon by impressing the executives with his willingness to embrace free trade and free markets." Nicholas D. Kristof and David E. Sanger, *NYTimes*, 2/16/99, p. 1.

CHARISMA

noun - a rare quality attributed to those who have demonstrated unusual leadership ability. *adjective* - CHARISMATIC.

"He [Gary Hart] has the makings of CHARISMA - the looks, the now polished style - but CHARISMA is something that is usually acquired after a candidate starts to look successful. (John Kennedy did not start out

CHARISMATIC, and it is probably forgotten that there was a time when Jimmy Carter was CHARISMATIC.)" Elizabeth Drew, *New Yorker*, 4/2/84, p. 77.

"Much of the media now has the hindsight to be embarrassed about being suckered by the political image making machinery of the Kennedy's and the ease with which so many reporters, columnists and editors were co-opted by the Kennedy CHARISMA and wealthy dazzle into feeding the Kennedy myths to their readers." Joan Beck, *Chicago Trib.*, 6/27/84, S 1, p. 18.

"At the New Zion Baptist Church in Louisville, KY., for a packed service last Sunday afternoon, Mr. Gore began, as he often does with a patter of parody about his own stiffness, a paean to the sad lot of the CHARISMATICALLY challenged. He said, for example, 'if you put a strobe light on Al Gore, it looks like he's moving.'" Kirk Johnson, *NYTimes*, 11/2/96, p. 9.

"Taft lacked the CHARISMA of Roosevelt; his career had instilled in him a passionate respect for law and authority, the very antithesis of the qualities of the CHARISMATIC personality." Donald F. Anderson, <u>William Howard Taft</u>, Cornell University Press, 1973, p. 60.

"Whether you agreed with Ronald Reagan or not, he had a clear and concise message. John F. Kennedy had brilliant speeches penned by Theodore Sorensen and others. Mr. Gore will never have the CHARISMA or the performance skills of a Reagan or Kennedy, but there is no reason for him to be unable to formulate and articulate a clear and compelling message." Bob Herbert, *NYTimes*, 5/27/99, p. A31.

"Mr. [George W.] Bush never tried to pass himself off as intellectual before. When you've got CHARISMA, who needs a Phi Beta Kappa key? But the shock of the early debates has been how charmless he's appeared. If Dan Quayle looked like a deer caught in the headlights when he was in front of the cameras, Mr. Bush sometimes resembles a possum cornered in the garage - hunched over, tense, eyes darting worriedly." Gail Collins, *NYTimes*, 12/10/99, p. A31.

"However, she said: 'I thought Gore was very CHARISMATIC. He's not often called that, but compared to Bradley, he was more CHARISMATIC. But as far as the issues were concerned, I thought Bradley did better in his answers because he was more direct.'" Michael Tackett and Lisa Anderson, *Chicago Trib.*, 10/28/99, S 1, p. 20.

CHARLATAN

noun - quack or fraud, MOUNTEBANK.

"He [Teddy Roosevelt] was, in his dealings with concrete men as in his dealings with men in the mass, a CHARLATAN of the very highest skill - and there was in him, it goes without saying, the persuasive charm of the CHARLATAN as well as the daring deviousness, the humanness of naivete as well as the humanness of chicane. He knew how to woo - and not only boobs." H. L. Mencken, <u>A Mencken Chrestomathy</u>, Vintage Books, 1982, pp. 239-240.

"In his strongest comments to date on the Louisiana governor's race, President Bush said today that State Representative David Duke was a CHARLATAN unfit to hold public office because he has espoused racist and neo-Nazi beliefs." Roberto Suro, *NYTimes*, 11/7/91, p. A12.

"Through [President Lincoln's door at the White House] had come swindlers, hypocrites, liars, CHARLATANS, and bootlickers." Benjamin P. Thomas, <u>Abraham Lincoln</u>, Knopf, 1952, p. 496.

"If he [the candidate] purported to know the right answer to everything, he would be either a knave or a fool. If he even had an answer to everything, he would probably be just a fool. If he had no emphatic views at all, he would probably be either cunning or a political coward, of which we have altogether too many. And, finally, if he should arrive at election time with almost everybody satisfied, then you should, by all means, vote against him as the most dangerous CHARLATAN of them all." Adlai Stevenson, Speech at Los Angeles, California, 9/11/52, Edward Hanna, Henry Hicks and Ted Koppel, <u>The Wit and Wisdom of Adlai Stevenson</u>, Hawthorn Books, 1965, p. 32.

CHEESY

adjective - cheap, shabby.

"It was the sort of day for the Bush Presidency that can only be described as CHEESY. What should have been a triumphant moment for President Bush, the East Room swearing-in ceremony of David H. Souter as an Associate Justice of the Supreme Court, was meager and barely noticed. Mr. Souter, Mr. Bush's first appointment to the High Court, was not even given a reception, because there was not enough White House staff on duty to set up the party." Maureen Dowd, *NYTimes*, 10/9/90, p. A1.

"What changed? In substance Whitewater may have little in common with Watergate - an abuse of power by a President in office - but in form Whitewater has now started to mimic Watergate as CHEESILY as 'Pretty Woman' replays 'Pygmalion.'" Frank Rich, *NYTimes*, 3/10/94, p. A17.

CHICANERY

noun - trickery.
Note: The MONIKER given Nixon by detractors was "tricky Dick"

"No other postwar president is likely to cast such a long shadow into the new century. There will be the JFK of myth, LBJ's triumphs and tragedies and the Reagan enigma, but as the years go on we will always return to the parable of Richard Nixon. A man of endless contradictions, he built his career on Red-baiting, then embraced Mao's China; he sharpened racial 'wedges,' then enacted affirmative action. Finally, at the hour of his greatest glory, 1972, the year of a massive re-election, he lost it all, undone by lies that transformed CHICANERY into a constitutional crisis." *Newsweek*, 8/16/99, p.21.

"TAKE HIM HOME, PLEASE—HE'S BEGINNING TO MAKE ME NERVOUS!"

Pat Oliphant

CHIMERA

noun - an illusion, impractical idea, dream.

"Asked if he [Ronald Reagan] was serious about sharing the research and technology of SDI with the Soviets, he replied, 'Why not? What if we did?... Why not do what I have offered to do and asked the Soviet Union to do? Say, "Look, here's what we can do. We'll even give it to you. Now will you sit down with us and once and for all get rid ... of these nuclear weapons, and free mankind from that threat?"' The President's suggestion was widely derided at the time as an old man's CHIMERA, but a spectrum of experts we interviewed thought that he was really on to something." Jack Beatty, *Atlantic Monthly*, 2/89, p. 62.

CHIVY

verb - to move in increments, to obtain by persistent small maneuvers, to annoy with petty attacks.

"For more than a week now, at his campaign appearances, Mr. Bush has faced hecklers costumed as giant chickens, bearing signs that mock the Republican candidate for refusing to debate Bill Clinton on terms set out by an independent commission. The CHIVYING seems to have worked itself a surprisingly far way under Mr. Bush's skin, and recently the world has been treated to the novel sight of the President of the United States getting testy with a fake fowl." Michael Kelly, *NYTimes*, 9/30/92, p. A11.

"As Reagan did during his transition from Jimmy Carter, Clinton is seeking ways to get around the national media, ways to communicate and garner national support without having his message filtered through talk shows, CHIVIED by opponents in Congress and rearranged in news reports." Nicholas M. Horrock, *Chicago Trib.*, 11/30/92, S 1, p. 1.

CHOCKABLOCK

adjective - crowded, jammed, squeezed together.

"Filibusters against major spending bills are almost unheard of; few Republicans would cut off money to an entire Cabinet department, CHOCKABLOCK with popular programs, just to protest the spending they don't like. And not Hillary Rodham Clinton's health-care package in all likelihood." Michael Wines, *NYTimes*, 4/13/93, p. A10.

"At the Progressive meeting - preliminary to a convention in August [at which Teddy Roosevelt was nominated] - 'every one was CHOCKABLOCK with a sort of camp-meeting fervor, cheering, emotional. We were out to 'battle for the Lord' with a vengeance." Carol Felsenthal, <u>Alice Roosevelt Longworth,</u> G.P. Putnam's Sons, 1988, p. 128.

"Perhaps all our lives would look just as random and jumbled if our most precious material possessions, gathered over a lifetime, were reassembled in one place. By any measure, however, CHOCKABLOCK Monticello resembled a trophy case belonging to one of America's most self-indulgent and wildly eclectic collectors. How did one square this massive treasure trove of expensive collectibles with a life at least nominally committed to agrarian simplicity and Ciceronian austerity? The exhibit suggested that Jefferson lived in a crowded museum filled with the kinds of expensive objects one normally associates with a late-nineteenth-century Robber Baron whose exorbitant wealth permitted him to indulge all his acquisitive instincts." Joseph J. Ellis, <u>American Sphinx</u>, Knopf, 1997, p.14.

CHURL

noun - an ill-bred, rude person; boor.
adjective - CHURLISH.

"He's back, and frankly, we're all ears. Henry Ross Perot wants $15 from every citizen so he can crank up something called 'United We Stand America.' Sure, it seems CHURLISH of the richest candidate in American history to demand 'multiple family memberships.'" Editorial, *NYTimes*, 1/14/93, p. A16.

CHUTZPAH (CHUTSPA, CHUTZPA) (Y)

noun - brazenness, gall, cheek, brass, effrontery.

"But be that as it may [Jesse] Jackson has repented, and better a week after the fact than not at all. Like any politician, he had to delay and choose the right moment. And Jackson did it as only he could - with CHUTZPAH, from the podium of a synagogue." Lenita McClain, *Chicago Trib.*, 2/29/84, S 1, p. 11.

"Perot has demonstrated that $100 million plus a large dose of CHUTZPAH buys you a place at the presidential starting gate. He has shown that name recognition can be gained virtually overnight; that call-in shows and talk shows can catapult a candidacy from the ridiculous to the menacing." William Safire, *Chicago Trib.*, 8/27/93, S 1, p. 23.

"During [Newt Gingrich's] early years as an assistant professor at sleepy West Georgia College, he developed a reputation for a sort of Wagnerian overreaching. Stephen Hanser, one of Newt's closest intellectual advisers, found himself in 1972 in a contest with Newt over the chairmanship of their department. Hanser was unfazed by the young, unpublished instructor's CHUTZPAH. 'Oh, I think Newt being Newt saw an opportunity to make some changes in the department, and the fact that he was 28 or 29 at the time didn't bother him." After only a few years on campus, he also pushed himself for the presidency of the college." Gail Sheehy, *Vanity Fair*, 9/95, p. 153.

"You have to admire the CHUTZPAH. Two weeks ago, just as a commission was being assembled to figure out how Medicare can deliver promised benefits to the baby boomers once they start to retire, President Clinton proposed a new entitlement that would enable millions of the near elderly, a group that ranges in age from 55 to 64, to qualify for Medicare." Stuart M. Butler, *NYTimes*, 12/8/97, p. A23.

"Like most of the universe, the press corps was fixated on the circumstance behind her candidacy, beginning with Monica Lewinsky (was Mrs. [Hillary Rodham] Clinton benefiting from her status as a victim?) and ending with the CHUTZPAH required for a person to have a Senate Exploratory Committee before she has a mailing address." Gail Collins, *NYTimes*, 7/8/99, p. A24.

"'Every environmental issue confronts us with a duty to be good citizens,' said [George W.] Bush during an appearance in Pennsylvania on Monday. 'As we use nature's gifts, we must do so wisely. Prosperity will mean little if we leave future generations a world of polluted air, toxic lakes and rivers, and vanished forests.' That odd noise you hear is coming from the governor's aides, who have been trying desperately to stifle their laughter. This is breathtaking, spectacular, Texas-sized CHUTZPAH. Mr. Bush's relationship to the environment is roughly that of a doctor to a patient - when the doctor's name is Kevorkian. Where to begin? O.K. Let's start here. Mr. Bush's Texas is the most polluted state in the union. It is an environmental disaster zone." Bob Herbert, *NYTimes*, 4/6/00, p. A29.

"Voters never got the chance to judge House Speaker Newt Gingrich, who surely deserves a place in the CHUTZPAH hall of fame for wagging his finger [FINGERWAGGING] at President Clinton during the impeachment debate. Mr. Gingrich was no longer in power when Americans learned that he was involved with a Congressional staff member at the same time." Melinda Henneberger, *NYTimes*, 5/14/00, p. 3. [Note: They have set a wedding date and are listed on the internet for those who would like to give wedding presents!]

CIRCUMLOCUTION

noun - use of an unnecessarily large number of words; excess verbiage; evasive speech; periphrasis.

"There are some questions worth answering, no matter the consequences. And that is the case in Texas, where George W. Bush, the leading aspirant for the Republican Presidential nomination, has evaded reporters' insistent queries on unsubstantiated rumors that he used cocaine in the distant past. He has employed such CIRCUMLOCUTIONS as, 'When I was young and irresponsible, I was young and irresponsible.'" Glenn C. Loury, *NYTimes*, 8/24/99, p. A19.

CLINTON (SL)

noun - a retreat from idealistic rhetoric to the politically profitable.
Note:Definition is by Paul Greenberg, an old Clinton enemy from Arkansas. This neologism has died aborning. No other writer seems to have picked this up.

"If even *New York Times* is catching on, it may no longer be necessary to explain what a CLINTON is - a retreat from idealistic rhetoric to the politically profitable course. The other day, the *Times*' Thomas L. Friedman presented a real-life, step-by-step lesson in how to pull a CLINTON. He simply retraced this administration's slick course on a difficult question. This time the subject was not Haitians or the middle class, but the saddest victim yet of hopes raised only to be dashed: the tormented people of Bosnia." Paul Greenberg, *Chicago Trib.*, 4/16/93, S 1, p. 27.

CLINTON FATIGUE

noun - weariness with everything Clinton

"Some conservatives, seduced by CLINTON FATIGUE, a desire to win back the White House and the Bush millions, are winking at Mr. Bush's leftward shift, hoping this is nothing more than rhetoric or political strategy. They have convinced themselves that, once elected, Mr. Bush will move right and govern as a conservative." Gary L. Bauer, *NYTimes*, 10/7/99, p. A31.

"President Clinton remains popular, especially with his core Democratic constituency, but the American public - or so the conventional wisdom has it - is afflicted with 'CLINTON FATIGUE.' It is tired of Mr. Clinton and his ways, especially his sexual adventures." R. W. Apple, Jr., *NYTimes*. 10/11/99. p. A12.

"Writing in *The New Republic* two months ago, Sean Wilentz declared 'CLINTON FATIGUE' to be 'an utter hoax' and 'the latest sign of the growing gap between what the public actually thinks and what the pundits claim the public thinks.'" Frank Rich, *NYTimes*, 5/6/00, p. A27.

"Mr. Gore's aides argue that the public no longer cares about continuing scandal investigations, and that there may even be an electoral backlash against Republicans who continue to push for more. 'The Republicans think this plays into CLINTON FATIGUE,' said Chris Lehane, Mr. Gore's press secretary. But the thing people are fatigued with is scandal.'" James Dao, *NYTimes*, 6/28/00, p. A21.

CLINTON HATER

noun - a person with an intense, almost irrational hatred for President Bill Clinton.

Note: President Clinton has probably experienced greater personal animosity than any President since Franklin Delano Roosevelt.

"Mr. Bennett was hired to argue the President's brief not in the courtroom but on television, and he did it again this afternoon - with vengeance. 'She has no case,' he said of Ms. Jones. 'She has suffered no damages. She was never harassed. The CLINTON HATERS are trying to hound him out of office, and filings such as today's are part of that scheme.'" John M. Broder, *NYTimes*, 3/14/98, p. 1.

"Back in 1994, the scholarly Media Studies Journal had already concluded that the uniquely 'savage nature' of media comment was damaging the [Clinton] presidency itself. *The American Spectator* magazine was listed as one of nine institutions besieging the White House. That was before it was known that Richard Mellon Scaife, whom *Time* magazine calls a 'billionaire super CLINTON HATER,' funneled as much as $600,00 a year into the *Spectator's* 'Arkansas project.' You can buy a lot of dirt - true or false - at those prices." H. Brandt Ayers, *Chicago Trib.*, 3/12/98, S 1, p. 25.

"Put it all behind you - the grand jury, the special prosecutor, the sense that seamy behavior occurred in the Oval Office between President Bill and Monica Lewinsky. Abandon all these levels of outrage and debate about whether the special prosecutor is crazy (the Blind Friends of Bill view) or simply using standard procedure in pursuing presidential crime (the apoplectic BLUE-NOSED Republican CLINTON-HATER view). Flee this cheap media churning and get on to the main course, to the heart of what modern America is always about. Are there huge dollars to be made in the marketing of Monica Lewinsky?" Charles Madigan, *Chicago Trib.*, 3/5/98, S 5, p. 1.

"First of all, only Clinton's most rabid critics would fail to see the difference between resignation and impeachment. One is an honorable departure. The other is the political equivalent of capital punishment. Either would be just fine with the hard-core CLINTON HATERS. They'd like to see Clinton gone, along with his wife, the first daughter and their house pets, too. By any means necessary." Clarence Page, *Chicago Trib.*, 12/16/98, S 1, p. 27.

"The most rabid CLINTON-HATERS in Congress are white Southerners, led by Bob Barr, who has spoken before the racist Council of Conservative Citizens." Frank Rich, *NYTimes*, 12/19/98, p. A31.

"Perhaps the most emphatic stipulation in Mr. Hyde's summary of the case was his insistence that the impeachment charges brought by the Republican-controlled House were not the work of 'CLINTON-HATERS.' 'This is a question of what we love, he declared, citing the rule of law in a patriotism-steeped peroration that ranged from Bunker Hill to Desert Storm." Francis X. Clines, *NYTimes*, 1/17/99, p. 22.

"Slobodan Milosevic blinked after it became apparent that no amount of whining by his unwitting allies within the United States - the Clinton-bashing newspaper columnists and talk-radio bullies, the pacifist Democrats and the hyperpartisan Republicans in Congress - would make Bill Clinton back off. The CLINTON-HATERS, of course, will try to put the worst possible spin on Milosevic's withdrawal." John McCarron, *Chicago Trib.*, 6/7/99, S 1, p. 15.

"The bombing of Yugoslavia worked. So now, what will the CLINTON-HATERS come up with next? Perhaps they'll catch Hillary moving illegally into a rent-controlled apartment in Manhattan. Or get some dirt on Chelsea's next boyfriend. And what, exactly, has Socks, the presidential cat, been up to lately? No good, I'll wager." John McCarron, *Chicago Trib.*, 6/7/99, S 1, p. 15.

CLOYING

adjective - excessively sweet; disgustingly sentimental.

"In 1952, the Vice Presidential candidate [Richard Nixon] survived a financial scandal only after he delivered his infamous Checkers Speech. Today, many people remember that televised address for its CLOYING reference to Pat Nixon's 'respectable Republican cloth coat' and Nixon's sweat-soaked vow to retain the family cocker spaniel." David Oshinsky, *NYTimes*, 2/12/98, p. A31.

COBBLE

verb - to put together hastily.

"Clinton, after all, still had to contend with the prickly Senator. Quickly, another compromise was COBBLED together. Nunn would hold the hearings, but the military would no longer ask recruits about their sexual orientation. The issue would be postponed for six months, during which time Clinton might hope that his political strength, drawn from elsewhere, would grow." Sidney Blumenthal, *New Yorker*, 3/8/93, p. 43.

"While Mr. Perot has been criss-crossing the country and unloading his zinging one-liners, United We Stand America, the organization that he COBBLED together for his 1992 Presidential campaign, has been steadily signing up new members." B. Drummond Ayres, Jr., *NYTimes*, 11/6/93, p. 8.

COCKAMAMIE (COCKAMAMY)

adjective - absurd, ridiculous, implausible.

"Gingrich is a figure I vainly urged to step down ever since his COCKAMAMIE book deal. He belatedly got the voters' message and did the right thing; liberals and Big Labor will miss their favorite punching bag the way hard-line hawks miss Brezhnev." William Safire, *NYTimes*, 11/9/98, p. A29.

"In cooking up its COCKAMAMIE explanation for [John] McCain's attractiveness to voters across the political spectrum, religio-pols expose the fears of Republican elders: that the dread 'they' - all those starry-eyed amateurs and reformist outsiders - may take over 'our thing.' As a result, conservatives have to confront the group with the old 'G.O.P. death wish.' That clubby set of single-issue power brokers prefers to float out to sea in a Viking's funeral than to present a candidate who can appeal across party lines and energize swing voters." William Safire, *NYTimes*, 2/14/00, p. A27.

CODA

noun - a concluding part or summary.

"Rep. Dan Rostenkowski (D-Ill.), chairman of the House Ways and Means Committee, called [Hillary] Clinton a 'marvelous witness' and, in an emotional CODA as the hearing was ending, said he was tempted to applaud; other committee members actually did." Elaine S. Povich, *Chicago Trib.*, 9/29/93, S 1, p. 4.

"The Reagan and Buchanan speeches were the CODA to a day dominated by conservatives. Under withering pressure from Bush staffers, abortion-rights supporters finally dropped their plan for a floor challenge to the platform, which calls for a constitutional amendment prohibiting abortions." Charles M. Madigan, *Chicago Trib.*, 8/18/92, S 1, p. 8.

"Nixon can make no reply to "The Haldeman Diaries." For the first time, he must suffer disgrace in silence. The diaries are a signal that his rehabilitation years must appear as a faded CODA to his vivid political career." Sidney Blumenthal, *New Yorker*, 8/8/94, p. 39.

"'Economic security is an essential element of freedom,' Mr. Clinton said. 'In China, the extraordinary strides you have taken in nurturing that liberty and spreading freedom from want will be a source of strength for your people in the 21st century. But true freedom must mean more than economic opportunity. In America, we believe that freedom itself is indivisible.' The Beijing University speech offered a CODA to a series of weekend meetings with President Jiang and other top Government leaders here." John M. Broder, *NYTimes*, 6/29/98, p. A8.

COJONES (SP)

noun - testicles; by extension, courage.

"Many of you have been wondering, I know, about the ophthalmological machismo that has lately dominated international relations and how it came to replace the better-known forms of COJONES competition. For many years, my preferred form of exercise has been rapid blinking, so I am in excellent trim to explain all this." Molly Ivins, <u>Molly Ivins Can't Say That, Can She?</u>, Random House, 1991, p. 89.

COLTISH

adjective - playful, frisky, like a colt.

"Press conferences have helped make some Presidents and break others. The COLTISH charm and quick wit of John F. Kennedy, the easy familiarity of Gerald R. Ford and the effortless command of that old theatrical pro, Ronald Reagan, helped them put their ideals across. Richard M. Nixon's evident defensiveness and nervousness, President Johnson's chronic whining and exaggeration and Mr. Bush's spaghetti sentences [BUSHSPEAK] all got in the way of effective communication." R. W. Apple, Jr., *NYTimes*, 11/13/92, p. A9.

COMEUPPANCE

noun - a deserved rebuke.

"Is this the needle that bursts the Perot bubble? Can the undeclared independent candidate keep his remarkable drive toward the White house on course amid a storm of charges that his agents have spied on President Bush, members of the President's family and even his own children? Those questions were the talk of political Washington last night and today. Republicans and Democrats alike chattered about 'Inspector Perot' and his COMEUPPANCE, though they pictured the Dallas billionaire turned populist politician as a more sinister figure than Peter Sellers' screen gumshoe." R. W. Apple, Jr., *NYTimes*, 6/25/92, p. A15.

COMME IL FAUT (Fʀ)

adjective - proper, socially required.

"...I think Barbara Bush found them [State Dinners] a little dreary, especially her last year, when her husband shoveled so many politicos and fat cat campaign contributors into the receiving line. But she endured them, because State Dinners were a White House tradition going back to George Washington. They were, don't you know COMME IL FAUT." Michael Kilian, *Chicago Trib.*, 6/30/93, S 7, p. 4.

COMMON SCOLD (SCOLD)

noun - a noisy, quarrelsome, cantankerous person who breaks the peace, punishable as a nuisance at common law; an abusive person.

"Donald Regan, who fought with her [Nancy Reagan] constantly thought her nothing but a brittle SCOLD, but Deaver, while admitting that she was 'very intense, sometimes brittle in her manner,' found her a great deal more approachable and more flexible than her husband." Frances Fitzgerald, *New Yorker*, 1/16/89, p. 91.

"'Off budget,' is as 'Let's Pretend' as the President's big drug market in Lafayette Square and news turned into good television by actors. One feels half ashamed, like a COMMON SCOLD objecting to these frauds since, to borrow the Nixon White House's old slander on a nice town, they seem to 'play in Peoria.'" Russell Baker, *NYTimes*, 9/27/89, p. 27.

"The words were barely out of Sen. Bob Kerrey's mouth and the SCOLDS were at his throat: 'Take it back!' demanded homosexual activists, who were outraged that the Nebraska senator, who is also a Democratic presidential candidate, would dare utter a joke about a couple of lesbians in a bar." Dave Shiflett, *Chicago Trib.*, 11/27/91, S 1, p. 17.

"The format, which had Tom Brokaw alternately playing quizmaster and SCOLD, made the four credible [presidential] contenders - Tom Harkin, Bill Clinton, Bob Kerrey and Paul Tsongas - look like bickering and posturing schoolchildren." Leslie H. Gelb, *NYTimes*, 12/18/91, p. A19.

COMPASSIONATE CONSERVATIVE

noun - a political conservative who is SQUISHY on issues and principles, i.e. a believer in inclusion, the Republican big tent of Lee Atwater.

Note: a COMPASSIONATE CONSERVATIVE is a close cousin of the "liberal Republican," who, one sage commentator noted, is defined as a rescuer who throws a 50 foot rope to a person drowning 100 feet off shore.

"During the Roaring Twenties, the electorate fell in love with Calvin Coolidge, a monosyllabic politician who barely had the energy to get out of bed in the morning. (Coolidge was also, as far as we know, the first Vice President to serve while his boss [Warren G. Harding] was having sex with a woman not his wife in a room just off the Oval Office. He never felt compelled to point out that this was outrageous.)

"Unlike Coolidge, Al Gore is an energetic politician, and you only have to listen to his speeches to know that there will probably be A LOT OF INITIATIVES in a Gore administration. Even though George Bush has been gloriously unspecific about his own agenda, it is already easy to see that the two front-runners for the Presidential nominations have very different outlooks. Mr. Gore, for all his worries about BUREAUCRATIC EXCESS, is a government activist, and Mr. Bush, for all his talk about being a COMPASSIONATE CONSERVATIVE, does not seem to really have many new initiatives in mind." Gail Collins, *NYTimes*, 6/21/99, p. A18.

"Has compassion become a Republican virtue? Seems like it. George W. Bush, in his Presidential campaign kickoff speech, positively wallowed in the stuff, not only calling for 'COMPASSIONATE CONSERVATISM,' but also declaring his intention 'to rally [the] armies of compassion,' to show 'mercy,' to 'take the side of charities and churches.' Governor Bush's compassion play annoyed his competitors, softened his image, distanced him from the

Republican Congress and was generally applauded in the press." Mickey Kaus, *NYTimes*, 6/25/99, p. A27.

"Tough as it is to believe now, George W. Bush, the former 'COMPASSIONATE CONSERVATIVE,' was initially programmed to be the candidate that Mr. McCain is - a moderate who might appeal to independents and independent-minded Democrats who were turned off by Bill Clinton yet found the puritanical perpetrators of the Starr report even more EGREGIOUS (and frightening)." Frank Rich, *NYTimes*, 2/12/00, p. A 29.

"Warren Beatty is said to be a liberal Democrat (which means his sister Shirley probably views him as an arch conservative) though he has declined or been unable to articulate his political positions. This would give him an advantage over those candidates who do articulate their political positions such as Al Gore, who claims he'd be a President for the next century (which is, after all, when the next Presidential term begins), and George W. Bush, who uses phrases like 'COMPASSIONATE CONSERVATIVE' which; puts me in mind of Ebenezer Scrooge giving Bob Cratchit an extra lump of coal at Christmas." Michael Kilian, *Chicago Trib.*, 9/9/99, S 5, p.4.

CONCUPISCENCE

noun - strong sexual desire.

"As though our President [Clinton] didn't have enough to worry about, with the confusion on Kosovo policy and the collapse of the China World Trade Organization deal, now he must finally face the music on being CONTUMACIOUS about his CONCUPISCENCE." Maureen Dowd, *NYTimes*, 4/14/99, p. A29.

CONTRARIAN

adjective and *noun* - a person who takes a contrary view, one who questions the conventional wisdom.

"Bruce Babbitt, at his demonstrated peril, was even more CONTRARIAN. He proposed cutting the federal deficit by imposing a 5 percent national consumption tax with provisions to lessen the impact on low-income people, and he called for increasing the income taxes on Social Security benefits for the well-to-do. There were other heresies obviously unforgivable to the voters, but those give you the idea." Editorial, *Chicago Trib.*, 2/19/88, S 1, p. 16.

"On many issues Biden sounds a lot like Hart, particularly when he criticizes the role of special interests in the Democratic Party. But there is a lot more feeling in Biden's critique. Biden has become something of a CONTRARIAN in the party." William Schneider, *Atlantic Monthly*, April, 1987, p. 41.

"Former Governor [and presidential candidate] Edmund G. Brown Jr. of California has always been a politician willing to take the big risk and the

CONTRARIAN course, and he manages his personal finances in exactly the same way." B. Drummond Ayres, Jr., *NYTimes*, 1/31/92, p. A10.

CONTRETEMPS

noun - an embarrassing occurrence, a mishap.

"I don't mean to suggest that Clinton is some latter-day paragon of intercultural fairness. The Jesse Jackson-Sister Souljah flap is a reminder that Clinton is not immune to the temptation to pit people against one another to his own advantage. Probably the best explanation of that CONTRETEMPS is that Clinton wanted to show moderate whites that he was no patsy for Jackson - a perception that had cost Michael Dukakis four years earlier." William Raspberry, *Chicago Trib.*, 11/9/92, S 1, p. 17.

Len Borozinski

"It's hard to remember that the biggest CONTRETEMPS in her [Hillary Rodham Clinton's] first day on the job came over something small and silly, reflecting the tired role of first lady she inherited: the disproportionate DUST-UP over the ugly hat she wore at the inauguration." Anna Quindlen, *Chicago Trib.*, 1/14/94, S 1, p. 17.

"He [George W. Bush] quotes a letter from George the Elder telling him not to worry about stories that 'contrast you favorably with a father who had no vision and who was but a place holder in the broader scheme of things' - a worry, in light of the recent CONTRETEMPS over George the Younger's lack of foreign policy expertise, that somehow seems beside the point." Michiko Kakutani, *NYTimes*, 11/22/99, p. A 24.

CONTUMACIOUS

adjective - disobedient, rebellious, contemptuous.

"In today's ruling, Judge Wright made several references to other 'CONTUMACIOUS' conduct by the President, which she said she chose not to address in the interest of bringing the matter to a reasonably swift conclusion.

She specifically cited Mr. Clinton's violation of her order not to discuss his deposition testimony with anyone outside his legal team. She noted that a day after giving testimony, Mr. Clinton summoned his private secretary, Betty Currie, to the White House to review his testimony with her." John M. Broder and Neil A. Lewis, *NYTimes*, 4/13/99, p. A20.

"This lawsuit involved private actions allegedly taken by the President before his term of office began, and the CONTUMACIOUS conduct on the part of the President was undertaken in his role as a litigant in a civil case and did not relate to his duties as President." Opinion of Judge Susan Webber Wright, *NYTimes*, 4/13/99, p. A20.

"Moreover, this Court is aware that it is obliged to use the least possible power adequate to the end proposed in selecting contempt sanctions and will base the imposition of sanctions on a principle of proportionality, recognizing that the President's CONTUMACIOUS conduct occurred in a case that was both dismissed on summary judgment as lacking in merit and in which the plaintiff was made whole, having agreed to a settlement in excess of that prayed for in her complaint." Opinion of Judge Susan Webber Wright, *NYTimes*, 4/13/99, p. A20.

CORRECTOGRAM (SL)

noun - a press release or statement pointing out factual errors in an administration statement.

"If it is deliverable, it's grammable: songgrams, balloongrams, and bellygrams. Now there is a 'Reagan CORRECTOGRAM,' delivered at no charge to the news media by the Council for a Livable World, a Washington based organization that supports nuclear arms control. The CORRECTOGRAM states that it conveys a 'public service message to correct factual misstatements or errors by the Reagan Administration on nuclear arms control and national security.'... John Issacs, a council spokesman, said, 'as November '84 draws closer, President Reagan will be speaking off the cuff more and making more mistakes. We will issue CORRECTOGRAMS every day, if necessary.' The White House had no comment." James F. Clarity and Michael deCourcy Hinds Briefing Column, *NYTimes*, 9/2/83, p. 12.

COSSET

verb - to coddle, pamper, treat as a pet.

"In 1992, James Carville beat back the Star story about Gennifer Flowers, shaming reporters for piggybacking on a paper that paid sources and wrote, as he put it, about two-headed space aliens. The tabloids lost when Bill Clinton won. Most Americans put aside scandalous stories about his personal life, even if they rang true. But now, it seems, the tabloids have also won, driving the coverage in '96 and dragging the rest of us along on scoops about kinky consultants.... In an era when Dick Morris goes from hounded pervert to COSSETED author in a weekend, we can no longer use the rationale that scuzzy stories are newsworthy because they might scuttle a candidacy." Maureen Dowd, *NYTimes*, 9/22/96, p 13.

"Senate Vietnam vets, including Democrats like John Kerry, are boiling. Privately, some offer riffs like this: 'While McCain was getting tortured, Bush was flying jets defending Texas against Oklahoma, Trent Lott was doing jumping jacks for Old Miss, and John Engler was eating Dunkin' Donuts to make sure he was too overweight to be drafted.'

"It's unbelievable that as 2000 arrives we're again obsessing about Vietnam. The presence of an inspiring war hero in the presidential race has given other candidates, including those with a COSSETED berth in the war, the willies about how they stack up against him." Maureen Dowd, *NYTimes*, 11/21/99, p. 15.

COUCH POTATO

noun - a passive person, especially one glued to the television set; a telesot.

"'Recently a Baby Boomer from fat city who was considered mediagenic was shown to millions of COUCH POTATOES some of whom nearly experienced a cafe coronary....' The announcement was typed on the letterhead of The Alternative, a New York company of 'media-placed specialists.' It went on to reveal itself as a breezy account of the day Vice President George Bush introduced U.S. Senator Dan Quayle, his surprise choice for GOP running mate, to an astonished daytime television audience." Clarence Petersen, *Chicago Trib.*, 11/7/88, S 5, p. 1.

"Then came the Neil Bush story. Like all these stories, it was complicated. But it had two arresting elements. [President George Bush's] son was one. The other was a loan of $100,000 somebody had made to the president's son. What caught the eye about this loan was that it didn't have to be repaid. The dimmest COUCH POTATO could understand this [aspect of the savings and loan scandal]." Russell Baker, *Chicago Trib.*, 7/17/90, S 1, p. 13.

"'We've got an excuse - I do - for being a COUCH POTATO at the Super Bowl,' [President] Clinton told the party leaders. 'I'm not good enough to play - or young enough, or strong enough. But we're all good enough to play in citizenship.'" Todd S. Purdum, *NYTimes*, 1/23/95, p. A8.

COUNTRY CLUB REPUBLICAN (SL)

noun - a Republican who is a member of the social elite and concerned about proprieties.

"Former Texas Agriculture Commissioner Jim Hightower, a populist Democrat who has few kind words for Bush, does not believe Bush will wear well in a presidential campaign's harsh light.

"'He has been anointed by the entire Republican Establishment and the media has basically gone along with it,' said Hightower, an Austin-based author and radio talk show host. 'The truth is that despite the facade of the "COMPASSIONATE CONSERVATIVE," he's just another crony capitalist.'

"'I think he's a nice guy,' Hightower said. 'I think it's true he's not a Newt Gingrich practitioner of hate politics. He is something of a COUNTRY-CLUB REPUBLICAN in terms of his social sensibilities. But if the question is what would the average American get out of a Bush presidency, the answer is zero.'" Michael Tackett, *Chicago Trib.*, 5/24/99, S 1, p. 16.

"[George W.] Bush's second masterstroke has been to straddle the divide between the Christian right and the economic conservatives in the Republican Party, and that is a doozy of a split. In Texas, the Republican Party is owned by the Christian right: the party chair, the vice chairs, and everybody on down. When they won in 1994 they kicked out all the old-guard Texas Republicans, those in the school of George Bush the Elder - somewhat patrician, WASP, faintly elitist or Eastern. On the Christian right, such folks are known sneeringly as 'COUNTRY CLUB REPUBLICANS.' Republicans don't like to talk about class, but there's clearly a class subtext to their internal fights. Molly Ivins and Lou Dubose, <u>Shrub, The Short but Happy Political Life of George W. Bush</u>, Random House, 2000, Introduction, p. XV.

CROESUS

noun - a very rich person.

"His [Ross Perot's] outsider imitation, CROESUS by way of Andy of Mayberry, seems marred not a whit by the fact that he has known every President since L.B.J." Anna Quindlen, *NYTimes*, 6/3/92, p. A15.

CURMUDGEON

noun - an ill-tempered man.

Brian Basset

"And now he [Senator Jesse Helms] is telling his Commander in Chief [President Clinton] to wear a bulletproof vest when he visits North Carolina. The difference is that he is no longer just another oddball CURMUDGEON whose outbursts are ignored. People listen to the chairman of the Foreign Relations Committee. The Republicans have a duty to see that the chairman is someone who deserves an audience." Editorial, *NYTimes*, 11/23/94, p. A14.

"There's a 'Grand Bargain' just waiting to be struck that could finally reshape America's foreign-policy apparatus, pay off the U.S.'s overdue bills to the U.N. and pave the way for Senate ratification of a global treaty that will ban chemical weapons. We're talking about a big, big deal, and it's just sitting there, ready to be had. All it needs is for three leaders to show leadership: Commander in Chief Bill Clinton, CURMUDGEON in Chief Jesse Helms and Republican in Chief Trent (Don't-Ask-Me-To-Do-Anything-Too-Hard) Lott." Thomas L. Friedman, *NYTimes*, 3/27/97, p. A23.

CUSP

noun - a point of transition, turning point, leading edge.

"After flattening parts of Florida, Hurricane Andrew has crashed into Washington, taking dead aim at George Bush's effort to portray himself as a decisive, domestic policy President at the very CUSP of his fall campaign." Michael Wines, *NYTimes*, 8/29/92, p. A7.

"With Hillary Clinton pondering a New York Senate run and with Elizabeth Dole on the CUSP of a Presidential run, there is a heady sense of dutiful political wives on the lam." Maureen Dowd, *NYTimes*, 2/17/99, p. A17.

CUTUP

noun - a clown or boisterous person.

"For [Vice President] Gore, the appearance on 'Late Show with David Letterman' last fall was more than simply a matter of promoting the National Performance Review, his blueprint for streamlining the Government, in an alternative forum or of trying to recast his image in 60 seconds from that of robot to CUTUP. That night, the Vice President became the most visible example of a bewildering trend in American politics when he volunteered to play a figure of fun, even of the absurd, in pursuit of popularity." Jennifer Senior, *NYTimes*, 3/7/94, p. B1.

"The word on Mr. [George W.] Bush, a graduate of Yale and the Harvard Business School, is that he is a CUTUP who lacks the intellectual heft to be president. But why doesn't anyone ever mention that Mr. McCain ranked fifth from last in the Class of 1958 at the United States Naval Academy? Or that, like Mr. Bush, he was known for preferring carousing over cramming?" Richard L. Berke, *NYTimes*, 11/28/99, S 4, p. 1.

DDD

DEEP-SIX (Sl)

verb - to discard or throw away. *noun* - place of disposal.

Note:This term became well known during the Watergate period because of the inclusion in the Nixon tapes of references to DEEP-SIXING documents that might be embarrassing or incriminating if made public. Apparently derived from the naval slang for "burial at sea."

"The President [Reagan] may yet have to acknowledge that the likeliest basing mode for the MX missile will be the DEEP SIX." Alistair Cooke, *New Yorker*, 3/14/83, p. 156.

DÉJA VU (Fr)

noun - lit., already seen; the perception that an experience is being repeated.

"I have been dismayed, as the nuclear debate intensifies, to hear politicians, bureaucrats and military men talking in exactly these terms, and looking chipper as they do. Such comments gave me a nagging sense of DÉJA VU: Where had I heard that sort of thing before? It was 19 years ago, at a press luncheon. Lyndon B. Johnson's people were telling us we were not going to lose the Vietnam War." Caryl Rivers, *NYTimes*, 2/2/84, p. 27.

"Mr. Bush vowed in the election campaign to master the deficit without raising taxes, a fiscal formula that he derided in 1980 as 'voodoo economics' when Ronald Reagan proposed it. As one Democrat on the House Budget Committee put it, "The Bush plan will be DÉJA voodoo.'" Susan Rasky, *NYTimes*, 1/9/89, p. 11.

DÉMARCHE (Fr)

noun - a political or diplomatic initiative or maneuver.

"Any member of the Security Council has a right to oppose the re-election of a Secretary General, as the United States belatedly decided to do earlier this year. But had the Clinton Administration showed political savvy, it would have consulted with other members of the Security Council, certainly the four other permanent members, rather than leaking its unilateral DÉMARCHE to the press." William Shawcross, *NYTimes*, 12/3/96, p. A15.

DENOUEMENT (Fr)

noun - the final outcome of a literary or dramatic work or of a complex situation.

"As the House amply demonstrated, bringing the Clinton case to a fair DENOUEMENT is exceedingly difficult in the politically supercharged atmosphere of Washington. The Senate should have a better chance of success for several reasons, including the wise constitutional arithmetic that requires

67 votes to convict Mr. Clinton and evict him from office." Editorial, *NYTimes*, 12/21/98, p. A30.

"The sad resignation of Speaker-designate Robert Livingston over Hustler magazine's revelations about his sexual life will play less of a role than either party expects in the DENOUEMENT of the Clinton case. Republican arguments that Livingston's resignation stands as a model for Clinton are undercut by reports that the Louisiana Republican was pushed to quit by a group of his colleagues, at least 18 of whom expressed second thoughts about his leadership. On the other hand, no Republican will be convinced by the Democrats' use of Livingston's troubles as an example of the 'politics of personal destruction.' For Republicans opposed to Clinton, the president's alleged crimes and Livingston's PECCADILLOS are not remotely comparable." E.J. Dionne Jr., *Chicago Trib.*, 12/22/98, S 1, p. 31.

DE RIGUEUR (FR)

adjective - necessary, proper, required by custom.

"Two factors are at work here. One is that the comments were made by [Vice President Dan] Quayle. It has become DE RIGUEUR for even serious analysts to snicker and ridicule in response to his utterances, whatever their import." Editorial, *Chicago Trib.*, 5/28/92, S 1, p. 24.

"During Theodore Roosevelt's Harvard days it was also DE RIGUEUR to earn nothing higher than the 'gentleman's C.' Still, the future president could not restrain himself. TR not only ran to classes when his more elegant classmates ambled, he also leaped to his feet to shout questions at professors, until one shouted back, 'See here, Roosevelt, let me talk. *I'm* running this course.'" Carol Felsenthal, Alice Roosevelt Longworth, G.P. Putnam's Sons, 1988, p. 15.

"Our aspiring chief executives are falling over themselves to be holier than thou, not to mention each other, as they ostentatiously declare their devotion to Jesus. We have come to expect such uplift from religious conservatives, but now it's DE RIGUEUR across the ideological spectrum, with moderates and liberals offering up a strange new brew that might be called Religious Right lite. Witness the pilgrim's progress of Al Gore. Though he has talked and written about his faith in the past - as have all his rivals - he has pumped up the volume big time as he seeks the Presidency. In late May he summoned reporters on the religion beat to break the news that he believes 'the purpose of life is to glorify God.'" Frank Rich, *NYTimes*, 9/11/99, p. A25.

DÉTENTE (FR)

noun - an easing of relations.

"Meanwhile Mr. Buchanan appeared to be heading toward a DÉTENTE with Lenora Fulani, a leader in the New York Reform (independence) Party who was once an ally of Louis Farrakhan...Mr. Buchanan has been courting Ms. Fulani because she controls a number of votes in the Reform Party. And

Ms. Fulani, who once withdrew her support from Al Sharpton. because she felt he was getting too mainstream, is sounding very enthusiastic about Mr. Buchanan. 'To go from Al Sharpton to Pat Buchanan would make a dead person suspicious' said Reverend Sharpton yesterday." Gail Collins, *NYTimes*, 9/21/99, p. A3

DETRITUS

noun - discarded material, debris.

"The Gore campaign has been sifting through the DETRITUS of the elder Mr. Bush's steamrollering of Gov. Michael Dukakis of Massachusetts and has unearthed useful lessons. Those lessons, for an incumbent vice president defending a relatively popular administration against a sitting governor, are becoming increasingly evident. The basic thrust: try to hamstring the opponent by raising questions about his record and his readiness to be president." Katharine Q. Seelye, *NYTimes*, 5/1/00, p. A18.

DEUS EX MACHINA (L)

noun - literally, a god from a machine; a person or thing that provides a contrived solution to a difficult or insoluble problem.

"The greatest myth of political innocence in our time is simply stated: the problems of contemporary politics and society are essentially a simple matter of process, and a purified process will yield good public policy. Hence a gimmick like public funding of campaigns or term limits becomes a DEUS EX MACHINA - a magic key to resolve the conflicts of values and interests inherent in our democracy." Eugene J. McCarthy, No Fault Politics: Modern Presidents, the Press, and Reformers, Random House, 1998, p. 7.

DICEY

adjective - risky.

"Bush dislikes the single moderator format and wants a panel of journalists to ask questions and chew up the clock. He is reluctant to give Clinton a forum that might lift his rival to the level of the presidency, and he worries that in the absence of a foursome of journalists, the president might have to raise all those DICEY questions about draft-dodging and marital infidelity." Steve Daley, *Chicago Trib.*, 9/27/92, S 4, p. 4.

"A Wall Street Journal/NBC News survey last week gave Clinton a job approval rating of 60 percent, while similar polls by *NYTimes*/CBS News and USA Today/CNN found that 54 percent of those asked approved of the performance. That's a slightly higher grade than Ronald Reagan earned at the end of his first year, and a little better than the public assessment of Jimmy Carter's first 12 months.... All of which demonstrates that snapshot surveys at any point in a president's tenure provide DICEY and uncertain analysis." Steve Daley, *Chicago Trib.*, 1/23/94, S 4, p. 5.

"Penetrating the mood of the President's [sic] and his inner circle is DICEY in the best of times, since the White House is at once a huge public stage and a place of deep secrets, as the Monica Lewinsky affair [with President Clinton] itself shows. Now more than ever, insiders keep their own counsel and outsiders are reduced to studying shadows and preferred peeks past the veil." Todd S. Purdum, *NYTimes*, 9/21/98, p. A16.

DICHOTOMY

noun - a division into two parts, classes or groups, especially two mutually exclusive groups.

"The President [Ronald Reagan], trying to drum up support for keeping the Pentagon budget intact, sought to present a DICHOTOMY between those [like himself] who favor a strong national defense and ... whom?" William Raspberry, *Chicago Trib.*, 3/7/86, S 1, p. 27.

"And that brings us back to the Dr. Jekyll and Mr. Hyde DICHOTOMY of George Bush as seen last Monday. That morning he was the epitome of a bland, noncontroversial, incumbent-like and mistake-proof campaigner as he worked the mountainous north country of New Hampshire." Thomas Hardy, *Chicago Trib.*, 1/31/88, S 4, p. 3.

"In his talk Tuesday [President] Clinton noted recent polls, which he said show that support for his [health care] plan rises as the details are explained and understood. He called this 'an interesting DICHOTOMY' and said it shows that 'in a funny way, the debate is only beginning.'" William Neikirk, *Chicago Trib.*, 4/6/94, S 1, p. 10.

"Jefferson showed a flair for, and an intuitive attraction toward, a narrative structure built around moralistic DICHOTOMIES. The empire 'then and now' set the theme. The story became a clash between British tyranny and colonial liberty, scheming British officials and supplicating colonists, all culminating in the clash at Lexington and Concord between General Thomas Gage's 'ministerial army' and 'the unsuspecting inhabitants' of Massachusetts." Joseph J. Ellis, <u>American Sphinx</u>, Knopf, 1997, p. 41.

DICTUM

noun - an authoritative statement or pronouncement.

"She sat in a booth and stared down at the sundae, teetering at the precipice of improvisation, perhaps recalling Jackie O's DICTUM: Never chew in camera range. 'Y'all are just waiting for this,' she smilingly accused the photographers. 'They can't wait. Here you go. Are ye-e-e-e-w ready?'

As she took dainty bites, a reporter asked her position on Diary Queen vs. Tastee Freeze. 'Anything sweet,' replied the woman whose sweet-talking Washington ways earned her the nickname 'Sugar Lips.'" Maureen Dowd, *NYTimes*, 5/5/99, p. A31.

"If anything is a truism in American politics, it is that people do not care about income inequality. And as most such truisms eventually are, this one may be about to be contradicted. The 1990's will be remembered as a time of Reaganism without Reagan. In an ironic confirmation of the conservative DICTUM that most consequences are unplanned, President Reagan's deliberate attempts to redistribute wealth to the rich now appear puny compared with what stock options and C.E.O. compensation have done under President Clinton." Alan Wolfe, *NYTimes*, 9/22/99, p. A27.

DISCOMBOBULATE

verb - confuse.

"'Even after his [Richard Nixon's] last maudlin and, in my opinion, stupid speech to his staff - why everyone was crying I never understood because it was so fragmented, so DISCOMBOBULATED - he walked to the South Lawn and gave this almost enthusiastic wave. It was so uncongruous, like he was going on another trip. That's what was so strange about him.'" Bernard Weinraub (quoting Alexander Butterfield), *NYTimes*, 5/30/95, p. B2.

DISINFORMATION

noun - false information which is disseminated purposely to deceive.

"He [President Reagan] has been embarrassed and his credibility damaged in recent weeks by the swap of journalist Nick Daniloff for a Soviet spy, the White House-engineered 'DISINFORMATION' campaign against Libya, the Hasenfus case - which indicated White House involvement in weapons deliveries to the Contras in Nicaragua - and his obvious confusion in the arms negotiations with Mikhail Gorbachev at the Reykjavik summit." Editorial, *Chicago Trib.*, 11/19/86, S 1, p. 20.

"I mean, consider Bud McFarlane, Reagan's national security adviser, who flew to Tehran with a chocolate cake, two .357 pistols, a suicide pill and a fake Irish passport. Remember how Bill Casey loved cloak-and-dagger nuttiness, 'DISINFORMATION' plots, mining Nicaragua's harbors. I can't discount any DOTTINESS from an administration that begat Iranscam and Ollie North." Sandy Grady, *Chicago Trib.*, 5/3/91, S 1, p. 23.

"The president is for it, if tepidly. Most Republicans in the House and Senate support it. Forty out of 50 governors want it (and the rest wouldn't respond one way or the other). But NAFTA, the North American Free Trade Agreement, is in trouble. ...And, of course, on the sidelines, with money to burn, is Mr. 'Giant Sucking Sound' himself, Ross Perot, ready to spread DISINFORMATION around the landscape." Mona Charen, *Chicago Trib.*, 9/1/93, S 1, p. 21.

DISINGENUOUS

adjective - lacking in candor.

Note: Adlai E. Stevenson, the Democratic presidential candidate in 1952 and 1956, set such a high standard of literacy and eloquence in his campaign speeches that he was accused by some critics of "talking over the heads" of the American people. When Stevenson was asked to comment on this criticism, his son, Adlai E. Stevenson III, told the author that his father replied "That's DISINGENUOUS."

"'He [Ross Perot] says the only reason he will come back is because of the issues, but if that is really his motive, why did he forsake the opportunity to fight for that all summer?'" Lifflander said. 'He started spending more money than when he was a candidate. It's DISINGENUOUS. He controls the grass-roots effort. He is the master puppeteer pulling the strings.'" Charles M. Madigan, *Chicago Trib.*, 9/30/92, S 1, p. 4.

"The Zoe Baird affair gave Mr. Inman [nominated by President Clinton for Secretary of Defense] plenty of time to put his books in order. The White House's explanation for his delay is DISINGENUOUS. It says Mr. Inman did not pay his back taxes because he was waiting to see if legislation pending in Congress would relax the $50 per quarter standard, substantially raising the threshold for taxable earnings." Editorial, *NYTimes*, 12/22/93, p. A12.

"Matalin's apology was DISINGENUOUS to its core. She was about as contrite as Hillary Clinton was when she apologized in April for bringing up persistent rumors that Bush had an extramarital affair. Despite Matalin's apology, the Bush campaign got what it wanted: a rehash of Clinton's rumored affairs on the front page of just about every newspaper in the country. Despite Hillary Clinton's apology, her husband's campaign got what it wanted: press attention to the unsubstantiated rumors of PHILANDERING by Bush." Editorial, *Chicago Trib.*, 8/5/92, S 1, p. 14.

"If [Newt Gingrich's] partisanship often can turn ugly as well, at least those of us he smears as abnormal 'McGovern-niks' know the McCarthyite side he's on. Noxious Newt may be a hypocritical moralist - witness his Clintonesque marital, draft and PAC-money histories - but he is incapable of the DISINGENUOUSNESS of Tricky Dick." Frank Rich, *NYTimes*, 11/17/94, p. A19.

"Platforms are supposed to be solemn, sincere public declarations of party principles and intentions. In fact, they are more often, in our times, DISINGENUOUS appeals to as many interests as possible to catch as many votes as possible. The people know this, by and large, and the result has been, it seems to, me, that platforms per se not only attract fewer and fewer votes, but have come to mean less and less to more and more, candidates included." Adlai Stevenson, <u>Major Campaign Speeches of Adlai E. Stevenson</u>, Random House, 1953.

DISTAFF

adjective - female, maternal.

"[Former chief of staff] Regan described Nancy Reagan as presiding over a 'shadowy DISTAFF presidency' and using 'adroit guerilla actions' to achieve goals in 'a genuine belief that she was the best judge of her husband's interests.'" News Story, *Chicago Trib.*, 5/9/88, S 1, p. 2.

DOG DAYS

noun - (1) the hottest part of the summer from early July to early September, (2) period of stagnation or inactivity.

"Ferraro appears to have thrown enough bones to the pack of media hounds baying after her financial disclosures to have survived the attack. This in itself is a rare political phenomenon, especially remarkable in the DOG DAYS of August when the media have little else meaty to chew on. Compare her hang-tough press conference performance to Richard Nixon's 'Checkers' speech when he was a vice presidential candidate and she makes Nixon look positively WIMPISH." Joan Beck, *Chicago Trib.*, 8/27/84, S 1, p. 12.

DOLLOP

noun - a blob, hunk or lump of some substance.

"Ordinarily, a comic strip is the last place you'd expect to find anything instructive about a political campaign. But Garry Trudeau, the fierce satirist who draws 'Doonesbury,' has injected a DOLLOP of harsh truth into his examination of the New Bush. He has invented an evil twin, Skippy, who, like Trudeau's Bush, is invisible and wrapped in an American flag, to explain behavior that puzzles reporters who knew the Vice President as 'such a nice, decent fellow.'" Editorial, *Chicago Trib.*, 9/28/88, S 1, p. 22.

"The Clintons' style of damage control has certain HALLMARKS that have been on clear display since the 1992 campaign. Phase one involves expressions of anger from President and Mrs. Clinton. Mr. Clinton's unseemly outburst at NBC correspondent Jim Miklaszewski in Prague was a classic example of his calibrated tantrums. The anger is usually followed by DOLLOPS of self-pity. The implied message is this: 'Why are you asking me these petty questions when I am working so hard to improve the world?'" Editorial, *NYTimes*, 1/18/94, p. A22.

DOMINATRIX

noun - a female who dominates.

"But perhaps the image that best links female power and primal fear is the cover of *Spy* magazine, which features Hillary Clinton's head pasted onto the zaftig body of a leather-clad DOMINATRIX holding a whip, with the cover line 'What Hillary Problem?' The message is not exactly a new one; that power in the hands of women is a thing of dread. Whether it's Medusa and her coiffure of snakes turning men to stone with a glance, the Sirens luring sailors to death on the rocks or Delilah seducing Sampson - powerful women are seen as ICONS of malevolence." Caryl Rivers, *Chicago Trib.*, 3/4/93, S 1, p. 29.

DONNYBROOK

noun - a riotous brawl, a rowdy free-for-all.

"Jackson is expected to continue campaigning. But even he has been speaking in more conciliatory tones lately. In an interview with the editorial board of the *Washington Post* on Tuesday he called for meetings among the three Democratic contenders to work out differences among them in order to avoid a 'DONNYBROOK' at the party's convention in July." Jon Margolis, *Chicago Trib.*, 5/3/84, S 1, p. 5.

"The cheering, whistling, foot-stomping audience seemed eager for a DONNYBROOK and Mr. Bush, who wrapped up the Republican Presidential nomination in March, pleased them when he berated his Democratic opponent as 'an articulate defender of a flawed world view.'" Maureen Dowd, *NYTimes*, 6/10/88, p. 11.

"But as [President George] Bush is realizing in the political DONNYBROOK about his new tolerance of tax increases, retail doesn't work indefinitely for presidents. The presidency is truly a "wholesale" office. Where the retail politician seeks to win 'customers' one by one, the wholesale politician seeks 'markets' by appealing to constituencies." Mark Shields, *Chicago Trib.*, 7/5/90, S 1, p. 19.

"Democrats are starting to voice concerns that they could suffer if either they or President [Clinton] are perceived as drawing out the impeachment proceedings into a long public spectacle featuring a parade of witnesses from Mr. Starr to Ms. Lewinsky. Representative Maxine Waters, Democrat of California, said 'Everybody is going to have to do the best job that can be done to keep this from being a DONNYBROOK that's unacceptable to the public.'" Alison Mitchell, *NYTimes*, 10/21/98, p. A22.

DOO-DOO

noun - excrement.

"Read my lips, I will bet you $5,000 that George Bush is feeding us a line of DOO-DOO, to use one of his favorite macho words. 'Be careful. I will not tolerate any insults directed at our Pollster-Designated Commander in Chief.' Don't change the subject. Are you a betting man or aren't you? 'You haven't even said what we will be betting on.' All right. Read my lips. I bet you five Big Ones that if George Bush becomes president, our taxes will go up." Mike Royko, *Chicago Trib.*, 11/3/88, S 1, p. 3.

"Asked why his followers had failed to show up for a straw poll in Iowa, [George] Bush said they must have been at debutante parties; asked what he would do about South Africa, he said he would call a 'confab'; seeking to describe someone in trouble, he spoke of his being in 'deep DOO-DOO.'" R. W. Apple, Jr., *NYTimes*, 8/18/88, p. 14.

"Sir George [Bush], now that your administration is underway, can you tell us your real policy on new taxes - Hey! Read my clips! How many times do I have to tell you guys - no new taxes! Contrary to what all the doom-sayers are putting out, there are no tough decisions to make! We won't have to cut defense or entitlements or raise taxes! Why? Growth! I believe the country will grow and grow and grow and grow its way out of all its problems! - What do we call this? Voodoo DOO-DOO! Yes, but kinder, gentler DOO-DOO!" Garry Trudeau, Donnesbury, *Chicago Trib.*, Comic Section, 1/1/89.

"Molly Ivins, a *Dallas Times Herald* columnist [said that, in reference to George Bush] 'no real Texan has ever described trouble as "DEEP DOO-DOO."'" Leah Lorber, *Albuquerque Journal*, 12/9/90.

DOOFUS (SL)

noun - a clumsy, silly, ridiculous person. cf. DORK.

"Much of this book is about how the country came to elect Bill Clinton in 1992, thus costing me twenty-five years' worth of eyewitness reporting on what a total DOOFUS George Bush can be. Damn, I miss him." Molly Ivins, Nothin' But Good Times Ahead, Vintage Books, 1993, p. 1.

"Please acquit me of partisan political vengeance: I was among those who thought Richard Nixon, whom I loathed as one of the few figures of real evil I ever saw in American politics, should have been pardoned. Both Reagan and Bush are, by comparison, merely amiable DOOFUSES." Molly Ivins, Nothin' But Good Times Ahead, Vintage Books, 1993, p. 191.

"The facts outlined in the Cox Committee report released last week on spying at national weapons' labs, he [Mike Malloy] says, 'stand in juxtaposition to Texas Gov. George W. Bush's strong criticism of [President] Clinton. . . . The boy Bush said 'There's only one administration that has been given the news about Chinese espionage at weapons labs. And that's the Clinton administration. The interesting question is, when did they know?'

"The host, Mike Malloy, improvising this monologue between callers, pauses for two seconds. 'Well, Dubbya,' he says, slipping into cowboy. 'They knew when your pappy was running the CIA, and then was vice president for eight years and then president for four. That's when they knew.' Another short pause: 'DOOFUS.'

"Oh, I know. Not nice to call names. Lowers the tone of civic discourse. But, well. Given the right-wing invective regularly broadcast at Clinton ('degenerate traitor,' is the least of it) and liberals in general ('degenerate traitors'), it's bracing to hear a little pointed mockery from the other side." Eric Zorn, *Chicago Trib.*, 6/1/99, S 2, p. 1.

DOPPELGÄNGER (GER)

noun - a lookalike or double.

"Much has been written about the President's dual - and dueling - personalities. The good Bill who promotes solid American values like V-chips and targeting deadbeat dads, and the bad Bill who cavorts with interns and lies about it. Saturday Night Bill and Sunday Morning Clinton, as Saturday Night

Dick Morris puts it. But now the DICHOTOMY has reached an absurd level with Impeachment Bill and State of the Union Clinton. The President and his DOPPELGÄNGER were side by side in Congress yesterday, but did not acknowledge each other's existence." Maureen Dowd, *NYTimes*, 1/20/99, p. A31.

"As Alessandra Stanley wrote in *The Times* in January 1998, the two [Hillary Rodham Clinton and Rudolph Guiliani] are opposite sex DOPPLEGÄNGERS. They are both accomplished, brainy lawyers, devoted parents, religious, relentless and, when they wish to be, charming." Maureen Dowd, *NYTimes*, 6/13/99, p. 17.

"How could such a man - the protagonist of such a gaudy, tumultuous, outsized life - turn out to have nothing inside? This was the question that drove Edmund Morris around the bend, where he collided with a writer's block of terrifying proportions. His stratagem for resuscitating himself and his book, as the world knows, was the creation of a DOPPLEGÄNGER. 'Edmund Morris' was born in Chicago, in 1912 (a year after the birth of Ronald Reagan); went to school in Canterbury, England, and summered in the vicinity of Dixon, Illinois (where Dutch Reagan went to high school and summered as a lifeguard); and attended Eureka College, in Eureka, Illinois (as a member of Reagan's class)." Hendrik Hertzberg, *New Yorker*, 10/11/99, p. 99.

"In Chapter 7 of his instantly notorious biography of Ronald Reagan, 'Dutch,' Edmund Morris does something infuriating. He proves he can write. The chapter, an insightful exploration of Reagan's early essays, short stories and handwriting, is blessedly free of the fictional DOPPLEGÄNGER that Morris uses to narrate the rest of this disorienting book." Carolyn Alessio, *Chicago Trib.*, 10/3/99, S 2, p. 1.

DORK (OM) (SL)

noun - a stupid, ridiculous person.

Note:The etymology may be a portmanteau or blend word combining dolt and jerk. See TWIT.

"Some have interpreted his stump [George Bush's] performance as evidence that he needs to stop taking Halcion because he's WIGGING out, but as a veteran Bush-watcher I can assure all hands that what we have here is merely George in his excess-of-exuberance mode. That's the one that frequently causes people to conclude that the man's a DORK, whereas he sees himself as simply being spirited and amiable." Molly Ivins, <u>Nothin' But Good Times Ahead</u>, Vintage Books, 1993, p. 53.

"BUSHSPEAK, the thing thing, that gloriously daffy streak he has - 'Read my lips,' 'ninety/ninety hindsight,' 'the manhood thing.' Lord, but I would miss that goofy, preppy, golden-retriever-like part of his personality, those moments of transcendent DORKINESS when we all stand there trying to believe he's just said what he did." Molly Ivins, <u>Nothin' But Good Times Ahead</u>, Vintage Books, 1993, p. 163.

"[Eddie Mahe, then deputy chairman of the Republican National Committee] well remembers the summer afternoon in the mid-70's when he first met the young politician. Hot sun was pouring through his office window; Newt [Gingrich] was dressed in sky-blue polyester pants and a madras jacket. 'How did this DORK get in here?' Mahe thought. Then the visitor began to speak: the unknown renegade sweating it out in polyester impressed the seasoned campaign strategist with a shrewd, concise ('Three points - boom, boom, boom') assessment of his Democratic foe in Georgia. Mahe saw a very live wire - and began to spread the word." Gail Sheehy, *Vanity Fair*, 9/95, p. 218.

"…writing in *Time*, Calvin Trillin memorably likened [Steve Forbes'] appearances to a comedy-club sketch of a 'DORK robot.' Forbes's opponents, meanwhile, mostly ignored him, perhaps assuming that his candidacy [in 1996] would sink under the weight of its own preposterousness." Elizabeth Kolbert, *New Yorker*, 11/8/99, p. 51.

DOTTY

adjective - crazy, eccentric, absurd.

"There's no evidence that Nancy Reagan's occasional interference in her husband's schedule, staff, or public presentation was ever anything more than protectiveness or perhaps over protectiveness. That [Ronald Reagan] was slightly DOTTY by the end of his second term was clear to everyone, and her fierce desire to protect him from demands beyond his fading abilities can only be considered commendable in human terms." Molly Ivins, <u>Molly Ivins Can't Say That, Can She?</u>, Random House, 1991, p. 108.

"WHY AREN'T YOU OUT THERE SAYING A LOT OF NEAT STUFF ABOUT PREMARITAL SEX AND ABORTION AND POT AND WOMEN'S RIGHTS . . . ?"

Pat Oliphant

"Indeed, his problem is less formidable than that faced by George Bush. In 1988, he had to offer himself as a substitute for the American family's revered, if somewhat DOTTY father figure [Ronald Reagan]. Mr. Gore has only to supplant the overindulged naughty brother." Editorial, *NYTimes*, 3/21/99, p. 14.

DOYENNE

noun - female senior member of a group.

"[Pamela] Harriman, the 73-year-old widow of Gov. Averell Harriman of New York, is the DOYENNE of Democratic politics and a leading fund-raiser and donor. It was to Mrs. Harriman's elegant Georgetown house, with its Van Goughs and Picassos, that the Clintons journeyed for their first gala dinner after arriving in the capital." Karen De Witt, *NYTimes*, 3/24/93, p. A8.

"Depending on whether you like the guy [Bill Clinton] or not, his trip to Washington, in which he mingled with small-business owners on Georgia Avenue and dined with the Democratic DOYENNE Pamela Harriman, could be seen as pluralism or packaging." Anna Quindlen, *Chicago Trib.*, 12/1/92, S 1, p. 23.

DRACONIAN

adjective - severe, cruel, harsh.
Note:From Draco, the seventh century B.C. Athenian lawgiver who recommended the death penalty for almost every offense.

"Mr. Clinton showed no desire to return to the health care issue in 1995 and fought Republican proposals to make sweeping changes in Medicare and Medicaid, the Federal programs for 70 million people who are elderly or poor, calling them DRACONIAN." James Bennet and Robert Pear, *NYTimes*, 12/8/97, p. A14.

"Nor do swing voters have to worry that Mr. McCain will owe Pat Robertson or Jerry Falwell a say in public policy or that he'll be policing anyone's sex life. (Indeed Mr. McCain has readily owned up to the tomcatting in his own past.) The Arizona senator has thrown in just enough pro-choice rhetoric to beguile voters for whom abortion is a secondary issue into believing that he's not DRACONIAN on Roe - and, taking the bait, the National Right To Life Committee is running commercials attacking him." Frank Rich, *NYTimes*, 2/12/00, p. A 29.

"Mr. Bush's tormentors have tried to dress up the propriety of the cocaine question ex post facto by linking it to his hypocrisy on public policy. As Governor, he has signed on to DRACONIAN laws in Texas that promote jail for first-time drug offenders caught in possession of minuscule amounts (though jail rarely befalls those of Mr. Bush's station, who can afford the right lawyers)." Frank Rich, *NYTimes*, 8/28/99, p. A25.

DROIT DU SEIGNEUR (FR)

noun - literally, right of the lord; the supposed right of the lord of the manor in feudal times to have sexual relations with a vassal's bride on the wedding night. While *Brewer's Dictionary* states that this custom may have existed to a limited extent in mediaeval Europe, it was more often the excuse for levying dues in lieu, i.e. extortion.

"Against this backdrop, Paula Jones sued Bill Clinton for sexual harassment. When the Supreme Court let her case go ahead while he was still in the Oval Office, a certain panic set in. The rules of power no longer out-ranked the rules of law. She mattered as much as he did. DROIT DU SEIGNEUR is dead. Women are citizens." Catharine A. MacKinnon, *NYTimes*, 3/5/98, p. A25.

"In Britain, where political sex scandals are the daily bread of tabloids and respectable newspapers alike, there was gleeful frontpage coverage of the most sordid details about Mr. Clinton's alleged relationship with Monica S. Lewinsky, leavened with wordy condescension on editorial pages. 'That 'DROIT DE [sic] SEIGNEUR' White House tradition of serial infidelity, as established by John Kennedy and Lyndon Johnson, may be as gross as it is foolish,' said an editorial in The Guardian, invoking the sexual imperative of feudal lords. 'But it is not yet the stuff of impeachment.'" Alessandra Stanley, *NYTimes*, 1/24/98, p. A11.

"Next, accept that impeachment cannot succeed solely for lying under oath about sex. We had an election about that and Clinton won. Even if Kathleen Wiley could produce DNA evidence of harassment, Clinton has established his DROIT DU SEIGNEUR and most voters think lying about it to a grand jury is no high crime." William Safire, *NYTimes*, 11/23/98, p. A23.

DUDGEON

noun - aggrieved or angered feeling; ill humor; resentment; commonly combined with high - "HIGH DUDGEON."

"Just as in the instance of DUDGEON - there is a plain 'DUDGEON' and there is 'HIGH DUDGEON' - so there is a distinction between a 'CANARD' and a 'base CANARD.' Currently, in the case of the Theodore Roosevelt Association, it is a matter of HIGH DUDGEON about what it holds to be a base CANARD started last May both by CBS News and by *People* magazine alleging that the 26th President of the United States, like the current occupants of the White House, sought guidance from astrology." David Binder, Steven V. Roberts, *NYTimes*, 8/3/88, p. 10.

"Every new President likes to make his own mistakes in dealing with the White House press, and Bill Clinton is obviously no exception. So he has let two months pass without holding a formal news conference. Wise politics for any President? Maybe, but it also edges the press toward DUDGEON." Russell Baker, *NYTimes*, 3/20/93, p. 15.

"In a series of speeches Brezhnev had made clear that the Kremlin was in HIGH DUDGEON over Carter's human rights policy." Strobe Talbott, Endgame, Harper & Row, 1979, p. 64.

"Let us stipulate that Newt Gingrich was not always a perfect husband. Neither were Bill Clinton, Ted Kennedy and Bob Dole. Neither, continuing in the bipartisan mode, were Franklin Roosevelt and Warren Harding. For all we know, neither were Abraham Lincoln and George Washington. Everyone who has always been a perfect spouse may now rise up in HIGH DUDGEON. Both of you." Jon Margolis, *Chicago Trib.*, 11/28/94, S 1, p. 17.

"Will President Clinton be caught in a character onslaught, as promised by Bob Dole for this week's second Presidential debate? If so, the President could do worse, and surely better, than Franklin Delano Roosevelt did when he nipped back at relentless Republican character attacks, offering up his 'Fala' speech of hilarious belittlement. ('These Republican leaders have not been content with attacks on me, or on my wife or on my sons,' Roosevelt declared in mock HIGH DUDGEON, his patrician cadence impishly slowed. 'They now include my little dog Fala.')" Francis X. Clines, *NYTimes*, 10/13/96, p. 6.

DUMP (OM)

verb - to treat someone unfairly, to give someone a dirty job to do (lit., to shit on one).

"The second New Hampshire Democratic presidential candidates debate was nothing like the first, which took place at Dartmouth College a month ago. Then it was great sport to DUMP on front-runner Walter Mondale. Now it isn't." Mary McGrory, *Chicago Trib.*, 2/28/84, S 1, p. 11.

"Maureen Reagan, the President's eldest daughter, said Wednesday the 'vendetta' her brother Michael is conducting against First Lady Nancy Reagan has left the President and his wife 'just agonized.' 'He thinks he can keep DUMPING on us,' she said. 'Now we're fighting back.'" *Chicago Trib.*, 11/29/84, S 1, p. 9.

"'If Reagan wins a second term,' Mr. [Vernon] Jordan told 3,000 delegates to the Urban League's national convention here. 'I warn you: Don't be poor, don't be old, don't be Hispanic, don't be black. The only way to make sure Reagan doesn't have another four years to DUMP on us is to elect Walter Mondale.'" James Barron, *NYTimes*, 7/31/84, p. 7.

"'My frustration level is going up in terms of sitting around and listening to Michael Dukakis and Jesse Jackson DUMP all over me and the Administration. So I'm beginning to get a little more combative [said George Bush].'" Maureen Dowd, *NYTimes*, 5/28/88, p. 7.

"'He [Bush] ought to stand up and fight for his record instead of DUMPING on me. Let's talk about what we're going to do for the American people over the next four years. ... I was in East Lansing to face the music and face the people,' [said Bill Clinton]." Mitchell Locin and George E. Curry, *Chicago Trib.*, 9/24/92, S 1, p. 5.

DUSTUP

noun - quarrel, commotion, row, BROUHAHA.

"In a conjugal DUSTUP in a television interview, President-elect George Bush and his wife, Barbara, have exchanged gibes about her weight and his dancing." Maureen Dowd, *NYTimes*, 1/20/89, p. 8.

"Now that Governor Clinton has dumped Jesse Jackson, President Bush may have to dump Dan Quayle. This has nothing to do with the Vice President's inability to spell 'potato.' George Washington was a terrible speller too, but a pretty good president nevertheless. On the other hand, President Bush needs a gesture that will make millions see him as decisive and politically courageous. Mr. Clinton showed the way by dumping Mr. Jackson in the now famous DUST-UP about Sister Souljah." Russell Baker, *NYTimes*, 6/23/92, p. A15.

"White House and Republican National Committee officials remained steadfast in their portrayal of Perot as a dangerous character who cannot be entrusted with the presidency. They have devoted the early summer to 'DUSTING UP' Perot, in the parlance of one top Bush strategist, in the expectation of running the independent out of contention in the three-way race between Bush, Perot and Democrat Bill Clinton." Thomas Hardy, *Chicago Trib.*, 6/25/92, S 1, p. 4.

"In 1992 and again this year the Clinton campaign's response to Republican charges of SKULDUGGERY often has been to express surprise, then strike back even harder. Case in point: the latest DUST-UP over potentially improper gifts of 'soft money' by foreign citizens and companies to the Democratic Party." Michael Wines, *NYTimes*, 10/26/96.

"...the Republicans have reverted to old tactics in South Carolina, where the two leading presidential candidates have hedged their bets for the Feb. 19 primary by supporting the right of South Carolinians to fly the Confederate battle flag over the State Capitol, despite the flag's association with segregation and the Ku Klux Klan...In previous presidential campaigns, the flag issue in South Carolina came and went quickly with little fanfare or lasting impact. This year's DUST-UP brought a demonstration by civil rights activists that included nearly 50,000 people, followed by the threat of an economic boycott against the state. In a development that should shame both Mr. Bush and Mr. McCain, a group of former state legislators who were serving when the flag went up recanted the decision and urged the current legislature to bring it down." Brent Staples, *NYTimes*, 2/15/00, p. A30.

DWEEB (SL)

noun - a boring, conventional person.

"There is a curious duality in people's reactions to Bush. Some listen to him and dismiss him instantly as a 'preppy DWEEB.' Others hear him on a good day and come away saying, 'This guy has a lot of knowledge and a lot of experience. He is not a lightweight.'" Molly Ivins, <u>Molly Ivins Can't Say That,</u> <u>Can She?</u>, Random House, 1991, p. 119.

EEE

EBULLIENT

adjective - enthusiastic, exuberant. *noun* - EBULLIENCE

"...Mr. Beatty can't stop talking about politics, and while he has yet to endorse a candidate, he couldn't contain his EBULLIENCE about Mr. McCain, whom he regards as a friend. Yes, the Arizona senator (like the other candidates of both parties) is well to the right of Bulworth - even on his signature issue of campaign finance reform. But still, Mr. Beatty avows: 'John is a good man.'" Frank Rich, *NYTimes*, 2/12/00, p. A 29.

EGGHEAD

noun - an intellectual, a double-dome.

Note:This word for an intellectual became popular during the 1952 presidential campaign when Adlai Stevenson was called an EGGHEAD by his detractors who claimed that he "was talking over the heads of the people." See DISINGENUOUS.

"Now, you might ask: Who cares what some columnist says about Bush? And if you were talking about 99.9 percent of our capital's syndicated pundits, you'd be right. But George Will [who had called Bush a 'SMARMY lap dog'] is more than a columnist. He is the chief EGGHEAD of conservatism." Mike Royko, *Chicago Trib.*, 2/10/86, S 1, p. 3.

"Or was he [George Bush] trying to pretend he wasn't one of those snobby, EGGHEAD Ivy League types who shop at boutiques instead of the feed and grain store, that he was just a country boy who loved feeling the mud between his toes?" Russell Baker, *NYTimes*, 6/15/88, p. 29.

"In fact, most political leaders prefer oral briefings to reading at length for themselves, and at least one, Adlai E. Stevenson, was seriously wounded by being caricatured as an EGGHEAD. But in modern times, such interests put Mr. Clinton in the company of, say, Woodrow Wilson, Franklin D. Roosevelt, Harry S. Truman and John F. Kennedy." William H. Honan, *NYTimes*, 12/10/92, p. B1.

"Writing against [Adlai] Stevenson, Alsop said that the candidate seemed to have the support of all the EGGHEADS, but, he asked, how many EGGHEADS could there be in the country? 'EGGHEADS of the world unite - you have nothing to lose but your yokes,' joked Stevenson in response." Michael Bonesteel, *Wilmette Life*, 9/13/90, p. D2.

"I think one of the greatest compliments that ever befell me was by the man who introduced me as a 'practical idealist', sort of a hard-boiled EGGHEAD, he said." Adlai Stevenson, Speech to a Convention of Textile

Workers Union of America, Chicago, Illinois, 6/1/60,Edward Hanna, Henry Hicks and Ted Koppel, The Wit and Wisdom of Adlai Stevenson, Hawthorn Books, 1965, p. 16.

EGREGIOUS

adjective - conspicuous for bad quality or taste; flagrant; extreme.

"Surely we Americans are strong enough to stand a few minutes of Russian propaganda, point of view or whatever you want to call it. Some of it may not be as misleading as some of Reagan's EGREGIOUS misstatements on a wide variety of issues." Julius Duscha, *Chicago Trib.*, 3/15/86, S 1, p. 11.

"He [General Grant] made costly and EGREGIOUS blunders, notably at Shiloh and Cold Harbor; he knew the sting of professional sneers; he quailed before Lee's sardonic eye. His eight years in the White House were years of tribulation and humiliation." H. L. Mencken, A Mencken Chrestomathy, Vintage Books, 1982, p. 225.

"Mr. Dukakis called the handling of the Meese case 'a particularly EGREGIOUS example' of what he suggested were flawed ethical standards in the Reagan Administration." Andrew Rosenthal, *NYTimes*, 7/27/88, p. 10.

"As EGREGIOUS as Mr. Bush's judgment was in these matters, his selection of Sen. J. Danforth Quayle III was potentially the worst decision of his sheltered career. In choosing Mr. Quayle, Mr. Bush played a cruel joke on the American people. The thought of the empty-headed right-winger becoming president is deeply disturbing, and no one is to blame for that prospect but Mr. Bush himself." Editorial, *St. Louis Post Dispatch*, 12/12/88.

"In 1960, Brady took and had widely reproduced a likeness of [President Abraham] Lincoln that he went to EGREGIOUS lengths to retouch, rendering the gaunt, gangly ectomorph as handsome as a matinee idol. Lincoln credited that picture and his famous Cooper Union speech with winning him the election. But the 'handsome' Lincoln is not the one who fixes the eye and mind here. It is Brady's unvarnished reflections of the grizzled, war-weary, aging Lincoln in which the towering intellect and monumental compassion shine through." Michael Kilian, *Chicago Trib.*, 2/12/91, S 5, p. 5.

"Mr. [William] Bennett took particular exception to the two commercials by the McCain campaign that likened Mr. [George W.} Bush to President Clinton, which Mr. Bennett said was the most EGREGIOUS crossing of the line between fair play and unwarranted warfare so far." Frank Bruni, *NYTimes*, 2/9/00, p. A 14.

ELLIPSIS

noun - the omission of a word or phrase necessary to complete construction of a sentence; a jump without transition from one topic to another.

"Twice the trade office's rebuttal alters quotes that might otherwise offend President Carlos Salinas de Gortari of Mexico, the Administration's close ally in the fight for Congressional approval. Mr. Perot's book, for example, contends that, 'Nafta gives Mexican investors, such as the 29 elite businessmen at the Salinas dinner, a distinct competitive advantage in the U.S.-Mexican trucking industry.' The [Clinton] White House repeats the quote but omits, without using ELLIPSES, the reference to the dinner and never explains that the dinner was an occasion for Mr. Salinas to seek political donations of $25 million apiece from businessmen who stood to benefit from the free-trade pact." Keith Bradsher, *NYTimes*, 9/16/93, p. A10.

ELMER GANTRY

noun - a hypocritical minister.

Note:From the eponymous leading character in the novel by Sinclair Lewis.

"By now Pat Robertson has made clear that he cannot be written off as an electronic ELMER GANTRY, a colorful distraction from the rest of the Republican Presidential field." Wayne King, *NYTimes*, 2/27/88, p. 1.

"Democratic National Chairman Ron Brown, appearing on ABC, said Perot's campaign rhetoric 'indicates a real lack of tolerance, almost a kind of an ELMER GANTRY approach, that you can get people kind of revved up to walk down a path, and they don't even know where that path is taking them.' ELMER GANTRY is an unscrupulous evangelist character in a 1927 novel by Sinclair Lewis." *Chicago Trib.*, 6/8/92, S 1, p. 4.

"One almost forgot that telling warning from Haley Barbour, the Republican national chairman, that Clinton was 'an ELMER GANTRY president, who can mount the BULLY PULPIT and say anything he thinks you want to hear.' (ELMER GANTRY was a fictional silver-tongued evangelist and fraud; the Sinclair Lewis novel and subsequent 1960 movie starring Burt Lancaster embedded the type into American mythology.) Clinton was a far more solid figure, but his southern origins and Baptist roots, his ability to talk and campaign his way out of trouble, his fluency that often flirted with the glib, carried a certain Gantry-esque echo." Martin Walker, The President We Deserve, Crown Publishers, 1996, p. 319.

"The crowd roared as [Patrick Buchanan] denounced President Clinton as 'our own ELMER GANTRY, whose desecration of the temples of our civilization and personal misconduct disqualify him' as the nation's leader." Francis X. Clines, *NYTimes*, 10/26/99, p. A23.

ÉMINENCE GRISE (Fr)

noun - a confidential agent, a person exercising unofficial or behind the scenes power.

"Chaos came to modern physics before it came to Washington. Astute scientists theorize that patterns may be discerned even within what appears to be the shambling whirlwind of chaotic events. This insight suggests that those who are waiting for the Clinton administration to organize itself, or be organized by David Gergen or some other GRAY EMINENCE, might as well be waiting for Godot. The Clinton administration is organized just the way it wants to be." Eugene Kennedy, *Chicago Trib.*, 6/21/93, S 1, p. 15.

"'It's more than a lawyer-client relationship,' said George Stephanopoulos, the White House senior adviser. 'It's less than father-son. If there is a GRAY EMINENCE in this Government, it is Warren Christopher. He serves as a counselor to the President, on more than just foreign policy.'" Elaine Sciolino, *NYTimes*, 6/1/93, p. A3.

"'I am a non-executive chairman,' [Donald] Rumsfeld said in an interview. 'Scott Reed is the executive of this campaign, and every piece of it operationally reports to him. I have no line operating functions.' Nor does he need any. At 64, Mr. Rumsfeld is the campaign's EMINENCE GRISE - a former fighter pilot, congressman, Cabinet member, White House chief of staff, secretary of defense, diplomat, corporate czar and onetime presidential aspirant who is Mr. Dole's peer and chief trouble-shooter." Michael Wines, *NYTimes*, 9/26/96, p. A15.

"Laughter eased the day at times, as when a needling question came from Republicans about early scandal strategizing by Dick Morris, the President's chronic ÉMINENCE GRISE. The defense lawyers [in the Clinton impeachment trial] looked at one another in obvious hesitation. 'I couldn't find any volunteers,' said Charles F.C. Ruff, the White House counsel, who finally fielded the question as if it were a penance for someone else's sin." Francis X. Clines, *NYTimes*, 1/23/99, p. A9.

EMOLLIENT

adjective and *noun* - soft, soothing.

"From the start President Clinton took a far more EMOLLIENT stance, pulling back from conflict with Congress. He went so far, especially in failing to stand up for his nominees when they were attacked, that he suffered serious political damage. Congress concluded that this President could be rolled." Anthony Lewis, *NYTimes*, 5/8/95, p. A13.

EMPTY SUIT

noun - a person who is all form and no substance. Cf. ALL HAT AND NO CATTLE.

"It was as if we were watching a cross between 'The Newlywed Game' and 'The Jerry Springer Show.' John and Cindy McCain were up there on the podium conceding the South Carolina primary on Saturday night, and they were smiling and nuzzling as if they had just won a dining room set from Bob Eubanks. But if you listened to Senator McCain's words, what you heard was rage and indignation. He basically called George W. Bush a fraud, a sleaze artist and an EMPTY SUIT." David Brooks, *NYTimes*, 2/21/00, p. A23.

"As a candidate [George H. W.] Bush was the QUINTESSENTIAL EMPTY SUIT." Jack Germond, Fat Man In A Middle Seat, Random House, 1999, p. 243.

"One of Mr. [George W.] Bush's political problems today is a perception among some voters that he is arrogant, an EMPTY SUIT smirking condescendingly at the world, and that perception seems to have first manifested itself at Andover. That is when he developed his smirk (which his friends insist is simply a self-deprecating smile), and even then it irritated some classmates who saw him as no more than an empty polo shirt." Nicholas D. Kristof, *NYTimes*, 6/10/00, p. A10.

ENOCH ARDEN

noun - a man who disappears for many years and is presumed dead but later turns up alive, sometimes to find his wife happily married to another man.

Note:The eponymous hero of Tennyson's poem "ENOCH ARDEN." ENOCH ARDEN laws are statutes existing in some jurisdictions providing for divorce or legalizing remarriage by a wife or husband after a specified number of years' absence, usually seven, of the missing spouse.

"I think it unfair to charge, as some critics have, that Nixon gave the interviews because he was offered money. I believe that he would have done it without pay. He was not paid for his 'Checkers' speech in 1952, or for the press conference after his defeat in the 1962 campaign for governor of California. If Nixon had been ENOCH ARDEN, after looking through the window and seeing the happiness of his former wife and children with her new husband, he would not have turned away and gone back to the sea forever. He would have tapped on the window until noticed. And he would have returned occasionally thereafter to tap on the window again and remind those in the house that he was outside, lonely, and suffering in the cold." Eugene J. McCarthy, Required Reading, Harcourt Brace Jovanovich, 1988, p. 237.

ENSORCELL

verb - to bewitch or enchant.

"I know exactly how the Republicans feel. They've ENSORCELLED themselves. They really, really want this relationship to work out. After eight lonely years they've eagerly invented the image of their desires, imbuing him with magical qualities. Their fantasy guy will sweep in and transform their humdrum little lives. They're banishing all doubts, ruling out all rivals, ignoring any disturbing intrusions of reality.

They are counting the moments until the Big Crush [George W. Bush] replaces the Big Creep [Bill Clinton]." Maureen Dowd, *NYTimes*, 6/9/99, p. A31.

ENTROPY

noun - (1) the degradation of the matter and energy in the universe to an ultimate state of inert uniformity, (2) disorganization or steady deterioration of a society.

"In consequence, the selection of presidential candidates and the election of a president have come to be based on, or at least strongly influenced by, considerations other than basic qualifications for the office. Primaries enable candidates to circumvent or overcome party controls. Television emphasizes the importance of criteria such as a candidate's appearance and projection of personality. Makeup persons become as important as speech writers, while the presidential selection process moves closer to a state of ENTROPY: disorder, randomness, and chaos." Eugene J. McCarthy, Required Reading, Harcourt Brace Jovanovich, 1988, p. 17.

"[Sen. Tim Wirth], too, reflects [Woodrow] Wilson's obsession with the presidential PERSONA: If a president is inadequate, stasis pervades the government, and the country is threatened by ENTROPY. Bush is a mediocre president, but most presidents have been mediocre. What is new is the notion that the nation's health is held hostage to the genius of the chief executive." George F. Will, *Chicago Sun-Times*, 5/28/92, p. 34.

ERUDITE

adjective - learned, scholarly.

"Carol Allin, who ran the now-defunct Capitol Book Store here for 11 years, said Mr. Clinton used to browse in her shop about once a month and 'never left without an armful of books.' Such avid reading habits make Mr. Clinton seem positively ERUDITE compared to George Bush, who appeared to freeze when asked on television in 1984 to name a book he had recently read. Eventually, Mr. Bush mentioned a 22-year-old best seller, 'The Guns of August,' by Barbara Tuchman." William H. Honan, *NYTimes*, 12/10/92, p. B1.

ESCHATOLOGY

noun - a branch of theology dealing with the end of the world or the ultimate destiny of mankind.

"Down the banks of the Potomac, where the Hundred Days seems to have given way to the End of Days, the opinion of the political ESCHATOLOGISTS is unanimous: on top of the haircut fiasco and the Travel Office snafu, President Clinton is in big trouble with the Pentagon." Comment, *New Yorker*, 6/7/93, p. 6.

ETHOS

noun - the distinguishing character, moral nature, tone or guiding belief of a person, group, institution or culture.

"The [Senator John] Glenn campaign tries to evoke the Kennedy ETHOS in a number of ways." Elizabeth Drew, *New Yorker*, 11/21/83, p. 104.

"In what amounts to a departure from the prevalent Democratic ETHOS, Gerry Ferraro seems to enjoy life, politics and America in no particular order... For the Democratic Party and for the American left, this can only be a good sign. There was a time when liberals and radicals partied all night, knew every word to every song, tried to drink each other under the table and won more elections than they lost." Jon Margolis, *Chicago Trib.*, 7/23/84, S 1, p. 15.

"Moreover, Gary Hart is from an affluent Western State where the ETHOS has more to do with growth than with the left-out and minorities, and the following he is attracting includes few blacks." Elizabeth Drew, *New Yorker*, 4/2/84, p. 73.

EUMENIDES

noun - avenging deities; goddesses of vengeance; the furies (Erinyes) in Greek mythology who pursued Orestes relentlessly for having murdered his mother (Clytemnestra).

"On the night that Lyndon Johnson announced he would not run for the presidency again, Senator Eugene J. McCarthy was just concluding a speech to a college audience. He later reported: 'I was on the stage about to start the question period when all of a sudden the reporters started swarming all over me. I had never moved the press that way. I was like Orestes overcome by the EUMENIDES.'" Bill Adler, <u>The McCarthy Wit</u>, Fawcett Publication, Inc., 1969, p. 57.

EUREKA

interjection - used to express joy upon a discovery (lit., in Greek, "I have found it").

Note:Attributed to Archimedes upon discovering, while bathing, the principle of water displacement and thus a method for determining the purity of gold.

"Unlike George Washington and Abraham Lincoln, President Reagan did go to college. He has a degree from EUREKA [in Greek 'heureka,' or 'I have found it'] College, named, I think after what EUREKA grads say upon being handed their diplomas." Michael Kilian, *Chicago Trib.*, 10/15/85, S 1, p. 18.

"...Mr. Rowan dubs Mr. Reagan 'one of the most intuitive politicians ever to occupy the White House - and one of the EUREKA Factor's best salesmen.' The 'EUREKA Factor' is what Mr. Rowan calls sudden, illuminating, intuitive flashes of insight that separate great managers from the nuts-and-bolts plodders." Wayne King, Warren Weaver, Jr., *NYTimes*, 4/29/86, p. 10.

"The research of the diplomatic historian consists of intense slogging. There is almost never a single dramatic find, one document, that leads to a cry of 'EUREKA!' Usually if a historic current is important, you'll find evidence of it elsewhere,' Mr. Beschloss said. But in the case of his new book, 'The Crisis Years: Kennedy and Khrushchev 1960-63,' there was the equivalent of what he calls a EUREKA archive." Adam Clymer, *NYTimes*, 7/25/91, p. A6.

"On the night that Edmund Morris first shared his EUREKA moment with the editor of his long-awaited Ronald Reagan biography, Robert Loomis suffered a rare but severe attack of the literary shakes. Over dinner at a Washington hotel, Mr. Morris handed Mr. Loomis, a prominent Random House editor, a handwritten prologue describing his autumn stroll through Mr. Reagan's alma mater, Eureka College, where an idea jolted the writer so suddenly that he almost tasted the electricity." Doreen Carvajal, *NYTimes*, 10/5/99, p. A1.

EXISTENTIAL

adjective - relating to existence, based on experience.

"George Herbert Walker Bush is an EXISTENTIAL Yankee - born in Milton Mass., reared in Greenwich, Conn., and now living in the moment - who never seems to understand why he cannot just be. He draws strength from his title. He is president, and therefore he is doing something right, he will tell those who challenge him." Maureen Dowd, *NYTimes*, 8/20/92, p. A1.

"There is a yawning hole in the psyche of America and Americans where our sense of common purpose, of community and connection, of hope and a spiritual satisfaction should be. It was easy to mock Mrs. Clinton's EXISTENTIAL gropings. But though she had no easy label, no glib diagnosis, in those gropings she spoke the truth about a vacuum at the heart of the American character." Anna Quindlen, *Chicago Trib.*, 10/19/93, S 1, p. 23.

"Mailer had become obsessed with the Kennedys and had written a couple of famous pieces for *Esquire* about them. The first, 'Superman Comes to the Supermarket,' had pleased John F. Kennedy by representing him as a true EXISTENTIAL hero (the greatest accolade Mailer could bestow on anyone)." Norman Podhoretz, <u>Ex-Friends: Falling Out with Allen Ginsberg, Lionel & Diana Trilling, Lillian Hellman, Hannah Arendt and Norman Mailer</u>, excerpted in *NYTimes*, 2/6/99, p. A19.

"Unlike others of his generation, like Bill Clinton or Al Gore, Mr. [George W.] Bush never wore his hair long, agonized over Vietnam, wrestled with EXISTENTIALISM or cranked up Rolling Stones songs to annoy his parents... " Nicholas D. Kristof, *NYTimes*, 6/19/00, p. A14

EXTANT

noun - still in existence, alive, surviving.

"'To be brutally frank, the choice is now between the president and his friends,' [Pat Buchanan told Nixon on May 16, 1973]. 'Haldeman, Dean, Mitchell, Stans, Kalmbach appear headed, perhaps with Colson in tow, for political abyss. If they are to survive, they have to do it on their own. The only

question EXTANT now, it seems, is whether we are going down as well.'"
News Story, *Chicago Trib.*, 5/29/87, S 1, p. 3.

"No reply [to an improper request for confidential information] from
Lincoln is EXTANT, but later letters from Smith indicate that he had felt the
sting of rebuke." Benjamin P. Thomas, <u>Abraham Lincoln</u>, Knopf, 1952, p.
468.

FFF

FANDANGO

noun - a lively Spanish dance, tomfoolery.

"Mr. Perot's remarks received immediate and sensational coverage - 'No
Way On Gays' was the headline in *The Daily News* in New York - and he has
been involved ever since in the sort of journalistic FANDANGO politicians
have become unhappily used to, seeking to rejigger a statement he never
particularly wanted to make." Michael Kelly, *NYTimes*, 6/4/92, p. A10.

FANNY

noun - buttocks, KEISTER, GAZOO.

"You're right. Vice President Poodle, er, Bush, became surprisingly
aggressive [in the Dan Rather interview]. He hasn't been that macho since he
boasted of kicking Geraldine Ferraro's FANNY." Mike Royko, *Chicago Trib.*,
1/27/88, S 1, p. 3.

FARRAGO

noun - a mixture, HODGEPODGE, MISHMOSH.

"Corny? Yes, but the whole show is corny. Did you catch Senator Orrin
Hatch threatening to investigate Attorney General Janet Reno's investigation
of Clinton campaign money?... Poor silly old Republicans! They are always
getting themselves out-witted, forever trapping themselves into situations that
make them look hostile to goodness, cleanliness, friendliness, courtesy and
kindness, not to mention common sense. The absurdity of this FARRAGO can
be enjoyed only by people who like their mirth sour. For every thigh-slapper in
the performance, there is something solemn and depressing." Russell Baker,
NYTimes, 10/14/97, p. A19.

"The new evidence hardly settled the impeachment question as Mr.
Clinton's critics and defenders each claimed material supporting their
contentions. But the voluminous material confirmed the White House scandal
as a heated FARRAGO of personal, legal and political clashes that has put Mr.
Clinton's incumbency at risk." Francis X. Clines, *NYTimes*, 10/3/98, p. A9.

"Ronald D. Rotunda, a law professor at the University of Illinois, was an
ethics advisor to Kenneth Starr. The other day he made an extraordinary attack
on federal judges in Washington. Writing on the op-ed page of *The Wall Street*

Journal, he said judges appointed by President Clinton had dealt improperly - politically - with cases important to him....Professor Rotunda's main target was U.S. District Judge James Robertson, and I know his high reputation for integrity, so I decided to look into Professor Rotunda's charges. I found that they were a FARRAGO of untruths." Anthony Lewis, *NYTimes*, 3/25/00, p. A27.

FAUSTIAN

adjective - sacrificing spiritual values for material gains, i.e., selling one's soul.

"While Democratic opponents may not know what is in Mr. Bush's mind [in judicial appointments], most of them assume the President has made a FAUSTIAN bargain with the Republican right. 'I don't know if he explicitly sat down and told the right wing, "I'll leave you the judges and social policy," but that's exactly what happened,' Senator Biden said." Neil A. Lewis, *NYTimes*, 7/1/92, p. A9.

"Ever since he began his political career in Houston in the early 1960's, when he appalled his moderate supporters by soothing the John Birch Society-types in the Goldwater movement, Mr. Bush has been making one FAUSTIAN bargain after another, veering between the right wing he needed and the moderate Republican wing that was his heritage." Maureen Dowd, *NYTimes*, 8/20/92, p. A9.

"Wright, a 30-year veteran of Congress, represented Newt's FAUSTIAN pact for fame and power. Newt's ultimately successful campaign to unseat the Texas Democrat began in 1987, when he unleashed an extensive round of ethics charges against the Speaker, but the first hostilities came in May 1984, inspired by Newt's recognition that the C-SPAN cameras in Congress offered his main chance for national exposure." Gail Sheehy, *Vanity Fair*, 9/95, p. 221.

"Those who identified with many of the domestic, and some of the foreign policies of the Clinton agenda made a FAUSTIAN bargain. We overlooked Mr. Clinton's past indiscretions - he was hardly the first politician with testosterone overload - on the condition that he pursue his agenda and postpone the next dalliance until after he left the White House." Thomas L. Friedman, *NYTimes*, 1/27/98, p. A23.

FAUX

adjective - false, imitation.

"We've all been exhausted by the FAUX culture wars of the Clinton era. Ever since Bill Clinton was elected, conservatives have been acting as though the Oval Office had been festooned with macramé and bongs, as if there were some crazy free-love, war-protesting, pig-hating, Bobby Seale-supporting, Carlos Castañeda-reading, Bob Dylan-grooving hippie running the country." Maureen Dowd, *NYTimes*, 4/7/99, p. A23.

"The country was enamored of FAUX candidates like Mr. Trump and Warren Beatty a few months ago, when it looked as though we were in for 10 or 11 months of Bush v. Gore and would need all the diversion we could get." Gail Collins, *NYTimes*, 2/15/00, p. A31.

FECKLESS

adjective - (1) helpless; (2) purposeless.

"And the [Reagan] Administration, like Administrations before it, had undertaken a FECKLESS military mission [in Lebanon] and by saying that United States prestige was involved in its success has made that so." Elizabeth Drew, *New Yorker*, 2/20/84, p. 129.

"Minutes after Ronald Reagan was sworn in as president on Jan. 20, 1981, Iran released 52 U.S. Embassy hostages it had held for 444 days. Thus was insult added to Jimmy Carter's injury. The freeing of the Americans at the start of Reagan's watch was a final illustration of the FECKLESSNESS that seemed to mark Carter's presidency in general and his preoccupation with the hostage crisis in particular." *Chicago Trib.*, 8/6/91, S 1, p. 12.

"One problem George Bush has is that while he sees himself as a rough-and-ready Texas oilman, the rest of the country sees him as an elitist in a tennis sweater - the yammering, FECKLESS type Jack Lemmon used to play in the movies." Richard Roeper, *Chicago Sun-Times*, 1/29/92, p. 11.

"Is no one at the White House reading the history of recent presidential scandals? These clumsy efforts at suppression are FECKLESS and self-defeating. This White House's attempts to maintain political control of the investigation into President and Mrs. Clinton's real estate dealings in Arkansas are swiftly draining away public trust in their integrity." Editorial, *NYTimes*, 1/7/94, p. A14.

"From the perspective of his reelection year, most of the rest of the world would judge Clinton as an initially troubling and FECKLESS, but finally admirable president." Martin Walker, The President We Deserve, Crown Publishers, 1996, p. 351.

"They did not fully trust Nelson Rockefeller, a man with considerable experience and leadership potential, because they believed that his willingness to seek a divorce in order to marry someone else demonstrated a FECKLESSNESS inappropriate to the responsibilities of presidential power.
"But there is another, far more popular approach to character. Followers of this theory pay little or no attention to a candidate's personal character and focus instead on what he stands for - his political character. Indeed, even though we now know about Franklin Roosevelt's mistress or John F. Kennedy's affairs, for most of us, our positive opinions of those Presidents have not diminished." Alan Wolfe, *NYTimes*, 6/28/99, p. A21.

"Throughout the century the party-bolters have formed an interesting, if usually FECKLESS, category in American politics. The latest American apostate, Patrick Buchanan, likes to compare himself to the noblest renegade of them all, Teddy Roosevelt. In his ideological zeal Mr. Buchanan also calls to mind a Democrat, former Vice President Henry Wallace, who quit his party to challenge Harry Truman from the left in 1948. But when it comes to rhetoric and even his jackhammer speaking style, Mr. Buchanan is most reminiscent of George Wallace." Editorial, *NYTimes*, 9/15/99, p. A30.

DR. FEELGOOD (SL)

noun - an incorrigible optimist; a Dr. PANGLOSS.

"Does any of that really matter? Maybe not. Mr. Reagan is campaigning effectively as DR. FEELGOOD, dispensing patriotism, optimism and eyewash, with nothing missing but rose-colored glasses and an Uncle Sam suit. He's so neatly packaged for TV he could be sponsored again by Borax.... Still, Mr. Reagan's vulnerabilities exist, somewhere under DR. FEELGOOD'S jolly performance." Tom Wicker, *NYTimes*, 10/5/84, p. 31.

"He [Lou Cannon] gives Mr. Reagan good marks for the intangibles - inspiring confidence in the American system, showing friendship and leadership in his foreign dealings, being what his critics called a 'DR. FEELGOOD,' a calumny that Mr. Reagan took as a compliment." Herbert Mitgang, *NYTimes*, 4/24/91, p. B2.

"The real scandal is that Ronald Reagan was Leader of the Free World for eight years. Any real or alleged bedroom PECCADILLOS or crystal-ball fantasizing are irrelevant compared to the fact that the American people elected him not just once, but twice, gleefully tolerating eight years of DR. FEELGOOD platitudinizing while the cities were allowed to decline, the economy stagnated to a degree that we eventually must come to terms with, and Americans of privilege were having a ball at the expense of the rest of us." *Philadelphia Daily News*, as quoted in *Chicago Trib.*, 4/13/91, S 1, p. 17.

FEMME FATALE (FR)

noun - a fatally fascinating woman, a seductive woman, a siren, a Zuleika Dobson.

"Donna Rice, the bouncy blond model and FEMME FATALE who temporarily knocked Sen. Gary Hart out of the Democratic presidential race, can't seem to get enough of Washington. She was back over the weekend and seen dining in the posh Vista Hotel's American Harvest restaurant. She was observed wearing a red leather miniskirt, matching red pumps and handbag, and a filmy black blouse." Michael Kilian, *Chicago Trib.*, 1/15/88, S 1, p. 20.

"Donna Rice, FEMME FATALE of the 1987 Gary Hart political debacle, has entered a new chapter of her life - marriage. Rice wed Jack Hughes of Washington on Saturday at the Monmouth Plantation, the *Natchez* (Miss.) *Democrat* reported. Hart's candidacy for the Democratic nomination for president sank in 1987 after reports surfaced that Rice had spent the night in Hart's townhouse and pictures were published of her sitting on his lap aboard a luxury craft called "Monkey Business." Newsmakers - Tribune Wires, *Chicago Trib.*, 5/9/94, S 1, p. 2.

"Mr. Clinton began in the capable hands of a world-class FEMME FATALE [Pamela Harriman]. He ended up in the clutching hands of a junior FATAL FEMME [Monica Lewinsky]. Maureen Dowd, *NYTimes*, 10/11/98, p. 17.

FICO

noun - an obscene gesture of contempt (giving someone the finger).

Note:Defined by Dr. Samuel Johnson in his famous dictionary as "An act of contempt done with the fingers, expressing a fig for you." To fig was defined by Dr. Johnson as "to insult with FICOS or contemptuous motions of the fingers." In one of his campaigns Governor Nelson Rockefeller, piqued by a campaign heckler during a political speech, responded with a FICO, giving him the finger.

"When a reporter suggested the President demonstrate which finger was destined for surgery - a move that could have produced the near universal gesture for contempt [FICO] - Bush laughed and said, 'Don't tempt me.'" Janet Cawley, *Chicago Trib.*, 10/6/89, S 1, p. 5.

FINAGLE

verb - to obtain indirectly or by tricky or dishonest means.

"*Things to avoid:*... Detailed explanations of the Whitewater issue, whether they show that the Clintons are utterly innocent of all FINAGLING or prove beyond argument that the Clintons are guilty as sin." Russell Baker, *NYTimes*, 12/3/96, p. A15.

FIN DE SIECLE (FR)

noun - characteristic of the end of the nineteenth century; decadent.

"The adroit [Pat] Buchanan, once considered a distinguished servant of the republic, may become a FIN DE SIECLE William Jennings Bryan, the once-lauded populist who fell on the sword of his own self-righteousness while defending what he understood as religion under threat at the Scopes 'monkey' trial in the 1920s." Eugene Kennedy, *Chicago Trib.*, 9/21/92, S 1, p. 11.

FINGERWAG (SL)

verb - to shake or point one's finger to admonish, get attention or emphasis.

Note:FINGERWAG was used frequently by news analysts and commentators, during the weeks prior to the impeachment vote on President William Clinton, to refer to his shaking his finger at his audience while making his public statement denying that he "had sexual relations with that woman - Monica Lewinsky."

"Amid a fog of smugness and sermonizing, Mary Fisher burst on the Republican National Convention on Wednesday night like a sudden flare of light and warmth. After nearly two days of FINGERWAGGING from puritans and SCOLDS (briefly relieved by an amiable Ronald Reagan), delegates might have been forgiven for starting to despair as the atmosphere seemed to grow more dour by the minute." Editorial, *Miami Herald*, quoted in *Chicago Trib.*, 8/23/92, S 4, p. 3

"Mr. Clinton, in a FINGERWAGGING performance last January at the White House, told the nation he did not have sexual relations with 'that woman,' Ms. Lewinsky. He denied sexual relations with her in a deposition in the sexual harassment case brought against him by Paula Corbin Jones." Alison Mitchell, *NYTimes*, 12/20/98, p. 26.

FLACCID

adjective - soft, flabby, lacking vigor.

"For Mr. Bush, the debate was the latest in a series of attempts at redefinition. He has failed so far to shed the image of a detached President who was powerful on issues of diplomacy and war that no longer seem so pressing, and who is FLACCID on more urgent domestic issues." Andrew Rosenthal, *NYTimes*, 10/12/92, p. A10.

"Under savage criticism from Republican officeholders and strategists for a tardy, FLACCID and unimaginative campaign, President Bush headed into the Midwest and on to Texas and California last week, putting some fire into his speeches for a change while aides in Washington distributed 'distortion of the day' attacks on the record of his opponent, Gov. Bill Clinton." R. W. Apple, Jr., *NYTimes*, 8/4/92, p. A8.

"All this [the Bush administration's cautious position on global warming] sounds like a retreat into the FLACCID inactivity of the Reagan Administration on acid rain, when for eight years it was claimed that not enough was known about its causes to do anything about its effects." Tom Wicker, *NYTimes*, 5/9/89, p. 31.

"At a news conference in Saluda on Monday, Mr. Bush acknowledged, after his FLACCID performance in New Hampshire, that South Carolinians have been pressing him about whether he is tough enough to win." Maureen Dowd, *NYTimes*, 2/16/00, p. A29.

FLAKE

noun - a GOOFY person, an oddball, a FRUITLOOP.

"Mr. Forbes seems at least as determined as he was in 1996, and possibly more so. Then, he came across as the champion of a single issue: his proposal for a flat tax. Now, he speaks just as loudly about conservative religious themes, like opposition to legal abortion, that seem to depart from past statements that the Christian Coalition did not speak for most Christians and that Pat Robertson was 'a toothy FLAKE.'" Frank Bruni, *NYTimes*, 8/20/99, p. A16.

FLAPDOODLE

noun - foolish, empty talk, writing or ideas; nonsense; balderdash; codswallop.

"What a lot of FLAPDOODLE! How can anyone know what Mondale will do when Mondale himself has in all likelihood not made up his mind? When he does make up his mind, he will tell us. Then we will know, probably all of us at the same time. Until then, none of this informed [hah!] speculation need be taken seriously." Jon Margolis, *Chicago Trib.* 6/25/84, S 1, p. 11.

FLUMMOX

verb - to confuse or perplex, to BUMFUZZLE.

"A few days and another debate later, Mr. [George W.] Bush was asked, rather cruelly, what lessons he had learned from his study of the Acheson era. The FLUMMOXED governor started out with a caution that the United States should not 'retreat within our borders.' He put in a good word for free trade, quoted a speech he gave at the Citadel, and concluded this way: 'The lessons of Acheson and Marshall are/is that our nation's greatest export to the world has been, is, and always will be the incredible freedoms we understand in the great land called America.' Later, Mr. Bush said it was hard to give a full book review 'in a minute's time,' but more time was the last thing he appeared to need. In fact, he looked like a ninth grader who had forgotten to do his homework; desperately free-associating and hoping the bell would ring." Gail Collins, *NYTimes*, 12/10/99, p. A31.

FOLDEROL (OM)

noun - nonsense.

"One of the things people require in their leaders is a highly developed sense of euphemism. If Bill Clinton had gone on '60 Minutes' during the 1992 campaign and said, 'Sure, I was playing around' instead of repeating that FOLDEROL about his marriage having gone through a troubled period, he would now be back in Little Rock wondering whether it was too late to start a career as a saxophonist who did federal-budget-policy patter between songs." Calvin Trillin, Too Soon to Tell, Warner Books, 1995, p. 265.

FOOFARAW

noun - a fuss over a trifle; frills and finery.

"Washington - Ross Perot is why we have politics. He is a living, preening argument for political parties and the New Hampshire primary and all the much maligned FOOFARAW the pedagogues all complain about every election season." Steve Daley, *Chicago Trib.*, 10/4/92, S 4, p. 4.

FOOL'S ERRAND

noun - an unnecessary mission.

"What Mr. Dole did in dispatching Mr. Reed to Dallas makes that job a great deal harder for him, and cannot help others on the Republican ticket. Although some Republicans suggested that Mr. Dole had intended to keep the approach a secret and had been victimized by a leak, many more characterized the whole enterprise as a FOOL'S ERRAND and argued that no one could have thought something so startling could be kept quiet at the peak of the campaign." R. W. Apple, Jr., *NYTimes*, 10/25/96, p. A10

FORNIGATE (SL)

noun - sex scandal (after Watergate, Irangate, etc.)

"[David Brock's] rage at women, meanwhile, invariably colors his view of men who commit what he calls 'HANKY-PANKY' with them. On 'Crossfire,' a smirking Mr. Brock called Bill Clinton 'a bizarre guy,' not recognizing that the FORNIGATE charges, if true, would make the President seem all too pathetically ordinary, not bizarre." Frank Rich, *NYTimes*, 1/6/94, p. A13.

FRENETIC

adjective - frantic, frenzied.

"Santa Barbara, Calif., Nov. 30 - What is it with Presidents these days? The first to fall to whatever afflicts them was George Bush. He seemed, at first, an unexceptional man in his habits of relaxation. He likes to fish a little, or play horseshoes or golf, or jog, or go out for Chinese food, or mess around in his boat. Soon, though, it became clear that the President was a bit unusual. He liked to do all these things at the same time. It was said, wonderingly, that he was the most FRENETIC President the nation had ever seen. But Bill Clinton may end up making George Bush look like a shut-in." Michael Kelly, *NYTimes*, 12/1/92, p. A10.

FRISSON

noun - chill, shudder, tingle.

"But I still get a FRISSON when I encounter a German-American who was raised, amazingly, to loath Woodrow Wilson for calling into question the loyalty of what he called 'hyphenated Americans,' for egging on those who loved democracy so much that they defaced the walls of German social and gymnastic and educational associations across the country, and refused to listed to German music or, even, to eat sauerkraut." Kurt Vonnegut, <u>Palm Sunday</u>, Dell Publishing Co., Inc., 1981, pp. 21-22.

Frank J. Young

"When Gary Hart's campaign folded, the Governor of Massachusetts inherited most of Mr. Hart's glamorous supporters in the entertainment industry. A FRISSON of doubt went through Hollywood, however, when it was discovered that Mr. Dukakis had not seen his cousin and booster, Olympia Dukakis, in 'Moonstruck' until the night before she won an Oscar for her performance in the film, which starred Cher." Maureen Dowd, *NYTimes*, 10/26/88, p. 12.

"As one Republican close to the White House put it: 'The difficulty with thrusting him [Dan Quayle] forward in the pictures is that it causes FRISSONS of terror each time you see him. You think, O, my God, he's not actually advising Bush, is he? This is serious life-and-death stuff, not business for Dan Quayle.'" Maureen Dowd, *NYTimes*, 3/4/91, p. A12.

FRUITLOOP (SL)

noun - a silly, nonsensical person.

"Some days, having Reagan for president was like finding Castro in the refrigerator: Remember the time he appointed thirteen people to a commission on AIDS - including a sex therapist who thought you could get the disease from toilet seats; some FRUITLOOP who claimed gays were engaging in 'blood terrorism' by deliberately donating infected blood...." Molly Ivins, Molly Ivins Can't Say That, Can She?, Random House, 1991, p. 105.

FULSOME

adjective - offensive to good taste, esp. as being excessive or insincere (i.e. FULSOME praise).

"He [Lyndon Johnson] still agreed FULSOMELY with Marsh's political analyses and prognostications on world affairs, and was the first to point out that Charles had been right again on some predictions. He still asked Marsh for advice - and was so grateful when Charles gave it that the older man gave more and more. Harold Young, who had watched Johnson 'play' many an older man, felt he had never played one better than he did Charles Marsh; never, he felt, had Johnson been more 'humble,' more the 'great flatterer.'" Robert A. Caro, <u>The Years of Lyndon Johnson: The Path to Power</u>, Knopf, 1982, p. 486.

"The candidate [Bill Clinton] wrapped up with the FULSOME but shapeless rhetoric of consensus government, expressed in his trademarked formula. 'We can have an America that is pro-family and pro-choice; pro-environment and pro-growth; pro-business and pro-labor if we have the courage to do it,' Mr. Clinton said." Michael Kelly, *NYTimes*, 10/21/92, p. A12.

GGG

GADFLY

noun - an irritating person who provokes and criticizes others.

"But [Tuesday's NAFTA debate with Vice President Al Gore] accomplished one thing. It ensures that, from now on, no one need afford Perot a platform from which to air what pass as his opinions. He's been called a demagogue, a populist and a GADFLY. What he is, is over." Anna Quindlen, *Chicago Trib.*, 11/12/93, S 1 p. 27.

"Whatever else the White House expects to get out of a mano a mano debate with Ross Perot over the North American Free Trade Agreement, the challenge has already given the GADFLY Texan more prime-time publicity than his millions could buy." B. Drummond Ayres, Jr., *NYTimes*, 11/6/93, p. 8.

"It was a good year for Sen. Bob Dole of Kansas, and a better year for radio GADFLY Rush Limbaugh." Steve Daley, *Chicago Trib.*, 1/23/94, S 4, p. 5.

GAFFE

noun - a social blunder or faux pas, a tactless remark.

"Mr. Reagan's GAFFE [when he declared South Africa to be free of racial segregation] was one of the worst by a sitting president since Gerald Ford declared in the heat of debate that the people of Poland and other Eastern bloc nations do not feel dominated by the Soviet Union." Editorial, *Chicago Trib.*, 8/29/85, S 1, p. 22.

10/12/76

"ARE YOU REALLY SURE YOU WANT TO GET INTO THIS?"

Pat Oliphant

"In addition, he [Dan Quayle] made several GAFFES that concern some Bush advisers, such as calling the Holocaust an 'obscene period in our nation's history' and then explaining, 'I didn't live in this century.'" Gerald M. Boyd, *NYTimes*, 10/5/88, p. 14.

"Verbal GAFFES that wouldn't even be noticed if someone else made them stick to him [Vice President Quayle] like putty." Jonathan Alter, *Newsweek*, 5/20/91, p. 23.

"The truth is, it isn't just the usual gang of liberal suspects who view Dan Quayle as a slow-witted, well-scripted lightweight. The dark secret of the Bush administration is that millions of Republicans are embarrassed by Quayle's GAFFES, by his serpentine SYNTAX and his kindergarten logic." Steve Daley, *Chicago Trib.*, 6/21/92, S 4, p. 4.

"The Senator and the President looked forward to the 1964 race, Mr. Goldwater because he could argue clearly defined issues, and Kennedy because he thought his rival's conservatism and verbal GAFFES would make the Arizonan an easy target and enable him to win the landslide he needed to pass legislation he sought in a second term. Kennedy would just let Mr. Goldwater rattle on." Adam Clymer, *NYTimes*, 5/30/98, p. A10.

GAGGLE

noun - a cluster or group of people.

"President Bush left town last week, trailing his reckless disregard for the law. He went off to Somalia, Saudi Arabia and Moscow, having pardoned a GAGGLE of pals and retainers for their involvement, alleged and proved, in the Iran-Contra fiasco." Steve Daley, *Chicago Trib.*, 1/3/93, S 4, p. 4.

GALLIMAUFRY

noun - hodgepodge of things or persons, potpourri, FARRAGO.

"[Social Security] was also [Senator Patrick Moynihan's] major concern when he worked as a counselor to President Richard M. Nixon, the third President he served (after John F. Kennedy and Lyndon B. Johnson and before Gerald R. Ford) in what he calls a GALLIMAUFRY of domestic and international positions." Adam Clymer, *NYTimes*.

"Instant analysts were bowled over by the very fact of his [Clinton's] State of the Union address. But this giddy GALLIMAUFRY was an appeal to detach ourselves from reality." William Safire, *NYTimes*, 1/25/99, p. A27.

GANDY DANCER

noun - a railroad track worker.

"Stripped to his shirtsleeves in a steamy delta drizzle and sweating like a GANDY DANCER, [George] Bush presented news that caused jaws to drop and many questions to be asked." Charles M. Madigan, *Chicago Trib.*, 8/21/88, S 1, p. 26

GASBAG (OM)

noun - a talkative person, an idle gossip, a person with LOGORRHEA, a WINDBAG.

"President Clinton's immediate pickle results because Monica Lewinsky, apparently a compulsive GASBAG, talked and talked and talked into a tape recorder on a friend's telephone." Russell Baker, *NYTimes*, 2/13/98, p. A27.

"The real problem - and it was true from the day 'Beloved' opened, before 'word of mouth' could be the culprit - was that the audience feared more sermon than drama from the increasingly more preachy Oprah. As Tom Shales wrote in *Washington Post*, 'Winfrey playing national nanny is getting to be a drag' - a sentence that could also describe TV's Clinton-scandal GASBAGS." Frank Rich, *NYTimes*, 12/12/98, p. A31.

"The latest agenda of the media GASBAGS - now that they're bored drumming up fake suspense about 'wavering Republican moderates' - is to head off this trial. If a last-minute deal can't save the day, we're told, then surely the impeached President will resign to spare us 'the ordeal.'" Frank Rich, *NYTimes*, 12/19/98, p. A31.

GAZOO

noun - the human fundament; wazoo, KEISTER.

Note:The author first came across the word GAZOO in a *New York Times* story in May, 1987. In a letter to the author, Senator Alan Simpson of Wyoming stated as follows: "Thank you for your inquiries into my 'GAZOO' statement. I appreciate this opportunity to give you what little background I have. I have heard the term GAZOO used in many parts of the United States, but most often in Wyoming. Dear old Dad used to use it quite often - although Mom didn't appreciate it too much. People from Wyoming might refer to a GAZOO as the Wyoming end of a horse headed for Idaho - at least, that is the definition the comedian, Mark Russell, gave it! However, I think it more appropriate to leave the definition up to the interpretation of the individual."

"Back in March, Senator Alan K. Simpson complained about an aggressive press corps that he said was seeking to 'stick it' in President Reagan's 'GAZOO.'" Briefing, *NYTimes*, 5/13/87, p. 12.

"He [Senator Alan K. Simpson] also scolded White House reporters for shouting questions at President Reagan over the whirring of helicopter blades, saying that they hoped Mr. Reagan would somehow look foolish and that they were trying to 'stick it in his GAZOO.'" Neil A. Lewis, *NYTimes*, 10/24/90, p. A12.

"And [Senator Alan] Simpson has yet to finish his book, 'In the Old GAZOO: A Lifetime of Scrapping With the Press.' GAZOO, he explained, is 'the south end of a horse going north.'" Elaine Sciolino, *NYTimes*, 10/27/96, p. 11.

GEEK

noun - (1) a WONKY person; a person disapproved of as being too serious and intellectual, (2) a carnival performer whose act usually includes biting the head off of a live chicken or snake; by extension, a wild and crazy person.

"The fuss over a controlled substance is, of course, distracting from the deeper question of the other kind of substance. W. [George W. Bush] is the kind of guy who doesn't want to know more than he has to know - the President of the fraternity who thought it was not cool to study too much or work as hard as the GEEKS in the library.
"He seems to have good instincts, and he knows how to get good advice. But does that qualify him to lead the country? That's the substance abuse we should worry about." Maureen Dowd, *NYTimes*, 8/18/99, p. A25.

"...it is clear that [Steve Forbes] is not the same GEEKY, hopelessly awkward plutocrat who tried to buy the Republican nomination four years ago. This is a GEEKY, hopelessly awkward plutocrat who has seen the light." Elizabeth Kolbert, *New Yorker*, 11/8/99, p. 50.

GEMÜTLICHKEIT (GER)

noun - cordiality, friendship.

"George Bush looked like he'd be a cozy president, old shoe, GEMÜTLICHKEIT." P. J. O'Rourke, <u>Parliament of Whores</u>, Vintage Books, 1992, p. 41.

GLITCH

noun - a minor error or mistake.

"And even with the more efficient White House operation, there were GLITCHES. The leak of a Pentagon memo indicating that Clinton may be preparing to retreat, at least partially, from his pledge to end the military's ban on gays stirred up controversy on a politically charged issue that the White House had been trying to down play until the budget plan was settled." Carol Jouzaitis, *Chicago Trib.*, 6/27/93, S 1, p. 3.

GLOP

noun - a tasteless, unattractive mixture.

"Now this is a Presidential campaign in which the Republican front-runner, George W. Bush, has yet to emerge from his Fortress of Solitude in Austin. There are plenty of men out there talking generalized GLOP, and Elizabeth Dole has made some surprising, and specific, position statements on gun control, abortion and the situation in Kosovo. We all know she is spontaneity-deprived, a heavily programmed candidate. But her husband's failure to come racing to her defense full throttle makes you want to get in there and argue for her side." Gail Collins, *NYTimes*, 5/18/99, p. A30.

GOLD DIGGER (OM)

noun - a person who uses charm and wiles to get money or favors from others.

"From the moment she [Paula Jones] first made her accusation against the President in a televised news conference on Feb. 11, 1994, his advisers dismissed her as a GOLD DIGGER in league with his conservative enemies. At the same time, but more quietly, his lawyers were trying to settle the lawsuit. Their efforts initially foundered on Ms. Jones's demand for an apology; Mr. Clinton said he had nothing to apologize for." James Bennet and Neil A. Lewis, *NYTimes*, 11/14/98, p. A10.

GOODY-GOODY

noun - an ingratiatingly proper person; a straight arrow; a GOODY TWO-SHOES.

"It's tempting. We rarely get so obvious a target as Phil Gramm, the Texas senator who wants to become president. Like most Republicans, Gramm is a champion of middle-class, grass-roots family values. But he's been blushing lately because it's come out that he once invested a few thousand dollars in the production of a soft-porn film. So it would be easy to needle Gramm about talking like a GOODY-GOODY after financially backing the sort of bare-bosom-and-butt movie that decent church folk condemn." Mike Royko, *Chicago Trib.*, 5/24/95, S 1, p. 3.

"I [Vice President Gore] was never supposed to go one-on-one with this guy. I thought I had scared or charmed other Democrats out of the race. Bradley was the only one I didn't target. So I miscalculated a little. But now things are getting totally out of hand.

"Suddenly people are falling in love with that GOODY-GOODY when they're supposed to be falling in love with this GOODY-GOODY." Maureen Dowd, *NYTimes*, 4/21/99, p. A27.

"What she [Hillary Clinton] symbolizes for [Peggy Noonan] - a Reagan speechwriter and conservative chick before the term was invented - is the high school GOODY-GOODY who ratted on the girls smoking in the locker room. The poster girl for Ronald Reagan fancies herself the working-class defender against the lady who had it too easy!" Ellen Goodman, *Sarasota Herald-Trib.*, 3/26/00, p. 3F.

"Al Gore's GOODY-GOODINESS deprives him of the messy imperfections that allow voters to get past their envy of the famous and powerful. Unlike Bill Clinton, who stole the show at a recent fund-raiser by mocking his own aging in office - 'I was always the youngest person who did everything. Now... I'm just kind of an old gray-haired redneck' - the vice president has scarcely aged in his seven White House years. No love handles or shoe-polish hair color. He is a fanatic about preserving a near-perfect physique." Gail Sheehy, *NYTimes*, 6/2/00, p. A25.

GOODY TWO-SHOES

noun - a person who is a GOODY-GOODY; a person who is unusually good.

Note: from GOODY TWO-SHOES, the heroine of a children's story.

"When he [George W. Bush] says, 'I'm not going to itemize my mistakes,' he gives the impression that they could fill several spicy volumes, but the reality may be that they wouldn't take up two lines in a small ledger.

"GOODY, TWO SHOES!"

Jim Dobbins

"That disclosure could be a serious blow to his prospects. Unlike his father, who sometimes came across as a GOODY TWO-SHOES, Bush has shrewdly cultivated a rakish air meant to appeal to the sort of voters who frequently enjoy detours from the straight and narrow." Steve Chapman, *Chicago Trib.*, 4/11/99, S 1, p. 19.

GOOFY

adjective - silly, ridiculous, NUTTY, crackers.

"Presidential aide Paul Begala responded Tuesday, 'If GOOFY ideas ever go to $40 a barrel I want the drilling rights to Dick Armey's head. This is further proof that the right wing of the Republican Party is using the Starr investigation [of President Clinton] for partisan advantage.'" *Chicago Trib.*, 4/8/98, S 1, p. 3.

"[Stark county, Ohio] is an easy place to find *a lot* of people who are deserting Mr. Perot in 1996. Their reasons break down into four basic categories. First, there is the 'GOOFY' problem. 'He had an original story that appealed to me last time,' said Frederick Mottice, a lineman for a power company. 'But now he might be a little GOOFY. He thinks people are out to get him.' Jim Lenart, a program analyst, mentioned this factor, too. 'I still like what he stands for,' Mr. Lenart said. 'But a lot of people are saying maybe he's a little GOOFY.'" Michael Winerip, *NYTimes*, 10/27/96, p. 12.

"The inexpressibly GOOFY trio of Texans - Armey, DeLay, and Archer - stand behind him [Newt Gingrich] like Huey, Dewey, and Louie, reminding us that things can always get worse." Molly Ivins, <u>You Got to Dance With Them What Brung You</u>, Random House, 1998, p. xxii.

"The worst of the testing tizzy is not [George W.] Bush's ignorance, but his GOOFY efforts to reassure us he isn't. No one wants to see a presidential candidate wave around his current reading material ('Titan,' the John D. Rockefeller biography - please note the 744 pages!). And no one wants him to sound a Nixon-like 'I am not a crook' note, as when Bush told *Time* magazine, 'I've never held myself out to be any great genius, but I'm plenty smart. And I've got good common sense and good instincts.'" David Broder, *Chicago Trib.*, 11/17/99, S 1, p. 31

GORBYMANIA (SL)

noun - fascination with Soviet General Secretary Mikhail Gorbachev. The anticipated traffic jam in New York when Gorbachev addressed the United Nations was called Gorbylock.

"The president elect's meeting with Mikhail Gorbachev this week may offer a glimpse of how [George] Bush will deal with the Soviets. Aside from a healthy distrust of 'GORBYMANIA,' Bush has provided only general ideas as to how he will confront the nation's central national security challenge." Hugh De Santis and Robert A. Manning, *Chicago Trib.*, 12/6/88, S 1, p. 17.

GOTCHA

verb - contraction of "I've got you" meaning "I've fooled or tricked you."

"His [Ross Perot's] style, by all accounts, is not an act, but that does not mean Mr. Perot has not pondered what he is doing. He has, and he finds it a good thing. Looking back at some of his more contentious television interviews, he described his questioners as engaged in a game of 'GOTCHA,' trying to 'prove their man- or womanhood by trying to trap' people into stupid or false answers. As he sees it, he is winning the game." Michael Kelly, *NYTimes*, 5/26/92, p. A10.

"'Don't you think that it would have been responsible for you to call me and say, "Ross, I'm going to ask you this question, bring all your stuff?"' he [Ross Perot] asked David Broder of the *Washington Post*, accusing him and his fellow panelists of 'sneak attacks' and 'GOTCHA' questions." Richard L. Berke, *NYTimes*, 8/2/93, p. A9.

"By mid-July, Dole was no longer associating with reporters. He did not grant the traditional pre-Convention interviews to their newsweeklies, and he did not offer 'exclusive' interviews to the local press on his visits around the country. Bringing down the curtain meant that Dole's GAFFES were fewer, and the press's GOTCHA! game ended." Ken Auletta, *New Yorker*, 11/18/96, p. 56.

"Although 'Dubyah,' as the Republican front-runner [George W. Bush] has become widely known, has been quite forthcoming about some aspects of his wild and woolly youth before age 40, he has repeatedly brushed off questions about whether he ever used cocaine. He refuses to play that 'Washington game' of 'GOTCHA,' he has said." Clarence Page, *Chicago Trib.*, 8/22/99, S 1, p. 17.

"The younger Bush [George W.] has acknowledged that at one time he drank heavily and that he made 'mistakes' in his youth. No evidence or even a credible allegation has been made that he ever used cocaine or any other illegal drug. When pressed, he has said he hasn't used illegal drugs in the past 25 years. His father said he is upset over how the media have questioned his son about rumors of cocaine use and believes it is right for him not to answer more questions on the subject. 'I do feel strongly about that, about "GOTCHA" politics, about intrusiveness', Bush said. The former President said he has not asked his son whether he ever used drugs. 'I wouldn't even consider to do that,' Bush said. 'I think what he's doing is correct and he has my full support.'" Associated Press, *Chicago Trib.*, 9/13/99, S 1, p. 9.

GÖTTERDÄMMERUNG (GER)

noun - violent collapse or destruction of a political or social order; lit., twilight of the Gods.

"The President [Bush] knows, a close friend said the other day, that 'this could be GÖTTERDÄMMERUNG.' At times, he said, the normally chipper Mr. Bush has been blue, but not so much since he bonded with Harry Truman." R. W. Apple, Jr., *NYTimes*, 8/20/92, p A8.

GRAVITAS (L)

noun - seriousness, importance.

"Quayle is a nice guy - good-humored and remarkably resilient. One hears stories of times he came up with a smart strategy in the inner councils. His puppylike demeanor has real appeal, but it's hard to picture him in the Oval Office. He just can't acquire GRAVITAS. Every time he seems to have steadied himself, he does something that turns him into a joke again. That's why his urging a young spelling-bee contestant to add an 'e' to 'potato' was so devastating. (Quayle's cue card had the 'e')." Elizabeth Drew, *New Yorker*, 9/7/92, p. 92.

"'If he [Bill Clinton] reaches the point where this is seen as an attempt to camouflage non-action on the economic front, it could be counterproductive,' [Kevin Phillips, a Republican political analyst] said. He also runs the risk of trivializing his mandate and damaging the GRAVITAS of the Presidency if he monkeys around too much." Michael Kelly, *NYTimes*, 11/30/92, p. A8.

"But this freewheeling humor carries a considerable risk. If the Vice President [Al Gore] is willing to play the class clown, won't the GRAVITAS of high elective office erode?" Jennifer Senior, *NYTimes*, 3/7/94, p. B4.

"He [George W. Bush] has faced questions about possible past drug use, and some have bluntly questioned his intelligence. One acid article in *U.S. News & World Report* began 'Is Dubya dumb?'...And voters will decide if Bush was treated unfairly by an overzealous reporter. 'I don't think in and of itself it's a big deal,' said Andrew Kohut, director of the nonpartisan Pew Research Center. 'Voters will say, especially Republicans, "there goes the press again trying to put a political candidate in a bad light."' 'On the other hand, if George W. has an Achilles heel, it is one of GRAVITAS,' Kohut said. 'Is he really up to the job? Is he enough of a leader? Does he have the background?...But I think it will take a lot more than not being able to name the leader of the Chechnyan province to sink his ship.'" Michael Tackett, *Chicago Trib.*, 11/9/99, S 1, p. 4.

"Karenna's younger brother and sisters have managed to stay out of the spotlight: Kristin, 22, is an aspiring writer; Sarah, 20, is a student at Harvard, and 16-year-old Albert III is still in high school. Karenna [Gore] herself shunned campus politics at Harvard, where she majored in American history and literature, and still seems to feel more comfortable as a student and mom. Over lunch with a *NEWSWEEK* correspondent last week, Karenna seemed a smooth blend of her mother's peppiness and her father's GRAVITAS." Debra Rosenberg, *Newsweek*, 8/16/99, p. 28.

"Signaling that he was ready to dive into a months-long battle with the two-term governor, Mr. Gore said repeatedly that Mr. Bush lacked the experience to be president, stoking questions that swirled in the primaries over his rival's GRAVITAS. He said this was evident in the governor's failure to put forth a 'presidential class' economic program." Richard L. Berke and Katharine Q. Seelye, *NYTimes*, 3/12/00, p. A1.

"Yet if the challenge for George W. Bush, the presumptive Republican nominee, is to prove his smarts, Mr. Gore's is precisely the opposite - to show that he is a regular guy despite a perceived surplus of GRAVITAS, which at least some Americans seem to find intimidating, boring, or, as he himself worries, just weird." Melinda Henneberger, *NYTimes*, 5/21/00, p. A16.

GUCCI COMMUNISM (SL)

noun - descriptive term for a brand of communist life style which emphasizes elegant clothes, attention to fashion and western cultural values.

"...it was Jesse Jackson who, as ever, knew how to create one of those quotes that reporters can't resist. Asked by NBC's Tom Brokaw whether Gorbachev was 'CHARISMATIC,' Jackson said 'When one looks at the suit and tie he's wearing, one sees a kind of GUCCI COMMUNISM.' Actually, Gorbachev looked more like a proper Wall Street lawyer. It was Jackson, in a double-breasted blue suit, who looked more Gucci-ish. But 'GUCCI

COMMUNISM' is what is known in the trade as a must-use quote, even if its meaning is uncertain, even if its meaning is nonexistent." Jon Margolis, *Chicago Trib.*, 11/20/85, S 1, p. 17.

GUSSY UP

verb - to dress up.

"Bill, Hillary, and Chelsea Clinton took a night off from the mundane cares and woes of the presidency Wednesday to get all GUSSIED UP and mingle with the SWELLS and cultural elite of the capital at the ballet." Michael Kilian, *Chicago Trib.*, 4/8/94, S 1, p. 24.

HHH

HAGIOGRAPHER

noun - a writer of the lives of saints, a synaxarist.

"But [William Jennings] Bryan made the grade. His place in Tennessee HAGIOGRAPHY is secure. If the village barber saved any of his hair, then it is curing gall-stones down there today." H. L. Mencken, The Vintage Mencken, Vintage Books, 1956, p. 163.

"Have you noticed that, in recent months especially, Harry Truman is being lifted up by the HAGIOGRAPHERS to the status of hero?" William F. Buckley, Jr., The Jeweler's Eye, G.P. Putnam's Sons, 1969, p. 301.

"His [Thomas Jefferson's] HAGIOGRAPHERS have depicted him as a man of perfect marble, swearing, in one historian's words, 'eternal hostility to every form of tyranny over the mind of man.'" Michiko Kakutani, Review of Jefferson by Max Byrd, *NYTimes*, 11/23/93, p. B2.

HALLMARK

noun - (1) a mark placed on an article to indicate its origin, purity, etc. and (2) a distinguishing feature or trait.

"They [White House officials] have been particularly shaken by the realization that the HALLMARKS of Mr. Reagan's personal popularity over the last six years - his adherence to certain fixed principles in foreign and domestic policy, his shrewdness in dealing with Congress and his credibility with the nation - appear to have been undermined." Bernard Weinraub, *NYTimes*, 11/19/86, p. 7.

"President Bush kicked off the budget debate with congressional leaders Tuesday, emphasizing the danger of the federal budget deficit and calling on them to reduce it without raising taxes, a pledge that was a HALLMARK of Bush's election campaign." Timothy J. McNulty and James O'Shea, *Chicago Trib.*, 1/25/89, S 1, p. 1.

"This tension between a yearning for action and a doubt that government can truly deliver has become a HALLMARK of the Clinton Presidency, and it will be at the center of the struggle over health care." *NYTimes*, 9/23/93, p. A11.

HANKY PANKY

noun - questionable activity, trickery, sexual play.

"The details about JFK's early campaign for Congress are fascinating, a portrait in ballot HANKY-PANKY and strong-arming but also in growing political maturity." Rick Kogan, *Chicago Trib.*, 9/20/92, S 5, p. 3.

"Rather than fill the drought with, say, further investigation into the White House campaign-finance scandals - how many Americans even knew that Charlie Trie was indicted last week? - the media instead try to strike lascivious sparks from damp wood. MSNBC trots out grainy newsreel footage of the Wilson and Harding Administrations in its search for novel Presidential HANKY-PANKY." Frank Rich, *NYTimes*, 2/4/98, p. A23.

"Partly, of course, the difference between [Watergate and the Clinton impeachment] is the difference between the nature of the alleged offenses: HANKY-PANKY with the Constitution vs. HANKY-PANKY with an intern." Neal Gabler, *NYTimes*, 12/13/98, p. 15.

HAPLESS

adjective - unfortunate.

"These are amusing sequences, rich with well-timed profanity, but no funnier than his equally successful efforts to persuade a San Antonio tailor to outfit his White House staff in ranch clothes (at wholesale prices) and a New York hairdresser to fly to Washington to do Lady Bird's hair and spruce up a few of his secretaries, one of whom has 'got to have a bale cut off if I'm going to look at her through Christmas.' Lyndon Johnson, worth eight figures at the time, says he is living from paycheck to paycheck, and would the hairdresser do it out of patriotism? 'This is your country,' the President says, 'and I want to see what you want to do about it.' 'Don't even worry about that, Mr. President,' says the HAPLESS hairdresser." Editorial, *NYTimes*, 10/11/97, p. A20.

"The Rodham saga [of Hillary's brothers Tony and Hugh], not to mention Roger Clinton's HAPLESS singing career, Ron Reagan's HAPLESS talk show career, Patti Reagan's HAPLESS writing career and Neil Bush's Silverado Savings and Loan fiasco, put one aspect of the current Presidential race in clearer focus. Legions of Americans have attempted to cash in on their relationship to the most powerful man in the world, but George W. Bush is one of the few who is actually succeeding at it." Gail Collins, *NYTimes*, 9/24/99, p. A27.

HARDSCRABBLE

adjective - marked by poverty or difficulty.

"Mr. [Gary] Bauer, 53, who is married with three children, grew up in Newport, Ky., a blue-collar, HARDSCRABBLE Cincinnati suburb. He said in an interview that his father, whose jobs included mopping floors, driving trucks and milling steel, alternately implored him to make more of himself and told him that he probably never would.

'He was a very mean drunk,' Mr. Bauer recalled." Frank Bruni, *NYTimes*, 8/17/99, p. A12.

HARPY

noun - a shrewish or predatory woman; an evil person, part bird and part woman, from Greek mythology.

"This tardy effort to rehabilitate Ms. Tripp - which arrives just as Kenneth Starr has hired his own new folksy P.R. spokesman - isn't for laughs. As the *Washington Post* has observed, 'If President Clinton falls it will be Linda Tripp who largely made it happen.' And if Ms. Tripp's evidence is to spur an impeachment proceeding, it wouldn't hurt politically if she were at least somewhat more sympathetic than say, Nurse Ratched or a finger-pointing HARPY out of a dinner-theater production of 'The Crucible.'" Frank Rich, *NYTimes*, 4/25/98, p. A23.

HATCHET MAN

noun - person hired to attack others, especially their reputations or character.

"Shedding, at least for now, concerns about reviving his lingering 'HATCHET MAN' image, Mr. Dole recited a catalogue of every scandal that has touched the Clinton White House as he accused the President of presiding over one of the most unethical administrations in the nation's history." Richard L. Berke, *NYTimes*, 10/16/96, p. 1.

"In a chapter titled 'Bob Dole, Pardon Advocate,' Mr. Walsh wrote [in his forthcoming book, 'Firewall: The Iran-Contra Conspiracy and Cover-up'] that the Senator from Kansas had become the 'HATCHET MAN' for Mr. Weinberger's lawyers. 'With a sardonic ruthlessness reminiscent of Joseph McCarthy, Dole hurled a continuous barrage of unsubstantiated charges at us,' Mr. Walsh wrote." Elaine Sciolino, *NYTimes*, 10/16/96, p. A 13.

"After Mr. Dole's statement about 'Democrat wars,' Mr. Mondale quickly hauled out the characterization that had already been slapped on Mr. Dole's career: 'I think Senator Dole has richly earned his reputation as a HATCHET MAN tonight.'" Katharine Q. Seelye, *NYTimes*, 10/17/96, p A11.

"There is no doubt that Bill Clinton has demeaned the Presidency. There is no defense for his actions or his lies. But the voters have chosen him twice by substantial margins and they stand behind him still. It is not up to the HATCHET MEN of the Republican Party to undo that." Bob Herbert, *NYTimes*, 12/13/98, p. 15.

HAYMAKER

noun - a powerful blow.

"It has been six years to the week since Gennifer Flowers, an Arkansas singer, rocked Gov. Bill Clinton's first Presidential campaign with accusations that she had been sexually involved with him. White House aides say that they have become accustomed to grappling with such periodic HAYMAKERS." James Bennet, *NYTimes*, 1/22/98, p. A21.

HEAVY

noun - a villain, an actor playing a serious role.

"Personalities also played a part [in the press downplaying Iran-Contra], I think. Ronald Reagan was not a HEAVY like Richard Nixon, and George Bush is surely not." Anthony Lewis, *NYTimes*, 5/11/90, p. A15.

HEAVY WEATHER

noun - to make HEAVY WEATHER is to make a task difficult or to experience difficulty in carrying on an activity.

"The Editorial writers who had the job of concocting mortuary tributes to the late Calvin Coolidge, LL.D., made HEAVY WEATHER of it, and no wonder. Ordinarily, an American public man dies by inches, and there is thus plenty of time to think up beautiful nonsense about him. More often than not, indeed, he threatens to die three of four times before he actually does so, and each threat gives the elegists a chance to mellow and adorn their effusions. But Dr. Coolidge slipped out of life almost as quietly and as unexpectedly as he had originally slipped into public notice, and in consequence the brethren were caught napping and had to do their poetical embalming under desperate pressure." H. L. Mencken, <u>A Mencken Chrestomathy</u>, Vintage Books, 1982, p. 251.

HECTOR

verb - to harass or intimidate.

.

"In 1992 would Mr. Clinton have turned away from his proposal for a middle class tax cut if Mr. Perot had not so effectively HECTORED him on the deficit?" Alan Brinkley, *NYTimes*, 9/16/99, p. A29.

HEDONISTIC

adjective - pleasure seeking.

"The girl [Alice Roosevelt Longworth] who had seemed so single-mindedly HEDONISTIC became one of her father's most valued sources of information and advice. Theodore recognized that, of his children, she had the most political savvy." Carol Felsenthal, <u>Alice Roosevelt Longworth</u>, G.P. Putnam's Sons, 1988, p. 116.

"Democrats want payback. And Republicans have been throwing stones from glass houses for so long, they can no longer recognize hypocrisy.

"Newt Gingrich's affair with a young Capitol Hill aide was an open secret in Washington all during impeachment, and all through his pompous lectures about America's cultural and moral decline.

"At the heart of W.'s [George W. Bush's] campaign is the notion that voters made a mistake when they turned out his father for a HEDONISTIC Bill Clinton. The Bushes, the subtext goes, will uphold the moral authority of the White House." Maureen Dowd, *NYTimes*, 8/18/99, p. A25.

HEEBIE-JEEBIES

noun - shakes, jitters, willies.

"Ross Perot rails so loudly against the special interests that it is easy to forget he is one. Mr. Perot made millions processing Government medical forms. Now he has offered the Republican National Committee at least $1 million to finance a prime-time network television program saying what kind of medical care policies the Government ought to have.... But this latest Perot indulgence is driven by personal psychology rather than policy. Mr. Perot needs a demon to make his life interesting. In 1992 George Bush was his demon, and Mr. Perot worked off his HEEBIE-JEEBIES by trashing Mr. Bush's chance for re-election. Now he is in the throes of a compulsion to demonize Bill Clinton, the nice young Democrat he was so bent on helping in the campaign debates." Editorial, *NYTimes*, 7/7/94, p. A12.

HEINOUS

adjective - abominable, evil.

"Still, Bill Clinton's moral and ethical sloppiness is less HEINOUS than the unforgiving and hypocritical behavior of Henry Hyde, Bob Barr and their lynch mob. It is worse to refuse to forgive than to need forgiveness." Maureen Dowd, *NYTimes*, 1/27/99, p. A27.

HELPMATE (HELPMEET)

noun - companion, wife, helper.

"Sen. Edward Kennedy will be a Good Catch for exactly the right young woman should he decide to remarry before the '88 presidential election...the presence beside the senator of a young, vulnerable HELPMATE would soften the press harping on the 1969 death of Mary Jo Kopechne at Chappaquiddick." Diana McLellan, *Chicago Trib.*, 12/28/86, S 6, p. 6.

"In an otherwise rosy depiction of life as the HELPMATE of a rising politician [George Bush], Mrs. Bush also states, almost as an aside, that she was so deeply depressed in the mid-1970's that she sometimes stopped her car on highway shoulders for fear that she might deliberately crash the vehicle into a tree or an oncoming auto." Michael Wines, *NYTimes*, 9/8/94, p. A1.

"Scorched by the fallout after Mrs. Clinton's leadership in seeking universal health care coverage, the White House has labored to play down her influence, describing a conversion from policy-maker to speech-maker, HELPMATE and goodwill ambassador - a seemingly docile role for an accomplished lawyer with more than two decades of experience in public life and no shortage of opinions." James Bennet, *NYTimes*, 1/20/97, p. A12.

"Just as Hillary Rodham Clinton is tiptoeing back into the public's view as her husband's HELPMATE and occasional conscience, questions about her role in some of the White House's more dubious dealings are dogging her steps once again." James Bennet, *NYTimes*, 3/7/97, p. A11.

"The young [Thomas] Jefferson promised his dying wife that he would not marry again. His wife's father was also the father of the slave Sally. Thus the 38-year affair was with his wife's half-sister, who may have shared many of her characteristics. Was it lifelong love or heartless domination? No examination of the Y chromosome can tell us. But many Americans can take pride in sharing this Founder's genes as well as those of the attractive HELPMEET [Sally Hemings] Callender derogated as 'this wench.'" William Safire, *NYTimes*, 11/2/98, p. A27.

"Politics: Taking the 'Help' Out of 'HELPMATE': If Elizabeth Dole seriously wants to be a Presidential candidate, the first thing she is going to have to do is lock up her husband.

'I'm her biggest fan and supporter,' Bob Dole told Richard Berke of *The Times* this week. Mr. Dole then went on to say that he was thinking about writing a check to Senator John McCain, Mrs. Dole's competitor." Gail Collins, *NYTimes*, 5/18/99, p. A30.

HELTER-SKELTER

adjective - confused.

"Just the other day, in Indonesia, the President suggested that he might support Mr. Gingrich's idea of a constitutional amendment permitting school prayer. Then the White House mounted a swift but unconvincing damage-control operation. The whole sequence recalled Mr. Clinton's HELTER-SKELTER early days and the artless flip-flops on gays in the military, on key appointments, on a host of environmental issues and, later, on health care itself." Editorial, *NYTimes*, 11/21/94, p. A12.

"Even with his comeback victory on the crime bill in the House, President Clinton's attack-and-compromise tactics continue to give his administration a HELTER-SKELTER quality that one presidential scholar calls 'government by the perils of Pauline.'" William Neikirk, *Chicago Trib.*, 8/23/94, S 1, p. 1.

HIJINKS (HIGH JINKS)

noun - horseplay, wild behavior, revelry.

"Kennebunkport, Me. - It's been one part summer camp, one part serious meetings and one part competitive HIJINKS for President Bush as he relaxes at his oceanside summer home here before heading for summit meetings in London and Houston." Janet Cawley, *Chicago Trib.*, 7/4/90, S 1, p. 3.

"HIGH JINKS on the campaign trail is nothing new, of course, and the Gore entourage has no monopoly on humor. But some Gore aides and reporters say the clowning on the Gore campaign in which sometimes even Secret Service agents participate, goes beyond other campaigns this year. And there seem to be a number of reasons for it." Steven A. Holmes, *NYTimes*, 9/14/92, p. A14.

"Many of you have called to ask for tips on how to distinguish Mr. Forbes from Mr. Hatch, each of whom resembles an assistant principal in one of those high school HIGH-JINKS movies. The answer is that Mr. Forbes is the one who doesn't blink, while Mr. Hatch is the one who looks as if he just smelled something awful." Gail Collins, *NYTimes*, 12/3/99, p. A29.

HIND

noun - a hick, rustic.

"When he [William Jennings Bryan] began denouncing the notion that man is a mammal even some of the HINDS at Dayton were agape. And when, brought upon Clarence Darrow's cruel hook, he writhed and tossed in a very fury of malignancy, bawling against the veriest elements of sense and decency like a man frantic - when he came to the tragic climax of his striving there were snickers among the HINDS as well as hosannas." H. L. Mencken, The Vintage Mencken, Vintage Books, 1956, p. 165.

HOBSON'S CHOICE

noun - no choice at all. Derived from Thomas Hobson, an English liveryman, who, in order to protect his horses, required each customer to take the horse who had been rested for the longest period of time.

Note:Frequently confused with the concept of a bad choice or a choice between two equally threatening alternatives, i.e., "Would you rather be shot or hung?" "Caught between Scylla and Charybdis."

"Mr. Clinton presented a searing HOBSON'S CHOICE to his lovely daughter. She dutifully blessed him with her protection, holding his hand on the way to the helicopter yesterday, even though he humiliated her mother with a girl close to her own age." Maureen Dowd, *NYTimes*, 8/19/98, p. A29.

"With [Senators] Lott and Gramm staring at him as he took the floor during debate, [Senator]McCain called the [$800 billion tax-cut bill] 'seriously skewed,' but said he would vote for it. The measure passed 50-49. Slumped in a chair outside the Senate chamber afterward, McCain asked, 'Why do we always face such HOBSON'S CHOICES?'" Newsweek , 8/16/99, p.4.

HODGEPODGE

noun - mixture, jumble, MISHMOSH.

"Her [Barbara Tuchman's] rogues' gallery in "The March of Folly" is a motley and arbitrary HODGEPODGE. It includes Lyndon Johnson, who blundered by stepping up American involvement in Vietnam, and Priam, who made the mistake of dragging a wooden horse through the gates of Troy." *Newsweek*, 3/12/84, p. 82.

"But he [Jesse Jackson] seemed spent (as well as distracted by a failed teleprompter), strayed far from his text, and pieced together a speech composed of a HODGEPODGE of his greatest hits from the campaign trail." Elizabeth Drew, *New Yorker*, 8/15/88, p. 75.

"If he [President Bush] had presented the capital gains tax as part of a real plan, instead of in a HODGEPODGE, the propriety of reducing taxes on 'gains' eaten up by inflation might have impressed the public." A. M. Rosenthal, *NYTimes*, 1/31/92, p. A15.

"Is the Clinton blend of market forces and regulatory controls a uniquely American system, as its architects argue, or a HODGEPODGE, as its critics assert?" *NYTimes*, 9/23/93, p. A11.

"Back in 1985, when President Ronald Reagan selected Edmund Morris as his official biographer, the writer vowed he would produce 'a substantial, scholarly book.' Fourteen years later, after years of worrying he didn't 'understand the first thing' about his subject, Mr. Morris has produced a book that is anything but scholarly or substantial. He has produced a bizarre, irresponsible and monstrously self-absorbed book - a Ragtime-esque 'memoir' featuring a self-annotating narrator out of a Philip Roth novel and childlike hero out of 'Being There.' Even worse, this loony HODGEPODGE of fact and fiction is being sold not as a novel but as 'the only biography ever authorized by a sitting President.'" Michiko Kakutani, *NYTimes*, 10/2/99, p. A15.

HOGWASH (OM)

noun - nonsense, balderdash, codswallop.

"Mr. DeLay is addicted to the thuggish tactics of the Gingrich era, and the Speaker-designate, Robert Livingston, seems afraid to confront him in public. Consider, for example, Mr. Delay's blustering misrepresentation of censure on CNN. 'It means nothing,' Mr. DeLay said. 'It's a piece of paper that said the President did something wrong.' That is pure HOGWASH. A suitable censure resolution would state that this President has earned lasting opprobrium for failing in his constitutional duty." Editorial, *NYTimes*, 12/1/98, p. A30.

"Meanwhile, the subject of Mr. McCain's temper has been explored in a recent New York Times article, which was cited in turn in a tough editorial in The Arizona Republic. The editorial dismissed as 'HOGWASH' Mr. McCain's contention that he does not fly off the handle. Like Jimmy Carter and Bill Clinton before him, Mr. McCain may discover that dark-horse candidates from smaller states find it especially hard to convince their old neighbors that they are ready for the big time." Editorial, *NYTimes*, 11/2/99, p. A30.

"So to embarrass Mr. Clinton, the Republicans have decided to pit the State Department budget against Social Security and to say that if you are for giving money to Ghana you are for taking it away from Grandma. The foreign operations budget, says Mr. DeLay, 'will come straight out of the pockets of American seniors.' HOGWASH. There is no more direct connection between Social Security and foreign aid than there is between Social Security and the Marine Band." Thomas L. Friedman, *NYTimes*, 10/20/99, p. A31.

HOMILY

noun - sermon; a moralizing discourse, esp. a long, dull one.

"That old master of the medium Ronald Reagan came on strong for 'families' in his State of the Union message. If you weren't used to his chicken-soupy sentiments and honeyed HOMILIES, you might feel like gathering up your family and barring the door against the feds." Joan Beck, *Chicago Trib.*, 2/13/86, S 1, p. 26.

"Next to Ross Perot, the President and Governor Clinton sounded like politicians giving scripted answers. That's paradoxical, because Mr. Perot's cracker-barrel HOMILIES are no less packaged. But at least they seem fresh, and in politics appearance is everything." Susan Estrich, *NYTimes*, 10/15/92, p. A15.

"An earlier letter to Polly strung together the same HOMILIES on hard work and then, in a particularly insensitive passage, seemed to say that his own love was conditional upon her measuring up. You must apply yourself, [Thomas] Jefferson lectured, 'to play on the harpsichord, to draw, to dance, to read and talk French and such things as will make you more worthy of the love of your friends. . . . Remember too as a constant charge not to go out without your bonnet because it will make you very ugly and then we should not love you so much." Joseph J. Ellis, <u>American Sphinx</u>, Knopf, 1997, p. 92.

While the God-fearing HOMILIES spouted by politicians do not necessarily guarantee Godly behavior in private, such as the post Columbine Congressional vote to allow the display of the Ten Commandments in public schools. 'Charitable choice', endorsed by Mr. Bush as well as Mr. Gore, has something to offend everybody." Frank Rich, *NYTimes*, 9/11/99, p. A25.

HOOTERS (SL)

noun - female breasts.

"'When they look at women like Hillary Clinton, Anita Hill, Kimba Wood, Zoe Baird, YUPPIE men become terrified. And they panic. So they rush to the nearest peep house to be reminded that women really are objects created solely for their pleasure.' There might be something in what she says. So I bounced her theory off Dr. I. M. Kookie, the renowned expert on lots of stuff. Dr.

Kookie said: 'Yes, I believe that there is some validity in her observations, especially about the insecurity of YUPPIE males, who have a lot to be insecure about. However, there is another possible explanation for the growing popularity of these ["gentlemen's clubs"].' What is that? 'Maybe some guys just like to look at HOOTERS.'" Mike Royko, *Chicago Trib.*, 3/10/93, S 1, p. 3.

HORNSWOGGLE

verb - cheat, honeyfogle, hoax.

"The British Laborite Dennis Healey once said that listening to the waffling Foreign Minister Geoffrey Howe was 'like being SAVAGED by dead sheep.' After sitting through Bill Clinton's acceptance speech, I felt as if wool from that sheep had been stuffed into his mouth - and my head. ... How can you persuade the most liberal-activist wing of 'th' Amurrican people' to swallow from a Democrat what might enrage them from a Republican? You HORNSWOGGLE them with dead-sheep language." Clancy Sigal, *NYTimes*, 7/23/92, p. A15.

HOWLER

noun - anything exaggerated or excessive, esp. a glaringly ridiculous and stupid blunder. *adjective* - HOWLING

"What the people saw - what the Presidential campaign was designed, as always, to exaggerate - was the more dashing and superficial aspects of the contrast: a natural optimist against a cautionary school principal; a confident purveyor of half-truths, and often of HOWLING boners [Ronald Reagan], which yet gave more hope (and more false hope) to more people than Carter's sober insistence that life is real and earnest and painfully complicated." Alistair Cooke, *New Yorker*, 3/14/83, p. 148.

"But they are afraid that if he [Vice President Quayle] is allowed to ad-lib, out will come HOWLERS such as his statement after the San Francisco earthquake that 'the loss of life will be irreplaceable.'" *Newsweek*, 5/20/91, p. 24.

"As we keep pointing out, he [George Bush] has no other option. He can't run as the candidate of change, and he has no ideas. Bush has become Mr. Bent Numbers. They're coming so fast and so phony the press can't even keep up. Undeterred by the complete absurdity of the 128 new taxes gig, Bush is still using that HOWLER along with a new, and equally specious, charge that Clinton's economic plan 'would cause 2.6 million jobs to be lost.'" Molly Ivins, Nothin' But Good Times Ahead, Vintage Books, 1993, p. 150.

HUBRIS

noun - excessive arrogance. *adjective* - HUBRISTIC

"'To begin with,' he said, 'even for a vice president who was not as underutilized or underprepared as Dan Quayle, it takes a fair amount of

HUBRIS to have a museum named in one's honor while one is alive.'"
Maureen Dowd, *Star Trib.*, 6/20/93, p. 14A.

"Three days before presenting President Clinton with a plan to transform the welfare system, dozens of his aides gathered behind closed doors on Saturday for a frank, sometimes anguished, debate about race, class, sex and the impact of their decisions on the lives of millions of poor people. Some officials likened their work to that of the civil rights pioneers, praising the merging plan as a historic opportunity to fight poverty and reverse family breakdown. Others call some of its provisions misguided, HUBRISTIC or downright mean." Jason DeParle, *NYTimes*, 3/21/94, p. A9.

"Perhaps the only value of 'In Retrospect' [by Robert McNamara] is to remind us never to forget that these were men who in the full HUBRISTIC glow of their power would not listen to logical warning or ethical appeal. When senior figures talked sense to [President] Johnson and Mr. McNamara, they were ignored or dismissed from government. When young people in the ranks brought that message, they were court-martialed. When young people in the street shouted it, they were hounded from the country." Editorial, *NYTimes*, 4/12/95.

"In the category of sound bites delivered under oath, the prize thus far goes to Michael E. Baroody, a longtime Republican consultant and fund-raiser who testified last week that he had early on warned Haley Barbour, the Republican Party chairman, against seeking out foreign funds for a Republican-sponsored research institute. Mr. Baroody invoked an allusion no less startling than the fall of Richard M. Nixon in Watergate. He testified that he had warned Mr. Barbour against HUBRIS and his exact words were: 'We could get the money, all right; that would be easy. But it would be wrong.'" Frances X. Clines, *NYTimes*, 7/28/97, p. A9.

"His [Lyndon Johnson's] suspicion and HUBRIS led him to abuses of the sort that got Richard Nixon forced out of office. He had the FBI monitor Bobby Kennedy, infiltrate civil rights groups and wiretap not only Martin Luther King Jr. but Johnson's own vice president." Steve Chapman, *Chicago Trib.*, 5/28/98, S 1, p. 21.

"Although Mr. Carter's constant efforts for world peace have generally won him admiration, they have sometimes exasperated diplomats and administration officials. 'It can be a problem when you have this free lance peace negotiator parachuting into the world's trouble spots,' Professor Brinkley said. 'Jimmy Carter has a valid intellectual stance in these situations, which is, "Let's stop fighting and then negotiate." But he wants to duplicate the Camp David accords, so sometimes the HUBRIS factor overflows.'" Sara Rimer, *NYTimes*, 2/16/00, p. 21.

HULLABALOO

noun - ruckus, uproar, commotion.

"In 1988, when he [George P. Bush] was 12, he was an unwitting participant in a short-lived HULLABALOO about the way his grandfather, then the vice president, introduced him and his two Mexican-American siblings to President Reagan. Vice President Bush affectionately called them 'the little brown ones.'" Frank Bruni, *NYTimes*, 4/18/00, p. A18.

HUMBUG

noun - something false, deceptive or misleading.

"...the spending cuts needed to reach the Dole target by 2002 would make Dracon of Athens look like a pussycat. Mr. Dole ruled out touching some of the biggest items: defense, Social Security, Medicare, Veterans' benefits. All other government activities would have to be cut not 5 but 37 percent. That figure comes from a study by the Center on Budget and Policy Priorities, and it is convincing.... You do not have to be an economist to understand that Senator Dole's economic plan is HUMBUG. But economists do not think much of it either." Anthony Lewis, *NYTimes*, 10/7/96, p. A19.

HUMONGOUS

adjective - huge, gigantic.

"But [Jim] Baker has assured top Repubs in Congress that the Prez [George Bush] won't promise any tax cut that would add to the already HUMONGOUS deficit." O'Malley & Collin Inc., *Chicago Trib.*, 8/24/92, S 1, p. 12.

HUNKER

verb - to crouch or squat; to make things secure, as in "HUNKER down."

"HUNKERED down at the worst moment of the Bush Presidency, White House aides seemed too stunned to explain what had gone wrong, but many freely acknowledged their predicament. 'Not a sunny day in the bunker,' one of them said." *NYTimes*, 10/11/90, p. A12.

"After he attended Baptist church services in Manhattan, the Democratic presidential candidate [Bill Clinton] HUNKERED down in his headquarters hotel, the Inter-Continental, to prepare the central focus of a week of otherwise predictable events, his acceptance speech Thursday night." Mitchell Locin and Thomas Hardy, *Chicago Trib.*, 7/13/92, S 1, p. 9.

"'George Bush is HUNKERED down there in the White House, in a state of political panic,' Gore said. 'He knows that on this issue, that this cable monopoly owns him lock, stock and barrel. But he also knows the American people are overwhelmingly on the other side of the issue. So he's trying to figure out what to do.'" George E. Curry, *Chicago Trib.*, 9/29/92, S 1, p. 5.

"Privately, Mr. McCain's mood was dark and 'rarely brightened,' according to his biographer, Robert Timberg. But publicly he never HUNKERED down, as did some of the other members of the Keating Five, the sobriquet Mr. McCain always hated because it did not differentiate among their different levels of involvement..." Jill Abramson and Alison Mitchell, *NYTimes*, 11/21/99, p. 32.

III

IACOCTION (SL)

noun - "An arrangement by which, in the name of free enterprise and private capitalism, a corporation is sustained by a combination of massive government loans, arrogance, hype, and the tolerance of competing companies." Eugene J. McCarthy, *Harper's*, 2/90.

Note: Inspired by the federal government's bailout of Chrysler Corporation and its President, Lee Iacocca, this is a coinage of former Senator Eugene McCarthy and the above definition by Senator McCarthy appeared in the February, 1990 *Harper's*. James Warren, *Chicago Trib.*, 1/25/90, S 5, p. 2.

ICON

noun - an image, idol or symbol.

"There was George Washington, the 'Father of Our Country,' who had the largest monument to patriarchal achievement in the world, dwarfing the memorials of the other American ICONS. Then there was Abraham Lincoln, who had a bigger memorial on the Tidal Basin than Jefferson and was usually the winner whenever pollsters tried to rate the greatest American presidents." Joseph J. Ellis, <u>American Sphinx</u>, Knopf, 1997, pp. 4-5.

"Jefferson was no longer just an essential ingredient in the American political tradition; he was the essence itself, a kind of free-floating ICON who hovered over the American political scene like one of those dirigibles cruising above a crowded football stadium, flashing words of inspiration to both teams." Joseph J. Ellis, <u>American Sphinx</u>, Knopf, 1997, p. 8.

ICONOCLAST

noun - one who destroys religious images or ICONS; one who attacks established beliefs or institutions; a radical.

"Carolyn Bessette-Kennedy, the very tall, very blond former Calvin Klein publicist, personal shopper for celebrities, dream date of Saudi princes, hockey players and Calvin Klein underwear models, is the new ICON for our celebrity-addicted age." Maureen Dowd, *NYTimes*, 10/3/96, p. A15.

"A very peculiar thing is happening. Just as she becomes the single most degraded wife in the history of the world, Mrs. Clinton is being promoted from celebrity into ICONICITY. The power elite is deep into Hillary hysteria, treating the glossy, domesticated, upswept, inauthentic version of the First Lady like a combination of Princess Di and Mother Courage. Dan Rather said she'd make a good Presidential candidate, and *Time* is considering beatifying her as Person of the Year." Maureen Dowd, *NYTimes*, 12/9/98, p. A31.

"Why is Mrs. Clinton hailed as 'a woman of stature, and an ICON to American women,' as the *Vogue* editor Anna Wintour puts it, only after she's been demeaned in this gross, horrible, painful way?" Maureen Dowd, *NYTimes*, 12/9/98, p. A31.

"In journeying to Las Vegas, Mr. [Ross] Perot came to the West where his ICONOCLASTIC appeal may be the strongest, and an area that Republican candidates have had a lock on since 1964." Steven A. Holmes, *NYTimes*, 6/5/92, p. A12.

"There is a curious thing about the John McCain phenomenon. Populist campaigns usually arise from adversity. In this time of unprecedented prosperity, one would expect voters to be fat and happy, contented with the status quo. Why, then, are so many turning to an ICONOCLAST, a candidate who promises to shake things up?" Anthony Lewis, *NYTimes*, 2/12/00, p. A 29.

IDIOT SAVANT

noun - a mentally defective person with an exceptional skill in a special field, i.e., music or mathematics.

"Let's face it: Perot is like a cross-wired IDIOT SAVANT whose yes-by-crackey insights and common sense about big business, government and the human condition are regularly interrupted by outbursts of pure political craziness. That's No. 1. His respectability as a candidate for president is as a slightly GOOFY billionaire who paid cash to get on the ballot nationwide and now is buying up hours of expensive time on television, babbling away about himself and uttering a few unvarnished truths about the national government that you could hear at any neighborhood bar. That's No. 2." Leonard Larsen, *Chicago Trib.*, 10/28/92, Sec 1, p. 19.

IMBROGLIO (EMBROGLIO)

noun - a complicated situation; a predicament; an embarrassing misunderstanding.

"Despite the tempests that have swirled around [Dan] Rather over the last year, he just completed his 17th consecutive week atop the A.C. Nielsen news ratings ladder. It is a statistic likely to bolster his standing inside CBS, despite the Bush IMBROGLIO." Steve Daley, *Chicago Trib.*, 1/27/88, S 1, p. 12.

"The brutal political reality [said Richard Nixon] is that standing tough against Jackson would help Dukakis with some whites, not only in the South, but in some of the key urban states in the North. Thus, to a certain degree the Jackson IMBROGLIO could be a net plus.'" Gerald M. Boyd, *NYTimes*, 7/15/88, p. 8.

"Tuesday, Santos blamed [Mayor Richard M.] Daley for the snub [not asking her to join the Illinois delegation] and said Arkansas Gov. Bill Clinton, the all-but-certain Democratic presidential nominee, ought to help straighten things out if he wants to get support from minorities and continue to mention Daley as a potential vice presidential candidate. Word of the IMBROGLIO in Illinois had not reached Clinton headquarters in Little Rock when a Clinton spokesman, Jeff Eller, was asked about it." Lynn Sweet, *Chicago Sun-Times*, 5/28/92, p. 16.

"Having survived impeachment, President Clinton and his defenders had hoped that the legal repercussions from the Monica S. Lewinsky IMBROGLIO were over. By holding Mr. Clinton in contempt, Judge Susan Webber Wright dashed those hopes." Jill Abramson, *NYTimes*, 4/13/99, p. A21.

IMMISCIBLE

adjective - incapable of mixing, as in oil and water.

"In 1948 the crystal ball was clouded [in the presidential contest between Thomas A. Dewey and Harry S. Truman]. Most of the experts - pundits, prophets, pollsters, prognosticators - were way off target when they forecast the behavior of the American voters on November 2. In America, politics and certitude may well be IMMISCIBLE." Paul F. Boller, Jr., <u>Presidential Campaigns</u>, Oxford University Press, 1996,p.268.

INAMORATA

noun - a woman with whom one is in love.

"[John F.] Kennedy has become the case study for sex in presidential politics... Yet there were no sightings of him arm in arm on a lonely night street, no public confessions by INAMORATAS, no telephone records or photos." Hugh Sidey, *Time*, 5/18/87, p. 20.

INCREMENTALISM

noun - a policy of social or political changes by degrees.

"Though often derided as political gestures, some of the little ideas from advocating school uniforms to insuring overnight hospital stays for new mothers, have had significant influence around the country. Taken together, Mr. Clinton's initiatives have produced coherent and substantial changes in health care, and to a lesser extent in education and social services. His ideas are screened by pollsters and picked in part to enhance his popularity. But brick by brick, Bill Clinton is proving himself to be the INCREMENTAL President, accomplishing piecemeal some of what he cannot do all at once." James Bennet and Robert Pear, *NYTimes*, 9/8/97, p. 1.

INELUCTABLE

adjective - inevitable, unavoidable.

"While Mr. Clinton all but acknowledged that the treaty would not be ratified while he is in office, he adamantly refused to sign a document formally asking that it be withdrawn and agreeing not to submit it again during his

Presidency. 'They want me to give them a letter to cover the political decision that they have made that does severe damage to the interest of the United States and the interest of non-proliferation in the world?' Mr. Clinton said angrily. 'I don't think so.'...Senator Daniel Patrick Moynihan, Democrat of New York, said the spread of nuclear technology would be 'INELUCTABLE' if the test-ban treaty was voted down by the United States. 'We must not reject the treaty,' Mr. Moynihan said. 'The word will be that we said "No," just as in 1919 we said "No" to the Treaty of Versailles." He was answered by Senator James M. Inhofe, Republican of Oklahoma, who characterized the treaty as 'nothing short of unilateral disarmament.'" John M. Broder, *NYTimes*, 10/9/99, p. A6.

INFOMERCIAL (Sl)

noun - a commercial that informs in an entertaining manner. cf. INFOTAINMENT.

"But Perot's support in national polls has doubled since the TV debates earlier this month. And he is spending enormous amounts of money - more than $2 million a day in October - on network TV ads, as well as his 30- and 60- minute 'INFOMERCIALS.'" Steve Daley, *Chicago Trib.*, 10/28/92, Sec 1, p. 1.

"By popularizing the INFOMERCIAL - the industry's cloyingly coy name for lengthy spots disguised as programming - Mr. Perot earned a dubious honor. Perhaps he might have improved his standing in the polls had he dumped Mr. Stockdale from the ticket in favor of the INFOMERCIAL celebrity Jay (The Juiceman) Kordich. 'No.'" Stuart Elliot, *NYTimes*, 11/3/92, p. C2.

"Perot also launched his latest television 'INFOMERCIAL,' titled 'Chicken Feathers,, Deep Voodoo and the American Dream,' on Sunday night. The half-hour program, in which Perot again brandished a 'voodoo stick' and flip charts, took aim at Bill Clinton's record as Arkansas governor and President Bush's stewardship of the economy but contained little new information about what Perot would do as president." Karen Thomas, *Chicago Trib.*, 11/2/92, S 1, p. 3.

INFOTAINMENT (Sl)

noun - information programs presented in an entertainment format; "news lite." cf. INFOMERCIAL. *verb* - INFOTAIN.

"We [in the United States] are overadvertised, over-INFOTAINED (a new word coined by a CBS executive to describe television news, combining information and entertainment)." Eugene J. McCarthy, Up 'Til Now, Harcourt Brace Jovanovich, 1987, p. 209.

"Perot is experimenting with innovative ways to communicate directly with voters and find new constituencies. He has appeared on 'INFOTAINMENT' TV shows such as 'Donahue' and 'Larry King Live,' which the president has disdained as undignified." Kenneth T. Walsh, *U.S. News & World Report*, 6/1/92, p. 28.

IVYSPEAK (SL)

noun - locutions popular in upper middle class circles on the East Coast, esp. among Ivy League graduates. cf. BUSHSPEAK.

"[George] Bush also uses a clumsy verbal shorthand - 'the vision thing' for world view, for example, and 'big mo' for electoral momentum. It is these verbal infelicities, this fondness for 'IVYSPEAK,' more than anything else, that has created his 'WIMP' image and prompted savage barbs from the press, from television comedians, from Democrats and, privately, from some Republicans." R. W. Apple, Jr., *NYTimes*, 8/18/88, p. 14.

"But those IVYSPEAK exclamations like 'whoopsie daisy' and 'by golly' still pop up in his [George Bush's] conversation, making him seem like a patrician vacationing at a dude ranch." *NYTimes*, 6/8/92, p. A8.

JJJ

JABBERWOCKY

noun - meaningless or nonsense speech or writing.
Note:JABBERWOCKY is the title of a nonsense poem in Lewis Carroll's Through the Looking Glass.

"These days, White House specialists are content with the modulated, unflappable, fact-and-slogan-crammed Presidential image that Mr. Clinton has adopted as his campaign alter ego. But the very thing his aides fear sounds much more interesting - 'high JABBERWOCKY' is their private term for it, Mr. Clinton's weakness for rambling uncontrollably after a long speaking day, jerry-building some hortatory bridge to Nirvana. His leap last week from the Internet to 'newborn babies with a genetic map in their hands' showed some promise. But it doesn't compete with the classic JABBERWOCKY of Gerald L.K. Smith, a preacher-ACOLYTE of [Senator Huey P.] Long's underclass exploitations, in his 1935 third-party warning to Establishment politicians that 'the arm wavin', baby havin', stump grabbin', sod bustin', go-to-meetin', God fearin' American people are about to take over the United States Government of America!'" Francis X. Clines, *NYTimes*, 10/13/96, p. 6.

"Such is Byrd's unique role, ensuring that he will be central during the upcoming trial of President Clinton. He has held more Senate leadership posts than anyone in history. He has written a two-volume history of the institution. He is the unchallenged master of Senate procedures, the final authority on its customs.... Byrd uses words so obscure that to most listeners, he could be making them up like Lewis Carroll in his poem JABBERWOCKY. Byrd has accused opponents of being 'ultracrepitarian critics,' of using 'MALEDICENT language,' of having a 'contumelious lip.'" Naftali Bendavid, *Chicago Trib.*, 1/10/99, S 1, p. 14.

JANUS-FACED

adjective - (1) looking in two directions; (2) deceitful, two- faced.

"[Jesse] Jackson is a JANUS candidate. With one face he confronts the future: American politics will not be the same when he is through, and he is unquestionably paving the way for some serious black candidate who will emerge before this century is out. But with his other face he looks to a racist past, and his unfortunate statements, his thoughtless insults to the person and the intelligence of the general voter, have alienated about twice as many voters as his CHARISMA has attracted. His verbal excesses terrify, and his threatening behavior repels." James A. Michener, *The New Republic*, 6/4/84, p. 17.

"U.S. President Bill Clinton continues to oscillate relentlessly between the characters of warbound Mars and the goddess of love, Venus. The United States has never seen such a JANUS-FACED president, bearing a war mask against Saddam Hussein and an expression of contrite repentance for the Monica Lewinsky scandal." *La Stampa*, Turin, Italy, quoted in *Chicago Trib.*, 1/16/99, S 1, p. 21.

JAPE

noun - joke, jest, wisecrack.

"[President Franklin D. Roosevelt said, 'Well, my dear, even the Republicans would agree that as a President, I'm a good bartender.' It wasn't much of a JAPE, but it was a presidential one." Herman Wouk, <u>The Winds of War</u>, Pocket Books, 1973, p. 431.

"The second Reagan-Mondale round in 1984 went to the elderly Mr. Reagan by consensus, owing to his JAPE about Mr. Mondale's comparative youth. This is informing the public?" Tom Wicker, *NYTimes*, 5/22/91, p. A15.

JEREMIAD

noun - a long lamentation or complaint.

"...Clinton mounted the pulpit to address a meeting of black ministers. The President wondered what Martin Luther King, Jr. would say if he were to return. In answering the question, the President presented a JEREMIAD: 'He would say, "I did not live and die to see the American family destroyed. I did not live and die to see thirteen-year-boys get automatic weapons and gun down nine-year-olds just for the kick of it."'" Sidney Blumenthal, *New Yorker*, 1/24/94, p. 41.

"Ross Perot is not one of those people who think free trade is fine as long as it's fair trade. ... No, Perot has a simple view of international trade: He's scared to death of it. That's the message of his latest 'INFOMERCIAL,' a lengthy JEREMIAD on the North American Free Trade Agreement (NAFTA) delivered Sunday." Stephen Chapman, *Chicago Trib.*, 6/3/93, S 1, p. 31.

JIHAD (JEHAD, JHAD)

noun - holy war, bitter strife or crusade (originally Islamic holy war).

"The MOUNTEBANK, Bryan, after years of preying upon the rustics on the promise that we would show them how to loot the cities by wholesale and *à outrance*, now reverses his collar and proposes to lead them in a JEHAD against what remains of American intelligence, already beleaguered in a few walled towns. We are not only to abandon the social customs of civilization at the behest of a rabble of peasants who sleep in their underclothes; we are now to give up all the basic ideas of civilization and adopt the gross superstitions of the same mob." H. L. Mencken, The American Scene, Ed. by Huntington Cairns, Vintage Books, 1982, p. 48.

"Kemp also said attempts to raise questions about marital fidelity have no place in the campaign for the Nov. 3 presidential elections. 'I do not want to see a religious war, a JIHAD, or some type of battle that splits America,' said Kemp, who is widely regarded as a potential presidential candidate in 1996." Reuters, *Chicago Trib.*, 8/24/92, S 1, p. 8.

"As long as the pragmatic Mr. Reed and his slick machine, the Christian Coalition, were the most visible G.O.P. theocrats, there was always some hope that backroom compromises or Sunday-morning-TV spin would soften or camouflage the most extreme JHADS of Pat Buchanan or Pat Robertson before they scared away the center of the American electorate." Frank Rich, *NYTimes*, 1/14/98, p. A15.

JIMBAKER (SL)

verb - to turn to someone who can effect compromises and solutions to difficult problems with great political skill.

"Jim Baker is more than mere mortal. He is the embodiment of a distinctive idea, a definition. As a verb, to JIMBAKER means to turn to someone who can pull together disparate forces with consummate political skill and forge a compromise acceptable to all. As a noun, a JIMBAKER is the product of this effort. 'JIMBAKERISH' is the adjective, 'JIMBAKERLY' the adverb. President Bush, JIMBAKERED the economy in the first presidential debate...." William Neikirk, *Chicago Trib.*, 10/14/92, S 1, p. 19.

"When Baker took over for Donald Regan as treasury secretary in the Reagan administration, he immediately engineered a fall in the value of the dollar that helped ease the pain on American manufacturing by boosting U.S. exports. Reagan achieved the distinction of being the first president to JIMBAKER the economy." William Neikirk, *Chicago Trib.*, 10/14/92, S 1, p. 19.

JUDAS GOAT

noun - a decoy who leads others to their death; a traitor.

Note:A JUDAS GOAT is a goat trained to lead other goats to the slaughter pen, veering off at the last minute to avoid their fate.

"At Berkeley, California, in March, as he [Senator Eugene J. McCarthy] was speaking before a large group of students, a hostile crowd of 'new leftists' began to heckle McCarthy. Jeering and booing, they delayed McCarthy's opening remarks. Finally he began:

"'Some say I was a JUDAS GOAT trying to lead the people back to President Johnson,' the senator said.

"'RIGHT!' screamed the new leftists.

"'And some say I was a stalking horse for Senator Kennedy,' McCarthy added.

"'RIGHT!' chorused the new leftists.

"'Right?' asked McCarthy in mock bewilderment. 'It's pretty hard to do both, I'll assure you!'" Bill Adler, <u>The McCarthy Wit</u>, Fawcett Publications, Inc., 1969, p. 25.

KKK

KEISTER (Sʟ)

noun - the buttocks; wazoo, GAZOO.

Note:President Reagan is not the only political leader to use the human posterior as a point of reference. The late Mayor Richard J. Daley of Chicago, responding to charges by critics, said that if they didn't like the way he was running Chicago they could kiss his "mistletoe," generally considered as a reference to the old wazoo.

"What seems to be happening in the [President Ronald] Reagan administration is that in response to the president's well-know irritation with leaks - he said at one point he'd had it up to his 'KEISTER' with them - interagency task force studies on secrecy have been launched under the direction of the Justice Department.... The Reagan administration's secrecy policy could do great harm to free expression and even to national security. This is a high price to pay because the president has a pain in his KEISTER." Morton Kondracke, *Chicago Sun-Times*, 4/7/83, p. 63.

"Reagan has in fact created an almost mythic figure: the regular guy who has 'had it up to my KEISTER' with all the perfidies of Washington - leaks, big spending, big government." Elizabeth Drew, *New Yorker*, 2/20/84, p. 118.

"New York, as *cher* Nancy's husband Ron would put it, is on its KEISTER." Michael Kilian, *Chicago Trib.*, 3/13/91, S 7, p. 4.

KERFUFFLE

noun - fuss, flap, disorder, disarray.

Note: Also spelled "CARFUFFLE" and "CURFUFFLE." A British expression which was a favorite of S.J. Perelman.

"Jeffrey Toobin caused a KERFUFFLE when he wrote in the *New Yorker* this week that Bill Clinton was interested in running for the Senate from Arkansas in 2002. If Mr. Clinton won in his home state and Mrs. Clinton won in somebody else's home state, they would make history as the first connubial Senate team." Maureen Dowd, *The NYTimes*, 6/30/99, p. A29.

"First it looked as if Bill [Clinton] was trying to help Hillary out on the Puerto Rican terrorist clemency deal. Then Hillary tried to capitalize on Bill's peace efforts in Northern Ireland, and rationalize with them. Now Hillary has waded into yet another ethnic KERFUFFLE with the Pakistanis, leaving the impression that she might be influencing Bill's policy decisions for a pot of gold [a Pakistani fundraiser for her New York senate race]." Maureen Dowd, *NYTimes*, 3/15/00, p. A29.

KINETIC (OM)

adjective - active, lively.

"The George Bush who 'froze' on stage with Reagan at the 1980 Nashua, N.H. high school debate was not the real George Bush, his friends say. Nor was the HyperKINETIC individual who debated Geraldine Ferraro in 1984 and then bragged that he had 'kicked a little ass.'" David Broder, *Chicago Trib.*, 3/31/86, S 1, p. 11.

"This whole city [Washington, D.C.] is focusing its collective KINETIC energy on what did the President know and when did he know it.'" Senator Warren B. Rudman, *NYTimes*, 12/22/86, p. 1.

"But his [Bruce Babbitt's] real strength is in small settings. Up close, the bobbing, KINETIC figure on the television screen transmogrifies into the modest hero of a Saturday afternoon Western. Woody Allen becomes Gary Cooper, Don Knotts turns into Jimmy Stewart." Wayne King, *NYTimes*, 1/28/88, p. 11.

KISSY-FACE (Sl)

noun - an insincere display of affection or friendship; making nice-nice.

"'Clinton is going to Beijing to play KISSY-FACE with the Chinese,' said John Mearsheimer, a University of Chicago political scientist. 'What does that tell the Indians?' It tells India that it is being encircled by an alliance of the United States, China and Pakistan, itself a customer for Chinese and American arms, Mearsheimer said. Two of these nations have the bomb, and Pakistan might be developing it. So, in this light, the Indian tests seem almost mandatory." R. C. Longworth, *Chicago Trib.*, 5/24/98, S 2, p. 4.

KLUTZ

noun - an awkward, clumsy, accident-prone person.

"The rumormongers in Washington have been spreading the story that President Bush might dump Dan Quayle. But Bush has put an end to that malicious talk by flatly saying he's not going to do it. And that's good news.

For one thing, it shows that Bush is not going to be swayed by polls. In Quayle's case, some polls currently show that 63 percent of Americans think he's kind of a KLUTZ. That's why some Republicans think he should be dumped. But Bush knows that polls can go up as fast as they go down. So all it would take is for Quayle to do something like spelling 'potato' *and* 'tomato' correctly, and his KLUTZ rating could drop to a more acceptable 62 percent." Mike Royko, *Chicago Trib.*, 7/23/92, S 1, p. 3.

KNEE-JERK

adjective - predictable, automatic, reflexive.

"Can President Clinton be serious when he complains to *Rolling Stone* magazine about never getting 'one damn bit of credit' from the 'KNEE-JERK liberal press'?... We are speaking of a person hardened to ridicule. Even his political label - 'KNEE-JERK liberal' - invites the world to think him moronic, the kind of numskull whose ideas are never passed through his brain for close examination, but are produced by rubber hammers tapping his knee." Russell Baker, *NYTimes*, 11/30/93, p. A15.

"Martin Luther King, Jr. and the rest of that vast black movement of the dispossessed who were being so inconsiderate of [President] Kennedy's problems were the ultimate in 'KNEE-JERK' and 'bleeding-heart-liberalism.'" Russell Baker, *NYTimes*, 11/30/93, p. A15.

KNOW-NOTHING

noun - an ignoramus; a person fearful of intellectuals and foreign influences.

"Millard Fillmore ran as the KNOW NOTHING candidate in 1856." Carl T. Rowan, *Chicago Sun-Times*, 4/10/92, p. 31.

"Why not, for one good example, stop apologizing because the American Civil Liberties Union has taken some positions Mr. Dukakis doesn't share? Hit back instead at George Bush for siding with Ed Meese in a KNOW-NOTHING attack on an organization that fights for every American's freedom of speech, religion, assembly, political views and right to be let alone." Tom Wicker, *NYTimes*, 10/11/88, p. 27.

"Perot starts the campaign without clear positions on most issues, and he says voters don't care. He argues that Americans simply want a strong leader who will use common sense to fix what ails the country. Some Democratic and Republican strategists fear that voters are so fed up with Washington's paralysis that millions will buy Perot's brand of KNOW-NOTHINGISM." Kenneth T. Walsh, *U.S. News & World Report*, 6/1/92, p. 28.

"'You have to remember that the '52 campaign was run in the shadow of the Cold War and there was Red-baiting by [Joseph] McCarthy and Nixon,' Schlesinger pointed out. 'Stevenson became a beacon for intellectuals, standing up against the onslaught of the KNOW-NOTHINGS.'" Michael Bonesteel, *Wilmette Life*, 9/13/90, p. D2.

"I am not a KNOW-NOTHING. . . How could I be? How can anyone who abhors the oppression of Negroes be in favor of degrading classes of white people? Our progress in degeneracy appears to me to be pretty rapid. As a nation we began by declaring that 'all men are created equal.' We now practically read it 'all men are created equal, except Negroes and foreigners and Catholics.' When it comes to this, I shall prefer emigrating to some country where they make no pretense of loving liberty - to Russia, for instance, where despotism can be taken pure, and without the base alloy of hypocrisy." Abraham Lincoln, speech quoted in <u>Bartlett's Quotations</u>, 15th Edition, p. 520.

KOOK

noun - an eccentric, a screwball, a strange person.

"Like Mr. Perot, he [R. Clay Mulforn, an original board member of the group] contends that the critics represent a tiny but noisy minority who have attracted attention from news organizations by raising the specter of Mr. Perot as an authoritarian KOOK." *NYTimes*, 6/1/93, p. A10.

KOWTOW

verb - to fawn, to be obsequiously deferential, to TOADY.

"It is those black voters whom Democrats want to go to Mondale in November, but not at the cost of driving away others - Southern whites, Northern ethnic whites and Jews - who would be displeased if they saw the party KOWTOWING to the fiery black preacher." Jon Margolis, *Chicago Trib.*, 6/24/84, S 1, p. 8.

"Lyndon Johnson's college classmates had thought that this talent with older men was nothing more than flattery, 'KOWTOWING, suck-assing, BROWN-NOSING' so blatant that 'words won't come to describe it,' but Corcoran, a King of Flatterers himself, knew it was much more. He knew a master of the art when he saw one." Robert A. Caro, <u>The Years of Lyndon Johnson: The Path to Power</u>, Knopf, 1982, p. 449.

"President Bush has made it clear that he's more concerned about helping Soviet leader Mikhail Gorbachev than KOWTOWING to the hard right in his party. In recent weeks, he has announced plans to normalize trade relations with the Soviet Union and to give the Soviets greater access to American technology." Editorial, *Chicago Trib.*, 5/12/90, S 1, p. 10.

"George Bush and Bill Clinton are willing to do almost anything [to appease Ross Perot]. Both campaigns sent heavyweights to Dallas Monday to KOWTOW to Perot and his followers." Editorial, *Chicago Trib.*, 9/29/92, S 1, p. 16.

LLL

LACKLUSTER

adjective - dull, boring, pedestrian, mediocre; lit. lacking in brilliance or luster.

"Mr. [Jesse] Jackson was kind about Mr. Gore's LACK-LUSTER start for 2000. 'I have lots of respect for him,' he said in a telephone interview. But he added something that should make Mr. Gore shiver: 'And for Bill Bradley.'" Maureen Dowd, *NYTimes*, 5/12/99, p. A27.

"But Taft could not change his personality and essentially judicial temperament overnight. When one irate Republican complained about the LACKLUSTER speeches he had been giving, Taft replied: 'I am sorry, but I cannot be more aggressive than my nature makes me. That is the advantage and disadvantage of having been on the Bench. I can't call names and I can't use adjectives when I don't think the case calls for them, so you will have to get along with that kind of a candidate." Donald F. Anderson, <u>William Howard Taft</u>, Cornell University Press, 1973, p. 48.

"Because of the accelerated primary schedule next year, the nomination for both parties may well be locked up by March. That leaves little time to churn through a full range of issues and personalities. Mr. George W. Bush's less-than-spectacular performance was of interest, not simply because of the voting but because he delivered a LACKLUSTER speech. He will almost certainly have to bring more focus to issues in the weeks ahead." Editorial, *NYTimes*, 8/17/99, p. A18.

"Ike (Dwight D. Eisenhower) eventually traveled 33,000 miles, mostly by plane, and delivered over two hundred speeches, forty of which were televised. But his early appearances [in the 1952 presidential campaign] were LACKLUSTER and disappointing to his followers." Paul F. Boller, Jr., <u>Presidential Campaigns,</u> Oxford University Press, 1996, p.282.

LACONIC

adjective - concise, terse.

"Within two weeks of the party, Senator Eugene McCarthy, carrying the antiwar banner, almost defeated President Johnson in the New Hampshire primary, and four days later Senator Robert Kennedy joined the Democratic presidential contest... McCarthy, the LACONIC poet from Minnesota, reacted with hostility to this fiery new arrival on the presidential scene. He said he alone had challenged Johnson at a time when others 'were willing to stay up on the mountain and light signal fires and dance in the light of the moon. But none of them came down, and I tell you it was a little lonely in New Hampshire. I walked alone.'" David Maraniss, <u>First in His Class: The Biography of Bill Clinton</u>, Simon & Schuster, 1995, p. 108.

"[Former Sen. Warren] Rudman takes a less benign view of the invective directed at him. 'There's no question in my mind that it's anti-Semitism,' he says....'Ralph Reed is a baby-faced assassin. He's silky smooth, butter wouldn't melt in his mouth, but he's a vicious guy.' Still, Mr. Rudman didn't sound too broken up about it. Referring to Pat Robertson, he said, 'You love to make enemies like him,' and pointed me to a 1997 incident in which Mr. Robertson ridiculed the last G.O.P. war-hero candidate, Bob Dole, as 'a LACONIC Kansan with a bad arm.'" Frank Rich, *NYTimes*, 2/26/00, p. A31.

LACUNA (PL. LACUNAE)

noun - a gap, hole or missing space.

"Has he [George W. Bush] grown up? Can we trust him? He wants us to believe that his gut instincts and moral framework can carry him over the LACUNAE in his knowledge of geopolitics. He wants us to believe that his transformation from rowdy late bloomer to mature statesman is complete and non-reversible. 'A lot of people around the world would find it rather frightening to envision a President of the United States, at the moment of probably America's greatest power in history, who seems completely uninformed on the state of the world,' says Alan Brinkley, a history professor at Columbia University. 'It's one thing to rely on the advice of aides because you have respect for their judgment. It's another to do it because you don't know enough to distinguish good advice from bad advice.'" Maureen Dowd, *NYTimes*, 9/15/99,p. A31.

"W. may have gone too far this time. Americans can forgive him [George W. Bush] not knowing that Gen. Pervez Musharraf seized power in Pakistan. But can we forgive him not knowing that Sarah Jessica Parker quaffs Cosmopolitans in Manhattan? So he thinks the Taliban is a rock band. We can live with that. But he's never heard of 'Sex and the City'? Now there's an ominous LACUNA. Americans actually care about TV." Maureen Dowd, *NYTimes*, 5/10/00, p. A29.

LAME DUCK

noun - an elected official whose term will end soon, i.e., one who has failed to be reelected and is serving out the remainder of his term until his successor is sworn in.

"To read the major newspapers and watch television, the race for President is over, with Bill Clinton easily being re-elected in the polls. Even the Doonesbury comic strip's Presidential character, the White House WAFFLE has started looking ahead to what it is going to be like as a second-term LAME DUCK." Michael Winerip, *NYTimes*, 9/30/96, p. 1.

LAOCOÖN

noun - a Trojan priest killed with his sons by sea serpents after warning the Trojans against the wooden horse in which the Greeks were hidden; a person struggling in a difficult position.

"For many months now, President Clinton has temporized on the war in Bosnia, finding one reason or another to avoid American involvement. Prudence, his backers call it. Dithering say his critics.... But it was unclear tonight, as he and his advisers wrestled with the question again, as hard pressed as LAOCOÖN and his sons struggling with the serpents, whether Mr. Clinton would finally decide to [act firmly]." R. W. Apple Jr., *NYTimes*, 2/8/94, p. A1.

LARGESSE

noun - generosity.

"With a stroke of his pen, Bush swept away six years of investigative work, one felony conviction, three guilty pleas and two pending cases, arguing that the actions of independent counsel Lawrence Walsh constituted 'the criminalization of policy difference.' Weinberger and company, however, were not charged with policy differences. They were accused of (or pleaded guilty to) lying to Congress - and, by extension, to the American people.... Happily, however, it appears the American public isn't buying Bush's logic or his lame attempt to cast the beneficiaries of his LARGESSE as patriots." Steve Daley, *Chicago Trib.*, 1/3/93, S 4, p. 4.

"Mr. Bush joked that it wasn't because of Justice Souter's Yankee heritage that the reception following the swearing-in would be 'without a lot of LARGESSE.' Referring to the impasse over enacting a new Federal budget, he said, 'I think we all know the reason.'" Neal A. Lewis, *NYTimes*, 10/9/90, p. A21.

"Using the legwork of other reporters from both the national and Texas press as a springboard for their commentary, Ms. Ivins and Mr. Dubose argue that as a candidate Mr. [George W.] Bush benefited, at crucial points in his career, from family influence and the LARGESS of corporate interests. They observe that most of the money for his failed oil business ventures was raised during the years when his father 'was either running for president or serving as Ronald Reagan's vice president'..." Michiko Kakutani, reviewing Shrub, The Short but Happy Political Life of George W. Bush by Molly Ivins and Lou Dubose, *NYTimes*, 2/18/00, p. B51.

LEITMOTIF (GER)

noun - a dominant or recurring theme.

"Clothing has become something of a LEITMOTIF in Mr. Starr's investigation. One of his potentially strongest pieces of evidence is a navy blue dress, bought at the Gap, that Ms. Lewinsky turned over to prosecutors. They are having it tested to determine whether it bears stains from a sexual encounter with the President. On Monday, during more than four hours of testimony at the White House, prosecutors asked Mr. Clinton why he chose to wear that particular tie [that Monica S. Lewinsky told prosecutors she had

151

given him] on that particular day, one Clinton adviser said." Don Van Natta, Jr. and James Bennet, *NYTimes*, 8/19/98, p. A20.

"As it had on Thursday, the question of calling witnesses [in the Clinton impeachment trial], with most Republicans in favor and most Democrats opposed, wound its way through the day's proceedings like a Wagnerian LEITMOTIF." R. W. Apple Jr., *NYTimes*, 1/16/99, p. 1.

LEVEE (OM)

noun - a reception.

"In fact, [President Abraham] Lincoln was an easy target. He freely walked Washington's streets, daily traveled to and from a summer cottage, held public LEVEES and greeted visitors to his office at frequent 'public opinion baths,' as he called them." Harold Holzer, Review of Come Retribution by William A. Tidwell, James O. Hall and David Gaddy, *Chicago Trib.*, 1/15/89, S 14. p. 5.

"Once a week, except in summer, the President held an evening reception or LEVEE. People came by the thousands to shake his hand and perhaps steal an opportunity to ask a favor of him." Benjamin P. Thomas, Abraham Lincoln Knopf, 1952, p. 471.

"The White House, usually the social Mecca of the capital, took on such an air of stern simplicity under [President] Polk, with no dancing or refreshment of any kind at the LEVEES, that one Senator declared: 'I had rather be whipped than go,' though he went none the less." Benjamin P. Thomas, Abraham Lincoln, Knopf, 1952, p. 116.

LEXICON

noun - the vocabulary of a person, group or society.

"Bill Clinton's campaign might as well have slapped a big, red 'Kick Me' sign on their candidate's back when a top aide told a Washington Post reporter about their highly organized efforts to suppress 'BIMBO eruptions.' The line immediately entered the LEXICON of the campaign when the newspaper quoted Clinton aide Betsey Wright using it. No self-respecting HATCHETMAN or hatchetwoman could let that one go by. And President Bush's didn't." Editorial, *Chicago Trib.*, 8/5/92, S 1, p. 14.

"In the ad, [Sen. John] Glenn says, 'We're just moving into a whole new time period that has tremendous advantages for the future, if we just set goals and go for it.' ('Go for it' and 'Thumbs up' are part of the Glenn LEXICON.)" Elizabeth Drew, *New Yorker*, 11/21/83, p. 186.

"When applied to Republicanism, 'moderate' is probably a cuss word in the ... LEXICON [of President Reagan]." Russell Baker, *NYTimes Magazine*, 8/16/87, p. 20.

LIBIDINOUS

adjective - lustful, lascivious.

"He [David Brock] quotes John Robert Starr, the conservative columnist and managing editor of The Arkansas Democrat: 'The difference between Bill and Hillary is that deep down Hillary is a good person.' This sentiment finds its fullest expression in Mr. Brock's detailed account of Bill Clinton's marital infidelities, which if true, suggests that he is promiscuous to a degree unrivaled even by the LIBIDINOUS J.F.K." James B. Stewart in a review of The Seduction of Hillary Rodham by David Brock, *NYTimes Book Review*, 10/13/96, p. 9.

LIBIDO

noun - sexual drive.

"Mr. Clinton has been plagued by stories of a legendary LIBIDO for years. He tacitly admitted in a national television broadcast in the New Hampshire primary campaign in 1992 that he had had an affair with Gennifer Flowers, a former nightclub singer. Betsey Wright, an aide to Mr. Clinton, spoke later about the need to suppress 'BIMBO eruptions.'" R. W. Apple Jr., *NYTimes*, 1/22/98, p. A21.

LILLIPUTIAN

adjective - a very small person.
Note:Derived from Lilliput, the country in Jonathan Swift's "Gulliver's Travels," inhabited by a race of tiny people, cf. BROBDINGNAGIAN.

"The President continued his campaign to present himself as a man of government, dealing with great issues, rather than a Gulliver immobilized by LILLIPUTIANS armed with subpoenas. Today, standing before a map of the world at the National Defense University at Fort McNair in Washington, he spoke of grand strategy, outlining a vision of the United States as global peacekeeper." Neil A. Lewis, *NYTimes*, 1/30/98, p. A12.

"His [Jefferson's] most damaging statement came in a letter to his Italian friend Philip Mazzei, in April 1796, that effectively ended his cordial relationship with Washington when it was picked up in the American press the following year: 'It would give you a fever were I to name to you the apostates who have gone over to these heresies, men who were Samsons in the field and Solomons in the council, but who have had their head shaved by the harlot England. . . . We have only to awake and snap the LILLIPUTIAN cords which they have been entangling us during the first sleep which succeeded our labors.' If, as everyone at the time assumed, Samson was George Washington and the reference to shaved heads was a comment on his support for the Jay Treaty, Jefferson's letter was both grossly unfair and extremely unpolitic." Joseph J. Ellis, American Sphinx, Knopf, 1997, p. 161.

LITANY

noun - a lengthy recitation or enumeration.

"He [Ross Perot] boasts of his unsuitability for television politics, poking fun at his Texas country-boy accent, his big, beaten nose, the great out-sticking ears that frame his face like cartilaginous quotation marks. He generally ends his LITANY of curiously likable flaws with the same shrugging summary. 'What you see,' he says, 'is what you get.'" Michael Kelly, *NYTimes*, 5/26/92, p. A1.

LOGGERHEADS (AT)

noun - a strong, obstinate, quarrelsome state of disagreement.

"Johnson himself, a Democrat who became the wartime Vice President on a Union ticket and ascended to the Presidency after Abraham Lincoln's assassination, provoked strong emotion. Senator Charles Sumner of Massachusetts, a Republican, called him 'the impersonation of the tyrannical slave power.' Johnson's resistance to the Republicans' stern reconstruction policy put him at LOGGERHEADS with Congress... After the [impeachment] vote, the Senate reconvened as a court only once more, 10 days later. The outcome on two more articles was the same. The trial was declared over. Andrew Johnson threw a party that lasted for days." Susan Sachs, *NYTimes*, 2/10/99, p. A20.

LOGODAEDALY

noun - cunning manipulation with words; verbal legerdemain.

"So for logolepts [word maniacs] who are incurably omnilegent [reading everything], here are some picks from this new collection of LOGODAELAUS [verbal legerdemain] by a columnist who is not an autologophagist [one who eats his own words]: ...'It's our fault. We should have given him better parts.' Jack Warner on hearing that Ronald Reagan had been elected governor of California." Joan Beck, *Chicago Trib.*, 9/15/86, S 1, p. 15.

"[Former Gov. William F.] Weld's new job had been a secret until he announced it today, but by this afternoon he was already well-ensconced, right down to the trademark stuffed armadillo on his shelf and the two-volume, unabridged Webster's International Dictionary (Second Edition - 'the one for the LOGODAEDALIAN,' he said, using a James Joyce word for a fancy speaker) on his table. Though he has often been mentioned as a possible Presidential candidate in 2000, Mr. Weld said today, 'I don't see running again, frankly.'" Carey Goldberg, *NYTimes*, 11/18/97, p. 12.

LOGORRHEA

noun - excessive wordiness (diarrhea of the mouth).

"Though a Bush aide insisted that the comment referred to Jackson's energy on the campaign trail, Jackson said it demonstrates in Bush a 'combination of constipation of the brain, a deficit of ideas and

[LOGORRHEA] diarrhea of the mouth.'" Mitchell Locin, *Chicago Trib.*, 5/9/88, S 1, p. 5.

"Jackson has, of course, become fabled for an inextinguishable loquacity verging on LOGORRHEA - the columnist Mike Royko has observed, 'He looks at a defenseless ear the way William (Refrigerator) Perry eyes a roast chicken' - and his compulsion to expound is not daunted by hopeless language differences." Marshall Frady, *New Yorker*, 2/3/92, p. 39.

"O.K., so there's no mint on the pillow, but there is one just blocks away. No, you can't sneak any dirty movies, but you can watch ESPN to your heart's content. And no, sadly, there are no 'magic fingers' - unless you count the ones that mysteriously extract tens of thousands of dollars from some guests' pockets without a promise of anything, no sir, not even a fluffy white bathrobe or a lousy bar of soap, in return. There are other drawbacks to passing the night at Motel 1600. There's the matter of the insomniac, LOGORHEIC host [Bill Clinton] who has been known in the wee hours to treat guests to lectures on health care and the Chilean social security system." James Bennet, *NYTimes*, 3/2/97, p. 1.

LOLLYGAG (LALLYGAG)

verb - to dawdle, to horse around or fool around.

"We will soon know if Indiana Guard slots were hard to come by in 1969, and what other influence was brought to bear [for Dan Quayle]. Then look for probes into poor grades, influence to get into law school, LOLLYGAGGING in the Guard, and any other matter to press the elitist charge." William Safire, *NYTimes*, 8/22/88, p. 19.

LOOPY

adjective - confused, nuts, crazy, eccentric, DOTTY.

"'Let's do this again,' said someone at the end [of the first news conference of his Presidency]. And why not? At the present rate, Mr. Clinton is on course to match the dubious record set by the Great Communicator himself, Ronald Reagan, who held a mere 0.5 news conferences per month. Even George Bush, LOOPY syntax and all, took the podium 2.9 times per month." Editorial, *NYTimes*, 3/24/93, p. A10.

"Even some of Mr. [Alan] Keyes's friends think that all these lonely years running for president as a black right-wing Republican have made him a little LOOPY. He does not seem to accept the fact that it is his own party that dismisses his candidacy as an oddity, useful only in enabling Republicans to make a perverse claim to diversity." Maureen Dowd, *NYTimes*, 12/5/99, p. 17.

"Gore seems never to have a spontaneous moment, though he does have a penchant for LOOPY, New Age rhetoric about environmentalism and personal fulfillment." John McCarron, *Chicago Trib.*, 1/10/00, S 1, p. 13.

LOOSEY-GOOSEY

adjective - unusually relaxed or laid back; mellow.

"Mrs. Dole, clad in a violet suit, black high heels and big gold earrings, knew what we were after. She decided to outfox us by proving she could get LOOSEY-GOOSEY. She added an 'impromptu' stop at Dairy Queen, where she let fly and ordered a cup of vanilla ice cream with fudge sauce and 'a little whipped cream and lots of nuts.'" Maureen Dowd, *NYTimes,* 5/5/99, p. A31.

LOWLIFE

noun - a person of bad moral character or inferior social position.

"No matter how hard the White House spins to the contrary, leaks are a legitimate source of news; without them, we'd never know what anyone in Washington was up to. But what about those phantom semen stains that have soiled the Lewinsky story from the start? If nothing else, they may help explain the greatest unsolved mystery of this scandal - why the public gives a President it regards as a lying PHILANDERER an approval rating rivaling the Pope's while it condemns the media and the independent counsel as LOWLIFES who should just get lost." Frank Rich, *NYTimes,* 2/11/98, p. A31.

"Part of the problem afflicting the debate is a shortage of historical parallels. Clinton's reprehensible LOW-LIFE follies are not Watergate revisited. The president did not dispatch henchmen to break into the office of Monica Lewinsky's psychologist. No one used the IRS to audit Ken Starr's tax returns. And had Richard Nixon's plumbers been on the job, they would have found a way to hotwire Linda Tripp." Walter Shapiro, *USA Today,* 9/25/98, p. 2A.

"This should be a comfort to President Clinton: He's got Woody Allen in his corner. Allen, who has first-hand experience with sex scandals, says Clinton is getting a 'raw deal' in the Monica Lewinsky case ... Allen, married to Soon-Yi, daughter of his one-time lover Mia Farrow, says Clinton was lucky that his accusers were 'such LOW-LIFES.' Allen threw GOP lawmakers Newt Gingrich, Trent Lott and Dick Armey in that category, calling them 'the bottom of the political barrel.'" Tribune News Services, *Chicago Trib.,* 11/17/98, S 1, p. 2.

LUGUBRIOUS

adjective - mournful, gloomy, melancholy.

"In any event, the last thing Al Gore needs is more ballast; the selection of a solid senior statesman (George Mitchell, of Maine, for example) would render the ticket so LUGUBRIOUS that Democratic partisans-who have a weakness for the rowdy when it comes to politics-might well sleep through Election Day." Joe Klein, *The New Yorker,* 7/3/00, p. 32.

MMM

MACHIAVELLIAN

adjective - Machiavelli's theory that in the amoral world of politics unscrupulous means to obtain or keep power are justifiable; hence, characterized by cunning or bad faith.

"Springing from unnamed sources, leaks of information about President Clinton and Monica S. Lewinsky have started a very public brawl among not only hotheaded partisans, but also normally tight-lipped, mild-mannered lawyers. To the rest of the country, the squabbling may sound like a sandbox spat. But within the Beltway, the leaks - and subsequent fingerpointing and name-calling - are being picked apart on talk shows and around dinner tables like grandmasters' chess moves, with ever more fevered theories of MACHIAVELLIAN strategy being spun to explain who is spreading the information, and why." James Bennet, *NYTimes*, 2/9/98, p.A15.

"The mayor's wife [Donna Hanover] has announced she will do a star turn Off Broadway in 'The Vagina Monologues,' a feminist meditation featuring just the kind of graphic sexuality that Rudy Giuliani has been trying to stamp out for years... Given Rudy's crusades against the Brooklyn Museum's 'Sensation' exhibition and X-rated businesses, Donna's decision to appear in a sexually provocative play certainly looks like a thumb in the eye... Some MACHIAVELLIAN types suspect Donna's theatrical surprise is all part of Hillary's plan - working brilliantly so far - to gaslight Rudy by getting under the control freak's skin and making him feel as if he has Lost Control of the Agenda. Did the First Lady's friends help her out by offering the wife of the sanctimonious mayor the role of a lifetime?" Maureen Dowd, *NYTimes*, 4/23/00, p. 11.

MACHINATION

noun - a scheme, plot or crafty action to accomplish something evil or improper.

"Only by manipulating the public ever more thoroughly was President Nixon able to save himself from his own MACHINATIONS." Sidney Blumenthal, *New Yorker*, 8/8/94, p. 34.

"The story that was taking shape in Jefferson's mind assumed the contours of a plot to reverse the course of the American Revolution, with the chief characters on the other side cast as villainous conspirators covertly commanded by the diabolical secretary of the treasury [Hamilton], whom he described to Washington as 'a man whose history, from the moment at which history can stoop to notice him, is a tissue of MACHINATIONS against the liberty of the country which has... heaped its honors on his head.' The hatred was PALPABLE." Joseph J. Ellis, <u>American Sphinx</u>, Knopf, 1997, p. 131.

MAIN SQUEEZE (MAIN MAN)

noun - a person's sweetheart or favorite date.
Note: If the MAIN SQUEEZE is a man, he is the MAIN MAN.

"And Ms. Matalin had to fall in line and write a statement expressing half-hearted regret at her outburst. (However, most observers suspect that she didn't regret it at all and wrote the apology with her fingers crossed.) But the most discomfort was exhibited by Mr. Carville. The poor guy didn't know what to say. There he is, loyally working for Clinton. At the same time, his MAIN SQUEEZE is ridiculing Clinton as a junk-food tubbo and a PHILANDERER." Mike Royko, *Chicago Trib.*, 8/5/92, S 1, p. 3.

"Officials began looking for new forms of testosterone testing and virility vying about six years ago. When your MAIN MAN is seventy-five, this gets a little DICEY, which is obviously why they decided to enter Reagan only in blinking contests. They wanted to try him in competitive napping as well, but it's not recognized by the International Olympic Committee." Molly Ivins, Molly Ivins Can't Say That, Can She?, Random House, 1991, p. 89.

"Goldwater, whose moment in the sun was in the days before you had to hold up a placard with an aborted fetus on it in order to get the Republican nomination, apparently didn't have much to say on the subject of abortion while he was the far right's MAIN MAN. Now he has publicly given his support to those Republicans who believe that the party ought to have room for people who are pro-choice - a position that the anti-abortion zealots treat as they might treat the decision of a prominent vestryman who announces that he is resigning his duties at the church in order to devote more time to his hobby of consorting with a pack of murderers." Calvin Trillin, Too Soon to Tell, Warner Books, 1995, p. 88.

MALADROIT

adjective - awkward, bungling.

"The latest political miscue also followed Mr. Clinton's unusually MALADROIT performance at the White House correspondents' dinner, when he used an occasion normally reserved for a little self-deprecating humor to attack the conservative commentator Rush Limbaugh and the Senate Republican leader, Bob Dole, in ways that made him look mean-spirited." Thomas L. Friedman, *NYTimes*, 5/24/93, p. A11.

"It [the announcement by LBJ that he would not accept the nomination of his party for another term] also led Vice-President Hubert Humphrey to enter the presidential race with the backing of LBJ. In a strife-torn nation, though, Humphrey's speech announcing his candidacy was singularly MALADROIT: it dwelt on 'the politics of joy.'" Paul F. Boller, Jr., Presidential Campaigns, Oxford University Press, 1996, p.321.

"From the very beginning, his [George W. Bush's] often MALADROIT maneuvering on gay issues has looked more like TRIANGULATION than principle. Before the early primaries he forswore meeting with a gay Republican group; then, just before California, he said he would reconsider." Jonathan Rauch, *NYTimes*, 4/17/00, p. A25.

"Yes, Mr. [George W.] Bush probably couldn't bring the Republican Party to a DÉTENTE with homosexuality in 2000, but he could move the party to the center, folding homosexuals into his vision of 'COMPASSIONATE CONSERVATISM'." Jonathan Rauch, *NYTimes*, 4/17/00, p. A25.

MALARKEY

noun - insincere or foolish talk, balderdash.

"President Reagan, it develops, is almost the only person at the White House who doubts the persistent stories of rivalry and intrigue among his principal aides. These 'tales,' he told several reporters in an interview, are 'a great exaggeration.' And indeed, it may all be MALARKEY." Edwin Yoder, *Chicago Sun-Times*, 5/10/83, p. 32.

"The President's no-new-taxes promise is MALARKEY, of course. On my home ground, which is probably much like yours, the gasoline tax has gone up five cents since the President [George Bush] made his famous pledge and the property tax is being raised at this very moment." Russell Baker, *NYTimes*, 4/11/90, p. A15.

"Mark Penn, [President Clinton's] pollster, said 'The public had already seen little logic to what was going on by this independent counsel, and with this [Paula Jones] decision the public will see even less logic in terms of pursuing an independent counsel investigation.' Another Democratic pollster, Mark Mellman, was slightly less enthusiastic. 'I don't think it dramatically changes things,' he said, 'but this signals to the public exactly what they've been thinking: there's a lot of false accusations, a lot of MALARKEY.'" Richard L. Berke, *NYTimes*, 4/2/98, p. A19.

MALCONTENT

noun - a dissatisfied or discontented person.

"While Mr. Clinton dismissed Mr. Perot yesterday as a MALCONTENT, Paul Begala, a top Presidential adviser, accused Mr. Perot of being 'desperate for attention,' adding: 'When he goes to a wedding, he wants to be the bride. When he goes to a funeral, he wants to be the corpse. He just wants to be the center of attention.'" B. Drummond Ayres, Jr., *NYTimes*, 5/28/93, p. A11.

MALEDICENT

adjective - slanderous, evil.
Note:a related word is malediction, the opposite of benediction.

"The last master of rococo cut is Senator Robert Byrd of West Virginia. A couple of years ago the Democrat took aim at the featherweight Republican Senator Rick Santorum, chastising him - without ever using his name - and others for calling the President a liar. Mourning the growing incivility of Congress, Sen. Byrd dressed down these rowdy colleagues for their 'MALEDICENT language,' 'contumelious lip,' and 'intellectual pemmican.'" Maureen Dowd, *NYTimes*, 6/21/97, p. 21.

MALEFACTOR

noun - an evildoer.

Note:Used by President Theodore Roosevelt in a speech at Provincetown, MA. on Aug. 20, 1907 in which he referred to the "MALEFACTORS of great wealth." Sometimes attributed to Franklin Delano Roosevelt who may have borrowed the phrase from his cousin, but attributed by Bartlett's to President Theodore Roosevelt.

MANDARIN

noun - a person of high standing in the artistic, intellectual and social communities, esp. the more traditional members thereof.

"Mr. Woolsey told the House Intelligence Committee that he could absorb a $1 billion cut in next year's budget but not much more - a snub of Mr. Clinton's campaign pledge to find $7.5 billion in cuts over five years. 'Precipitous' cuts, Mr. Woolsey warned, 'will cripple us in the long run.' It's understandable that a new President might waver when faced with mysteries, political connections and massed inertia of the national security MANDARINS. But it defies common sense, with no Soviet threat in prospect, to believe that the intelligence agencies can't make do with less than $28 billion." Editorial, *NYTimes*, 3/18/93, p. A14.

MANICHAEAN

adjective - philosophic dualism; a view of the world as a basic conflict between good and evil, light and dark.

"Detractors of [former President Richard M. Nixon] will decry the book's obsession with potency and winning, with geopolitical giants who are variously 'fragmented,' 'reluctant' and 'awakened,' as well as a MANICHAEAN view of the world that he sees as divided between the bad Soviet Union and the good United States. Admirers will applaud his vast knowledge of world affairs, his experience with international leaders and the way he combines hardheadedness with idealism." Christopher Lehmann-Haupt, *NYTimes*, 4/11/88, p. 21.

"What about President Reagan - where does he stand on MANICHAEANISM? The sociologist Robert Nisbet, writing in *Reason* magazine, referred to 'Reagan's MANICHAEAN division of the world into the Good and Evil empires,' although the president's visit to Moscow subsequently cast that vivid differentiation in subtler tones." William Safire, *The Kansas City Star*, 6/12/88, p. 5H.

"...there was an undertone to several of last week's speeches which indicated that several Republicans are convinced that if God is not a registered Republican, at least the devil must be a Democrat. Forgetting for a moment the problem of MANICHAEANIST heresy involved here, these Republicans seem uncomfortably reminiscent of their predecessors in the early 1950's who implied, if they did not directly charge, that their opponents were not simply misguided but doing the will of the Kremlin." Jon Margolis, *Chicago Trib.*, 8/23/88, S 1, p. 19.

"With the coming of Ronald Reagan to power, Nixon tacked hard right - an old instinct. During the summer of 1980, he published a polemic entitled 'The Real War,' which reflected a MANICHAEAN view of United States-Soviet relations: an implicit repudiation of his own Presidential approach, it was packaged as a reiteration - 'hard-headed détente.'" Sidney Blumenthal, *New Yorker*, 8/8/94, p. 37.

"Next we see Robert F. Kennedy as the MANICHAEAN bare-knuckled Senate staff counsel of the 1950's, first in the service of the Red-hunter Joseph McCarthy, later as the obsessed foe of the head of the Teamsters, James R. Hoffa." Sean Wilentz (reviewing In Love with Night by Ronald Steel), *NYTimes* Book Review, 1/30/00, p.13.

"The first lady and Blumenthal talked often. After enduring six years of investigations about everything from the Whitewater investments to her health-care task force, Mrs. Clinton had grown bitter about the accusatory nature of politics in Washington. Blumenthal's MANICHAEAN outlook - his sense of the world as divided between the Clintons' supporters and their implacable and obsessed enemies - had come increasingly to appeal to the president's wife." Jeffrey Toobin, A Vast Conspiracy, Random House, 1999, p. 241.

MANQUÉ

adjective - frustrated.

"Bush played Hoover to Reagan's Coolidge. Although it was a portrait of Coolidge that graced Reagan's Cabinet Room, it was F.D.R. he called his true hero. Ironically, it is primarily Reagan as a Roosevelt MANQUÉ that blocks Clinton from claiming F.D.R.'s mantle." Sidney Blumenthal, *New Yorker*, 3/8/93, p. 41.

MANTRA

noun - a word or formula to be recited or sung; a hymn to be chanted or intoned; a sacred formula believed to possess magical power.

"He [Gary Hart] accused Gephardt of advocating 'misguided' trade policies and deceiving voters with populist rhetoric. And he said Dukakis 'chants phrases like "Massachusetts miracle" and "presidential leadership" like a MANTRA.'" *Chicago Trib.*, 2/15/88, S 1, p. 9.

"Asked about the poll on Friday by Bill Nigut of WSB-TV in Atlanta, Mr. Quayle dismissed it as 'nonsense, ridiculous,' and repeated verbatim a defensive MANTRA often used by Mr. Bush: 'Don't pay any attention to the polls. Just listen to the President. Watch what I do. Watch what he does. And listen to what he has to say.'" Maureen Dowd, *NYTimes*, 3/4/91, p. A12.

"But Mr. [Ross] Perot and what he tells us about ourselves - as opposed to the little he tells us about himself - is not going anywhere, at least for a while. His name has become synonymous with 'Throw the bums out,' a slogan that has become the voters' MANTRA lo these last 12 months." Anna Quindlen, *NYTimes*, 6/3/92, p. A15.

"The MANTRA for President Clinton's visit [to Moscow], Treasury officials say, is: more Russian reform in return for more Western money more quickly." Thomas L. Friedman, *NYTimes*, 1/13/94, p. A4.

"To counter such a view, Mr. Clinton has repeated this MANTRA: no new income taxes for the middle class." Richard L. Berke, *NYTimes*, 8/6/93, p. A8.

"And, now, is it Clinton's turn? Will the administration that came into office on a MANTRA of 'change' be able to get enought of a grip on it to save itself in '96?" Clarence Page, *Chicago Trib.*, 2/8/95, S 1, p. 19.

"When reporters ask about the First Lady's marriage, Ms. Berry repeats the MANTRA authorized by her boss: 'She [Hillary Rodham Clinton] has made it clear that she supports her husband, she loves him and she forgives him.'" Elaine Sciolino, *NYTimes*, 9/21/98, p. A16.

"Gov. George W. Bush began his quest for the presidency in a blaze of promises and good intentions, carrying an emphatically articulated vision of the new image he planned to establish for the Republican Party and the new voters he intended to woo. 'I'm a uniter, not a divider,' Mr. Bush, the Texas Governor, said at the outset of a nine-month trek to this critical juncture, and he repeated that MANTRA each step of the way." Frank Bruni, *NYTimes*, 2/19/00, p. A1.

MARE'S NEST

noun - a real mess; a jumble; a place of confusion or disorder.

"On February 26th, the Tower Commission report came out, its conclusion absolving the President [Reagan] of all but negligence in regard to the MARE'S NEST of covert operations carried out by the N.S.C. staff [in the Iran-Contra matter]...." Frances Fitzgerald, *New Yorker*, 1/16/89, p. 92.

MAVEN (Y)

noun - expert.

"...Mrs. Clinton is expected to emerge in a more open way, working in tandem with her husband in selling their ever-changing health-care reform package. Interview MAVENS Barbara Walters, Diane Sawyer and Connie Chung may get their moments, with the First Lady [Hillary Rodham Clinton] expected to make frequent TV appearances." Steven Daley, *Chicago Trib.*, 9/16/93, S 5, p. 1.

"[George W.} Bush himself seems to think it will be sufficient to rely on key advisors. He told New York *Times* columnist Maureen Dowd that the crucial thing was to know which foreign policy advisors to trust and which to 'kiss off.'.... Does George know where he stands, or which advisors to 'kiss off'? Is he his father's son or a Reaganite?...It will be tempting for Bush to wrap himself in the foreign policy mantle of the 'great communicator.' Yet Ronald Reagan was no MAVEN of foreign policy detail. He had one big idea: The communist Evil Empire must be contained, rolled back if possible. He built a highly successful foreign policy on an ideological crusade." Trudy Rubin, *Chicago Trib.*, 11/11/99, S 1, p. 27.

MEA CULPA

noun - a formal acknowledgment of error or guilt.

"So is now the time for a MEA CULPA - a confession that George Bush was right and those of us who opposed the war wrong? Sorry, but no. The ease and popularity of the triumph don't change the fundamental fact: This was not a war the United States needed to fight - and when it is not necessary to fight, it is necessary not to fight." Stephen Chapman, *Chicago Trib.*, 3/7/91, S 1, p. 27.

"By offering a swift MEA CULPA, the Democratic front-runner was clearly hoping to minimize the incident as quickly as possible as he [Governor Bill Clinton] tries to focus on strengthening his sudden position as the seemingly unassailable leader in what is now a two-man race for the Democratic Presidential nomination." Andrew Rosenthal, *NYTimes*, 3/21/92, p. 8.

"Mr. [C. Boyden] Gray, President Bush's longest-serving senior aide, has mastered the deft MEA CULPA in three years of being Mr. Bush's chief counsel, a period in which he has seen more than his share of political controversy." Michael Wines, *NYTimes*, 11/25/91, p. A11.

"Richard Nixon, ruminating about Watergate in his last years, grudgingly acknowledged 'that what happened was my fault,' a young aide says. 'The cover-up wasn't only illegal but stupid,' she says he told her. Nixon's MEA CULPA, a confession he could not bring himself to utter as he sought to preserve his presidency, is reported in 'Nixon in Winter,' a second book by Monica Crowley, 28, who worked for Nixon from 1990 until his death in 1994." *Chicago Trib.*, 5/29/98, S 1, p. 18.

"It was just over four minutes long, barely 500 words, the shortest big speech of Bill Clinton's Presidency... But in its tone and content, in its blend of unapologetic UMBRAGE and tightly conditioned admission, the President's MEA CULPA was minimal, and deeply personal. Begun in his own backward-slanting handwriting, annealed with the iron-willed anger of his wife, the

163

speech was pure Bill Clinton, for better or worse." Todd S. Purdum, *NYTimes*, 8/19/98, p. A22.

"Mr. Gore appeared to hope that by acknowledging his involvement in fund-raising situations that raised questions, and proclaiming that he was redoubling his efforts to change the system, he could head off Mr. Bush's effort to portray him as unprincipled. At the news conference today, Mr. Bush emphasized his response: nothing that Mr. Gore proposes - and no amount of MEA CULPAS - can erase the taint of the Clinton administration's ethics record." Clifford J. Levy, *NYTimes*, 3/13/00, p. A16.

MELLIFLUOUS

adjective - having a smooth melodic flow.

"For all his reputation as the Great Communicator, President Reagan, MELLIFLUOUS with a prepared statement, often bumbled into incoherence when required to extemporize. In the last four years, PARSING President Bush has become a competitive sport, turning up gems like, 'I just am not one who - who flamboyantly believes in throwing a lot of words around.'" Editorial, *NYTimes*, 11/13/92. p. A12.

MÉNAGE À TROIS (FR)

noun - a sexual relationship among three people; usually while living together; literally, a household for three.

"That inaugural night Jack [Kennedy] had his choice of the young party girls and movie starlets at Alsop's party. One European ambassador offered his niece to the new president. Six attractive young starlets, supplied by actor Peter Lawford, Jack's brother-in-law, volunteered to sleep with the new president of the United States. Peter lined them up, and after inspection Jack selected one or two to take to bed. One account says he selected two and took them into a spare bedroom at the same time for a MÉNAGE-À-TROIS-type sexual encounter." Wesley O. Hagood, Presidential Sex, Carol Publishing Group, 1995, p. 138.

"As Nixon lost the debates of 1960 by looking sweatier, jowlier and less clean-shaven than Kennedy, so he had lost posterity. In our Hollywood culture, star quality is everything. A handsome, charming, witty man who has a fling with Marilyn Monroe is as close to a god as we have. He's always going to trump a gloomy Gus [Nixon] in a bad suit whose only MÉNAGES À TROIS were those platonic ones in which he drove the woman he would later marry to her dates with rival suitors." Frank Rich, *NYTimes*, 11/15/97, p. A23.

MERCURIAL

adjective - characterized by rapid and unpredictable mood changes; QUICKSILVER.

"Mr. Byrd is...interested in Jefferson as a personality, as a highly gifted and conflicted individual who happened to play a formative role in the founding of this country. His Jefferson is an elusive, MERCURIAL fellow: a romantic who conceals his emotional vulnerabilities behind a mask of cordiality; a lonely widower, who is ill at ease in the public world of banquets and speeches; a doting father who refuses to accord his daughters the freedom he promotes for the masses, and a chilly moralist and master of self-control who finds himself unexpectedly falling in love." Michiko Kakutani, Review of Jefferson by Max Byrd, *NYTimes*, 11/23/93, p. B2.

"The snub to Nixon, a strong supporter of Yeltsin and his controversial reforms, had all the trappings of the jarring, shoot-from-the-hip gestures for which the MERCURIAL Russian president has become famous." James P. Gallagher, *Chicago Trib.*, 3/10/94, S 1, p. 1.

"'Well, Mr. Perot never declared, so how can he have dropped out?' said Marie-Rose George, Utah coordinator for the Perot Presidential campaign, a MERCURIAL movement that, she and her fellow volunteers now know with unyielding certainty, he never really quit and will, in any event, soon be rejoining." Francis X. Clines, *NYTimes*, 9/26/92, p. A6.

MERITOCRACY

noun - a society, group or governing body in which persons are moved into leadership positions based on ability.

"[Theodore] Roosevelt was less concerned with MERITOCRACY and more inclined to treat the lower classes fairly in their station." Naomi Bliven, *New Yorker*, 8/26/85, p. 86.

"'Dartmouth is a microcosm of the national debate, encouraged by the Reagan Administration, over the ideals of equity versus MERITOCRACY,' he said. 'The issue is how broad we want our definition to be of educating the best and brightest in our society.'" Edward B. Fiske, *NYTimes*, 10/8/86, p. 9.

"Mr. Walker sees [President] Clinton as the perfect symbol of the great American MERITOCRACY that blossomed after 1945 thanks to the G.I. Bill, the sexual revolution and the civil rights movement..." Douglas Brinkley, *NYTimes Book Review*, 9/22/96, p. 14.

"He [Bill Clinton] came from the South, a part of the country that had gone from backwardness to unprecedented prosperity, from chronic population loss to population growth within his lifetime. His mother had worked and educated her way into the new mass middle class, and he had won scholarships and university credentials that catapulted him into the ranks of the American elite. He was a MERITOCRAT at a time when American society was uniquely tailored to reward merit." Martin Walker, The President We Deserve, Crown Publishers, 1996, p. 346.

MICAWBERESQUE

adjective - unrealistically and eternally optimistic; based on Wilkins Micawber, the character in the Charles Dickens novel, David Copperfield.

"In foreign affairs START's competitors for the top of the agenda fall into a narrow band of possibility between the merely imponderable and the unquestionably disastrous. Events might thrust crises before President Bush from which he could try to extract a 'win.' But this MICAWBERESQUE vision of foreign policy - something might turn up - is a formula for drift, not mastery. Moreover, the something that might turn up, whether in the Middle East, Eastern Europe, or Central America, is more likely to cost political capital than to provide an occasion to gain it." Jack Beatty, *Atlantic Monthly*, 2/89, p. 59.

"Today David E. Kendall, [President Clinton's] personal lawyer, scored points in senators' smiles of appreciation as he turned several of the prosecutors' own words against them: they had previously assured the House that there was no need for witnesses. Mr. Kendall belittled the prosecutors in quick order as desperate blackjack players, a programmed barbershop chorus and a pack of Mr. MICAWBERS fruitlessly hoping for something fresh to turn up. He caused a bipartisan guffaw when he quickly added, beaming in all insincerity, 'I don't want to be uncharitable to the House managers.'" Francis X. Clines, *NYTimes*, 1/27/99, p. A20.

MICROMANAGE

verb - to manage with attention to the smallest details.

"Psychologist Nancy Stark, president of a consulting firm in Oakland, Calif., also hadn't heard of MICROMANAGEMENT, 'and I read a lot of books about management.' She was shuffling through a shelf of them as we spoke, 'Microcosm, macrosystem, microprocessor - those words make a lot of sense. I'm trying to figure it out. If there's a micromanagement, is there a macro-management? Is Reagan a macromanager?' When I called Harold Leavitt, professor of organizational behavior in Stanford's business school, I got 'Ho boy!' and a laugh. 'It must be a pop phrase,' he said. 'I guess it means close supervision, as opposed to a more distanced, delegated style...'" Linda Witt, *Chicago Trib.*, 8/17/87, S 1, p. 11.

"I was stuck in traffic listening to the Iran-Contra hearings when Adm. John Poindexter's sonorous voice suddenly interjected a new word into my vocabulary. 'I did not MICROMANAGE Ollie North,' he testified... MICROMANAGE wasn't the first bit of business-sounding jargon I learned from being an Iran-Contragate junkie. I was already familiar with 'CYA.'" Linda Witt, *Chicago Trib.*, 8/17/87, S 1, p. 11.

"San Antonio, Tex., Aug. 25 - Vice President Bush attacked Congress today as having 'tied the President's hands' and seeking to 'MICROMANAGE' Administration efforts in the Persian Gulf and Central America." Bernard Weinraub, *NYTimes*, 8/26/87, p. 11.

"President Lyndon Johnson demanded that politicians and aides swim with him in the raw. President Richard M. Nixon was not the sporting type, though he did bowl. President Gerald R. Ford liked to take people golfing and skiing.

President Jimmy Carter was so into tennis (or MICROMANAGING) that he personally controlled who played on the White House courts." Richard L. Berke, *NYTimes*, 7/26/93, p. A6.

"In addition, some aides said, Mr. Gore was prone to MICROMANAGING his campaign, initially run not by one strong manager but by a succession of people with varying responsibilities. As a result, the operation was rife with disorganization, which led to excessive spending and made it harder for Mr. Gore to raise money." Richard L. Berke, *NYTimes*, 10/9/99, p. A8.

MILQUETOAST (MILKTOAST)

noun - a meek, timid, retiring, unassertive person; a doormat.

Note:Based on Caspar MILQUETOAST, the comic strip character in *The Timid Soul* by H.T. Webster. From milk toast, a bland dish.

"For a while, Ronald Reagan broke the pattern. As Mr. Right he hardly needed a conservative running mate. And anything he thought needed saying, he could say very well himself. So Reagan didn't need an Agnew. If anything, he needed Mr. MILQUETOAST, which is about what he got." Robert Gillmore, *Chicago Trib.*, 1/29/87, S 1, p. 25.

"No evidence has surfaced indicating that the young Mr. Clinton ever took part in any violent political actions or was an important anti-war organizer, or was ever radicalized in the process. Many of those involved with him at the time recall him as something of a MILQUETOAST by the fire-breathing standards of late 1960's radicalism, a young man driven by a desire to remake his country, not to reject it." Michael Kelly and David Johnston, *NYTimes*, 10/9/92, p. A13.

"The independent counsel [Kenneth Starr] not only recognized that he lacked experience [for the Clinton investigation] but hated that the public saw him as a fleshy, MILQUETOAST kind of person. One day he mentioned how angry he was that some of his adversaries in Little Rock were spreading the false rumor that he was having an affair on his visits there; what really teed him off was that everyone - everyone! - thought the rumor was inconceivable." Jeffrey Toobin, <u>A Vast Conspiracy</u>, Random House, 1999. P. 271.

MINIMALIST

noun - a believer in the doctrine of MINIMALISM, that in art and architecture simple forms are best, i.e. "less is more."

"The debate begins with the question of why President Bush lost. Did he lose simply because the economy was bad and his campaign LACKLUSTER (the MINIMALIST explanation), or because Republicanism itself had fallen out of synch with the times? Did he lose because he had broken with the conservative dogma or because he had been co-opted by it?" Robin Toner, *NYTimes*, 11/11/92, p. A16.

"George Stephanopoulos, Mr. Clinton's director of communications and one of the very few former campaign officials with any apparent connection to Mr. Clinton these days, presents daily briefings for the public that are portraits in MINIMALISM. Tiny shreds of information about Mr. Clinton's activities and thoughts are padded out and embellished to make the puny sound Presidential." Thomas L. Friedman, *NYTimes*, 11/11/92, p. A1.

"If Mr. [George W.] Bush can be faulted, it is not for the longstanding problems of Texas, but for his MINIMALIST approach to leadership. He believes that his role is to identify a few priorities and spend his political capital on those alone. After President Clinton's well-received State of the Union address last year, in which the President laid out a laundry list of proposals, Gov. Bush told me, 'Anyone who tries to do everything ends up doing nothing.'" Paul Burka, *NYTimes*, 4/28/00, p. A21.

MISHMOSH (MISHMASH) (Y)

noun - a HODGEPODGE, mess, jumble.

"[President Clinton] began by reading (too fast and without feeling) a statement about supporting reform in Russia, then vitiated its effect with a long, dull pitch for his economic program. This MISHMASH was presumably intended to show a domestic president unconsumed by foreign affairs; instead it showed him self-conscious about appearing to be." William Safire, *Chicago Trib.*, 3/26/93, S 1, p. 23.

"'You know, we didn't ask for this trial,' said Senator Patrick J. Leahy, a Vermont Democrat. 'We didn't ask for the President [Clinton] to conduct himself the way he did, and we didn't ask for the House to make a MISHMASH of this thing. But all that's happened and now we have to preserve the Senate and give the country a sense of credibility.'" Alison Mitchell, *NYTimes*, 1/9/99, p. 1.

"Virtually every minute of [President Clinton's] day is scripted, from the first meeting of the morning (usually around 9) until what the official schedule calls 'good night.'...Some days can be a MISHMASH of disconnected events - like last Tuesday's speech to insurance agents, which was followed by a conference on raising teenagers and a talk to a roomful of experts on Latin America. Five minutes of every day is set aside to brief Mr. Clinton on the schedule." Marc Lacey, *NYTimes*, 5/8/00, p. A14.

MISOGYNY

adjective - hatred and distrust of women *noun* - MISOGYNIST.

"But the suspicion [by the Religious Right] of Hillary Rodham Clinton reaches even deeper and into the dark recesses of MISOGYNY, the age-old hatred of women. ... Buying into the 19th Century cult of domesticity, where the woman confined her influence to the home and took responsibility for little except the spiritual nurture of her children, the Religious Right regards with extreme suspicion any woman who breaks out of those confines." Randall Balmer, *Chicago Trib.*, 4/21/93, S 1, p. 27.

"To his fans, David Brock, the writer who ruined the Clinton's Christmas, is a hard-hitting investigative reporter. To everyone else, he is a smear artist with a right-wing agenda. But a reading of Mr. Brock's oeuvre in the conservative journal *The American Spectator* suggests that his motives are at least as twisted as his facts. It's women, not liberals, who really get him going. The slightest sighting of female sexuality whips him into a frenzy of MISOGYNIST zeal." Frank Rich, *NYTimes*, 1/6/94, p. A13.

"While it might seem ironic coming from the writer who once called Anita Hill 'a bit nutty, and a bit slutty,' Mr. Brock is right that Hillary Clinton has been demonized at times by MISOGYNISTS and right-wing fanatics." James B. Stewart in a review of The Seduction of Hillary Rodham by David Brock, *NYTimes Book Review*, 10/13/96, p. 10.

"Mr. Ginsburg depicted Ms. Lewinsky as a victim poised between two powerful forces, a young, vulnerable neophyte in the Washington political culture. 'If the allegations are true that there was a sexual relationship with the president [Clinton],' said Mr. Ginsburg, 'Then he's a MISOGYNIST and I have to question his ability to lead. If they are not true, then why is the independent investigator ravaging the life of a twenty-three old girl?'" Francis X. Clines and Jeff Gerth, *NYTimes*, 1/22/98, p. A20.

MISOLOGIST

noun - a person antagonized by intellectual matters.

"Add 'MISOLOGIST' to your vocabulary, if you can find any use for it. It's a person who can't stand thoughtful conversation about intellectual matters. The MISOLOGIST does not do well in Advanced Philosophy II. The MISOLOGIST can be identified by frequent use of such imperatives as 'Can it!' and 'Knock it off!' and 'Aw, shut up!'" L. M. Boyd, The Grab Bag, *SF Chronicle*, 9/10/83, p. 29.

"[Geraldine] Ferraro has said she prefers to be identified as 'Ms. Ferraro.' But MS-SOGYNISTS and MS-SOLOGISTS in the media who refuse to Ms-represent her can call her 'Mrs. Ferraro,' she has conceded, although that is not legally or socially correct. The candidate from Queens is, in fact, Mrs. John Zaccaro. But she prefers to use her maiden name to honor her widowed mother, she explains. She objects to 'Miss Ferraro' - a form chosen by many career women even after marriage - because she reasons 'Miss' would indicate she is not married." Joan Beck, *Chicago Trib.*, 8/8/84, S 1, p. 14.

MOBOCRACY

noun - government by the mob or rabble.

"There is in [Perot's central governing idea of an 'electronic town hall'] a large step toward plebiscitary government, and a whiff of MOBOCRACY. It is a formula ripe for demagoguery , and Perot has already shown some demagogic tendencies." Elizabeth Drew, *New Yorker*, 5/18/92, p. 88

MODICUM

noun - a small quantity, dab, DOLLOP.

"The politics that followed, at the conventions and in the autumn campaign, had been set in motion in June of that year. That pattern should worry Perot, hearten Bush and comfort Clinton with a MODICUM of hope." Thomas Hardy, *Chicago Trib.*, 6/28/92, S 4, p. 4.

"Don Imus, the radio personality who likes to torture politicians, says that Steve Forbes spent $100 million to make himself a laughingstock....As for the [Forbes] campaign, it would be kinder to call it a quixotic venture that taught some worthy civic lessons. One lesson is that even in the era of dollar-driven politics, it is impossible to purchase a political base for a candidate who lacks reasonable policies and some MODICUM of personal appeal. Mr. Forbes should not be ridiculed for his lack of charm and his poor speaking ability, but neither should the electorate be expected to use its imagination in supplying the threshold qualities required of a presidential candidate." Editorial, *NYTimes*, 2/10/00, p. A 30.

MODIFIED LIMITED HANGOUT

noun - a partial disclosure of the truth.

Note: In the Watergate scandal, President Richard Nixon and his principal aides, Robert Haldeman and John Ehrlichman, discussed partial disclosure of the details of the Watergate burglary and the events that followed as a MODIFIED LIMITED HANGOUT, i.e., a limited disclosure as distinguished from "letting it all hang out," a complete disclosure.

"Maybe that's what Bush wants voters to do, letting him defuse the issue by making it clear he did use drugs without having to reveal what they were or how often he used them. He's hoping Americans will decide 1) they know enough about his past and 2) what they know doesn't disqualify him.

This plausible strategy was undone by the too-clever way Bush has addressed the issue. A firm refusal to discuss drug use might have worked - but the MODIFIED, LIMITED HANGOUT strategy won't." Steve Chapman, *Chicago Trib.*, 8/22/99, S 1, p. 17.

MODUS OPERANDI

noun - method of operation or procedure; operating manner.

"In the spring of 1977, [Anne Manning] was in Washington to attend a census-bureau workshop when Gingrich took her out to dinner at a Vietnamese restaurant. He met her back at her modest hotel room. 'We had oral sex,' she says. 'He prefers that MODUS OPERANDI because then he can say, 'I never slept with her.' Indeed, before Gingrich left that evening, she says, he threatened her: 'If you ever tell anybody about this, I'll say you're lying.'

She tells me this, she says, because she fears that Newt might become president someday. 'I don't claim to be an angel,' she says, but she is repelled by Newt's stance as Mr. Family Values. 'He's morally dishonest. He has gone too far believing that 'I'm beyond the law.' He should be stopped before it is too late.'" Gail Sheehy, *Vanity Fair*, 9/95, p. 154.

Note:Both Gingrich and Manning were married when this incident occurred.

"Another Republican who announced he will vote for both articles, Sen. Robert Bennett of Utah, said at first he was skeptical about the allegation of lying under oath, then changed his mind as the evidence came in and as he remembered 'my experience with the Clinton political apparatus and its MODUS OPERANDI.'" William Neikirk and Mike Dorning, *Chicago Trib.*. 2/12/99, S 1, p. 23.

MONIKER

noun - personal name or nickname.

"He [Bill Clinton] did his best, with a low-key speech that emphasized humble beginnings and quoted from scripture to convince people that he doesn't deserve his 'slick' MONIKER." Editorial, *Chicago Trib.*, 7/18/92, S 1, p. 20.

"Introduced by Colorado Gov. Roy Romer as the leader of 'a new Democratic Party,' Clinton said the MONIKER 'means no more trickle-down economics but not tax-and-spend economics. It means we ought to have invest-and-grow economics.'" Mitchell Locin, *Chicago Trib.*, 10/22/92, S 2, p. 5.

"And incidentally, although he did not coin the phrase, Jesse Jackson was the most identifiable and vociferous proponent of using the term 'African-American' as a historically accurate MONIKER for black Americans." Adonis E. Hoffman, *Chicago Trib.*, 9/8/93, S 1 p. 19.

"He [Bill Clinton] was thirty-three, and his nicknames had regressed from the juvenile to the infantile. Where during his Fayetteville days he was sometimes referred to as 'Wonder Boy' or 'the Boy,' he now occasionally answered to 'Baby' - as in 'Baby's getting too big for his britches,' or 'Maybe Baby's growing up!' - a MONIKER given to him by Frances Walls, a longtime Democratic activist in northeast Arkansas. Even a friendly cartoonist portrayed the child governor riding around on a tricycle or peering from the turret of a tank." David Maraniss, First in His Class: The Biography of Bill Clinton, Simon & Schuster, 1995, p. 364.

MORPH

verb - to change into a different form.

"The White House, which was least scathed in the Brill version of the Clinton/Lewinsky media saga, gloated as the Diogenes Watch MORPHED cannibalistically into Les Liaisons Dangereuses. News addicts not already numbed by the growing specialty of media-watchdogging-cum-hotdogging could pay the $3.95 and read Mr. Brill's full 25,000-word JEREMIAD, providing they had the stamina of a doctoral candidate." Francis X. Clines, *NYTimes*, 6/21/98, p. 3

"You wouldn't know, for instance, that Mr. Brill tracks down exactly how a false 'one-source story from a fifth-hand source,' about a Secret Service agent's supposed witnessing of a Monica-Clinton tryst, was spread as fact by all too many of the country's major news operations. Or that he unearths the genesis of the illusory semen-stained dress and details just how it MORPHED into the holy grail of scandal coverage." Frank Rich, *NYTimes*, 6/17/98.

"When it comes to politics, it's smart to play your cards straight. George W. Bush's problem is that he hasn't done that, and voters know it. How can Governor Bush turn back John McCain? He must stop trying to MORPH into McCain Jr. (the 'reformer with results') and start using his strong point - that he is part of the Republican establishment." Charles E. Cook Jr., *NYTimes*, 2/24/00, p. A27.

"...Mr. Gore is now adopting various costumes while vice president, trying to buff his image by throwing off drab Washington duds for snazzier suits (if sans Mylar) as well as chinos and polo shirts. In his search for an 'authentic' identity - a journey 'from wooden to plastic,' in the words of a New York *Post* headline - the man has MORPHED into a male model out of a Dockers or Home Depot ad." Frank Rich, *NYTimes*, 10/23/99, p. A27.

"Mr. Morris's batty book [the authorized Reagan biography] is surely destined for commercial success. There's a lot of nostalgia for Reagan and Reaganism. And we have become a culture of MORPHING. Entertainment has overwhelmed truth, and the universities are riddled with professors who deny that objectivity is possible." Maureen Dowd, *NYTimes*, 9/22/99, p. A27.

"Mr. Gore celebrated his victory Tuesday night by MORPHING into Mr. McCain. Admitting past sins, he embraced campaign finance reform - for real this time, cross my heart - and embarked on a series of town hall meetings in the heartland." Gail Collins, *NYTimes*, 3/10/00, p. A23.

MOT JUSTE (FR)

noun - the right or most appropriate word to convey the exact meaning or nuance intended.

"I have finally hit upon the MOT JUSTE (for you Arkansans, that means 'right word') to describe the social life of Bill and Hillary Clinton. Le MOT, or if you will, the word, is 'sneaky.'" Michael Kilian, *Chicago Trib.*, 6/30/93, S 7, p. 4.

MOUNTEBANK

noun - an unscrupulous cheat, impostor, CHARLATAN, swindler.

"He [William Jennings Bryan] was, in fact, a CHARLATAN, a MOUNTEBANK, a zany without sense or dignity." H. L. Mencken, The Vintage Mencken, Vintage Books, 1956, p. 164.

"For the more one studies his [Teddy Roosevelt's] MOUNTEBANKERIES as mob-master, the more one is convinced that there was a shrewd man beneath the motley, and that his actual beliefs were anything but nonsensical." H. L. Mencken, A Mencken Chrestomathy, Vintage Books, 1982, p. 240.

Frank J. Young

"One day he [Clarence Darrow] urged poor Bryan into the folly I have mentioned: his astounding argument against the notion that man is a mammal. I am glad I heard it, for otherwise I'd never believe it. There stood the man who had been thrice a candidate for the Presidency of the Republic - there he stood in the glare of the world, uttering stuff that a boy of eight would laugh at. The artful Darrow led him on: he repeated it, ranted for it, bellowed it in his cracked voice. So he was prepared for the final slaughter. He came into life a hero, a Galahad, in bright and shining armor. He was passing out a poor MOUNTEBANK." H. L. Mencken, The American Scene, Vintage Books, 1982, p. 232.

MOXIE

noun - energy, pep, verve.

"At [John F.] Kennedy's inauguration, Frost, 86 years old, struggled in 22-degree weather, the wind riffling his white hair, to recite an earlier poem, 'The Gift Outright.' He also wrote a poem for the event, 'Dedication Poem,' which he did not read. Ms. [Maya] Angelou remembers being affected by it. 'Robert Frost was such a fine poet,' she said. 'He was white and male, but he stood for me, and for Spanish people and Chinese people and fat and thin. He was old and soon to die and couldn't see his own notes. 'He had the MOXIE to push on and recite what he knew. That further endeared him to me.'" Irvin Molotsky, *NYTimes*, 12/5/92, p. A8.

"The evening conversation turned to politics. 'If only' the Democrats had a contender with Bill Clinton's haystack hairdo and Kennedyesque sex appeal, Mario Cuomo's eloquence, Bob Kerrey's Medal of Honor, Paul Tsongas' or Bill Bradley's grasp of tax and economic issues, Tom Harkin's fiery populism and the MOXIE of Jesse Jackson or Jerry Brown." Thomas Hardy, *Chicago Trib.*, 5/18/92, S 5, p. 3.

"I went up against Pat [Buchanan] on aid to Israel in Nixon's '68 campaign on the issue of the sale of Phantom jets to Israel. Buchanan argued it would get us no Jewish votes; although Nixon agreed that Jewish Americans would oppose him overwhelmingly, he urged the sale of the jets anyway because he thought the Israel of Golda Meir was a strategic U.S. asset with admirable MOXIE." William Safire, *NYTimes*, 9/16/99, p. A29.

MUGWUMP

noun - a political independent, a person with his "mug" on one side of the fence and his "wump" on the other; a fencesitter.

"But commentators across the country are dusting off H. L. Mencken's words to describe the heights of HORNSWOGGLING, the MUGWUMP mendacity they find in Mr. Perot's renewed flirtation with the campaign. Even one of the best foreign observers of the American scene, The *Economist* magazine, could not resist irreverent cynicism in the headline, 'Ears 2: The Return.'" Francis X. Clines, *NYTimes*, 9/26/92, p. A6.

MUSHROOM CAMPAIGNING (SL)

noun - a campaign characterized by demagoguery, OBFUSCATION.

"John Sharp, a member of the Texas Railroad Commission and chairman of the Dukakis campaign in Texas, asserted that Mr. Bush had been practicing 'MUSHROOM CAMPAIGNING' on the voters - 'putting them in the dark and throwing manure on them.'" Robin Toner, *NYTimes*, 10/7/88, p. 10.

NNN

NABOB

noun - a wealthy, luxury-loving person.

Note:Used by Vice President Spiro Agnew in the phrase "NATTERING NABOBS of negativism" to attack those of liberal political persuasion with whom he disagreed. The phrase was coined by William Safire, a speechwriter.

"In 1968, Spiro Agnew became what former Sen. Eugene McCarthy called 'Nixon's Nixon.' While Nixon undertook to play Eisenhower - at least until

Watergate - Agnew took on the 'communists' of his day: 'radiclibs' and 'NATTERING NABOBS of negativism.'" Robert Gillmore, *Chicago Trib.*, 1/29/87, S 1, p. 25.

"Some U.S. NABOBS have even accepted honorary British knighthoods: Caspar Weinberger, Colin Powell, James Baker and, as of last week, George Bush." Michael Kilian, *Chicago Trib.*, 12/8/93, S 5, p. 3.

"Obviously humble, Middle American Bill and Hillary didn't want America to see them in glittering gowns and $200 Hollywood haircuts, carrying on like NABOBS and SCHMOOZING with hated, ick, *Washington insiders*. They wanted to be taken as simple Wal-Mart folk, drudging away into the wee hours preparing reports and plans on joblessness, health care, Somalia and whatever remains of Bosnia." Michael Kilian, *Chicago Trib.*, 6/30/93, S 7, p. 4.

"These days, the candidates see NABOBS of negativism everywhere. At a debate this week, former Senator Bill Bradley said Vice President Al Gore had gone negative on him. Mr. Gore called this accusation a 'negative attack' on his integrity." Peter Marks, *NYTimes*, 1/29/00, p. 1.

NAMBY-PAMBY

adjective and *noun* - wishy-washy, insipid, without vigor, FLACCID.

"Jackie [Kennedy] ran a tight ship. Those kids weren't NAMBY-PAMBYS, but they weren't hell-raisers either. Jackie made sure they didn't overdose on the Kennedy stuff.'" Harrison Rainie, *Chicago Trib.*, 5/14/85, S 5, p. 1.

"Carter would never have gotten away with this. When his press secretary, Jody Powell, contended that patience and persistence offered a better hope than military action in obtaining the safe release of the 52 Americans held in Iran, Carter was painted as a WIMP by Reagan and Republican conservatives who formed Reagan's hard-core support. Surprisingly, the administration's NAMBY-PAMBY response to such terroristic going's-on has not evoked hoots of derision and questions about Reagan's manliness from Democrats on Capitol Hill." James G. Wieghart, *Chicago Trib.*, 6/21/85, S 1, p. 27.

"So with Democrats putting the boot into [George] Bush by telling people he is a 'WIMP,' is soft on drug-king Noriega, and so forth. This is simple, old-fashioned dirty pool, and letting political technocrats get away with perfuming it under a NAMBY-PAMBY word like 'negatives' shows how easily we can be led around by these swine." Russell Baker, *NYTimes*, 11/2/88, p. 27.

NARCISSISTIC

adjective - preoccupied with self-love, egocentric.

Note:From Greek mythology when a beautiful young man falls in love with his own reflection in the water, dies and is turned into the Narcissus flower.

"His [Newt Gingrich's] childhood shaped by the rejection by not just one but two fathers, and the manic-depressive illness of his mother created a psychic need so great that only the praise that attends a savior can fill the vacuum inside him. He drives himself monomaniacally, obsessed only with his goal. No amount of personal deprivation - 100-hour workweeks, no vacations, no time with his wife - diminishes his NARCISSISTIC vision of the global glory that will ultimately be his prize." Gail Sheehy, *Vanity Fair*, 9/95, p. 152.

"'When you spend years in solitary, you get to know yourself very well' [John McCain said]. And what did you learn? 'NARCISSISM,' he says drily. 'I do have a confidence in myself. You talk about trying to become an alpha male. I never heard of such a thing. I know my strengths and failings. I'm very well prepared for whatever difficulties the rest of my life brings. And being crazy,' he concluded, 'ain't one of them.'" Maureen Dowd, *NYTimes*, 11/21/99, p. 15.

"Curiously, Morris has in fact succeeded where he claims to have failed. Despite his protestations of bafflement, he has shed new light - harsh, bright light - on Reagan's character. That character turns out to be roughly as we knew it to be. The public Reagan is the affable performer, docile on the set, but stubbornly attached to a few large, simple notions. The private Reagan, too, is affable, docile, and stubborn. He is also, as Morris shows with great acuity, NARCISSISTIC, egocentric, happy, trustful, childish, and oblivious. He is intellectually inert, a terrible bore, a practitioner of denial, and a cold, unimaginative man who has no interest in, curiosity about, or genuine compassion for other people." Hendrik Hertzberg (Review of Edmund Morris, Dutch: A Memoir of Ronald Reagan), *New Yorker*, 10/11/99, p. 102.

"The senator [John McCain] went beyond making the case that the Bush campaign played out of bounds. He took the SMARMY tactics too personally, and tried to make the case that he was good and everyone who opposed him was evil. His righteousness slowly MORPHED into a kind of NARCISSISM, in which he became the personification of everything worth voting for." Maureen Dowd, *NYTimes*, 3/8/00, p. A27.

NATIVISM

noun - policy of favoring native inhabitants over immigrants.

"Let's face it: We have a third party in place, financed by Ross Perot, its ear tuned to great sucking sounds. NATIVISM is its wellspring, populist revolt is its style, autocratic technocracy is its essence." William Safire, *Chicago Trib.*, 8/27/93, S 1, p. 23.

"In Enid, Okla., last week Mr. Bush said Governor Clinton believed in 'social engineering' and 'an elite central government.' Those were old European ideas, Mr. Bush said, and Mr. Clinton was for them because 'he and a number of his advisers studied them at Oxford in the 1960's.' Why did President Bush go in for such crude NATIVISM? Because he is running behind in the South, and even Oklahoma, and because the latest Baker strategy is to smear Governor Clinton." Anthony Lewis, *NYTimes*, 9/21/92, p. A15.

"So far only three politicians of national stature have dared to take on this KNOW-NOTHING NATIVISM [in Ross Perot's opposition to NAFTA] - Jimmy Carter, Bill Bradley and Jack Kemp." Tony Snow and James Carville, *NYTimes*, 11/2/93, p. A15.

"But [Jack] Kemp expressed concern that extending the restrictions of Prop 187 to the federal level would paint the GOP as NATIVIST and anti-immigrant. He argued that Republicans had alienated European immigrants at the turn of the century and had made another critical mistake in the 1950s and '60s, stepping away from the voting-rights debate. 'I believe there is no chance for the Republican Party to be a majority party in this country without being a party of inclusion,' Kemp said." Steve Daley, *Chicago Trib.*, 11/22/94, S 1 p. 9.

"'America is for Americans,' Bob Dole said in California. It is by overcoming such NATIVISM and anti-immigrant paranoia that we have become a great country." Anthony Lewis, *NYTimes*, 11/1/96, p. A15.

"In place of the Soviet military threat, Mr. [Pat] Buchanan has installed the Chinese economic threat. But whatever the outside villain, the psychology of this kind of third-party politics has remained remarkably steady across the years. It usually involves a melange of NATIVISM, populism and protectionism, plus the idea that the vast majority of Americans are being duped by an oligarchical conspiracy that stages fake political feuds designed to perpetuate both sides in office." Editorial, *NYTimes*, 9/15/99, p. A30.

NATTER

verb - (1) to complain, grumble, nag, scold; (2) to chatter idly.

Note:An alliterative phrase coined by William Safire as a speechwriter for Vice President Spiro Agnew was "NATTERING NABOBS of negativism." See PUSILLANIMOUS.

"'You say something here about 'the prattling pundits of positivism.' 'Parody of Agnew.' You've been reading his SCREEDS about the NATTERING NABOBS of negativism.'" Peter DeVries, The Glory of the Hummingbird, Popular Library, 1976, p. 128.

"The president [Ronald Reagan] startled the world with what he said next. At least, he startled the hell out of me: 'I read every comic strip in the paper, so when it came back, I starting reading him [Doonesbury}. I have to tell you, I think some of your readers are absolutely right.' Man, this is the leader of the free world, and two or three other things, coming right out and saying he *reads every comic strip in the newspapers*.... There he is, bless his heart, chuckling and eating jelly beans, following the adventures of 'Mandrake the Magician' and 'Boner's Ark.' Sure, sure. Lots of readers right now say, 'Humph! There he goes, another NATTERING NABOB of negativism, knocking our leader." Bill Granger, *Chicago Trib.*, 11/5/84, S 2, p. 1.

"Mr. Clinton is happier on the road, where he is treated like the celebrity he is and runs fewer risks of being bogged down with endless meetings and NATTERING from members of Congress." Gwen Ifill, *NYTimes*, 2/17/94, p. A13.

"Three of his four children - his children, no less! - have come out with books attesting to his emotional distance as a parent. The theme of Reagan's out-of-itness has been explored in a shelf of books about the Iran-Contra affair, among other places. His ignorance about nuclear weapons, his alarming NATTERINGS about ARMAGEDDON, his inability to recognize members of his own Cabinet, his failure to distinguish between movies and reality, even his promiscuity between marriages - if any of these things were ever secret, they long ago stopped being so." Hendrik Hertzberg (Review of Edmund Morris, <u>Dutch: A Memoir of Ronald Reagan</u>), *New Yorker*, 10/11/99, p.97.

NERD

noun - a dull, boring, insignificant person.

"'What kind of person were you like in high school?' someone asked. 'Well, I wasn't a jock,' [President] Clinton replied. 'A lot of people probably would have said I was a NERD. But I liked my friends, I liked music, I liked the activities, but I liked to study too.'" Tribune Wires, *Chicago Trib.*, 7/24/94, S 1, p. 20.

"At the end, [Al Gore] refused to be dragged off stage. ('Can I say one more word? I would like to stay!') He bore an uncomfortable resemblance to the kid who asks the teacher for more homework. Mr. Bradley, lounging on his stool, arms folded across his chest, looked like the high school athlete watching the class NERD volunteer to stay and clap erasers." Gail Collins, *NYTimes*, 10/29/99, p. A31.

NESTOR

noun - a senior leader or counselor.

"A bunch of old-timers who had got into the Geritol the other night started arguing about which was the most brutal beating they had every seen laid onto some poor, miserable, wretched President of the United States. This was a natural outgrowth of somebody saying he had never seen a President subjected to abuse as cruel, unrelenting and bloody-minded as Mr. Clinton is now undergoing. Cries of 'Nonsense!' and 'Pish tush!' as well as 'Pshaw!' and 'Horsefeathers!' greeted this statement. It was a fearful thing to see the agitation of these NESTORS for they were all of that age at which, in the words of the incomparable S. J. Perelman, you can 'hear arteries snapping like pipe stems.'" Russell Baker, *NYTimes*, 8/16/94, p. A15.

NEWSY (SL)

noun - a journalist.

"Mrs. [George] Bush, who had some NEWSIES to lunch last week to talk about her first year in the White House, expressed concern for her son Neil, who has been linked to the nation's savings and loan scandal through his involvement as a board member of Denver's troubled Silverado Banking, Savings and Loan, whose collapse threatens to cost taxpayers $1 billion." Michael Kilian, *Chicago Trib.*, 1/21/90, S 5, p. 5.

"President Clinton and Mrs. Clinton welcomed NEWSIES to four Christmas parties Tuesday and Wednesday, which is enough to test anyone's holiday cheer." O'Malley & Collin INC., *Chicago Trib.*, 12/16/93, S 1, p. 24.

"Not only did Hillary Clinton accompany Barbara Bush on a friendly tour of the White House after the election, but she was not inclined to leave.... A mob of NEWSIES flocked to the White House to be present at the meeting of the two women." Michael Kilian, *Chicago Trib.*, 11/29/92, S 5, p. 5.

NIGGARDLY

adjective - sparingly, grudgingly, miserly.

Note:NIGGARDLY is an ancient word of Scandinavian origin and etymologically has no racist overtones. Nevertheless because of its similarity to an offensive racist homophone, its use is not considered P.C. by some. Frank Rich is obviously not intimidated, although the new African-American Mayor of Washington, D.C. was. Even Julian Bond, the president of the NAACP and a leading African-American intellectual was "NIGGARDLY" in his criticism of the resignation forced by the use of the word.

"When Ms. Currie failed to make the witness list, there was bafflement from Republicans like Susan Collins as well as Democrats like Charles Schumer - not to mention much of the press - and no credible on-the-record explanation for this omission from the prosecutors [in the Clinton impeachment trial]. But the NIGGARDLY, not-for-attribution mutterings were clear enough: The 13 white men cowered at the prospect of throwing hardball questions at an African-American woman who might break into tears." Frank Rich, *NYTimes*, 1/30/99, p. A27.

"An unfortunate incident reached an unfortunate conclusion in the office of the Mayor of Washington D.C., Anthony Williams, this week. Mr. Williams, who is black, permitted his newly appointed ombudsman, David Howard, who is white, to resign after using the word 'NIGGARDLY' in the presence of two co-workers who looked shocked at the phrase. The word means 'miserly,' and Mr. Howard, explaining how tight his office budget was, said 'I will have to be NIGGARDLY with this fund because it's not going to be a lot of money.' The context was clearly finance, but to one of Mr. Howard's co-workers who is black, the context was clearly race. Mr. Howard resigned, and Mr. Williams hurriedly accepted his resignation.... Washington is a racially polarized city, so officials must choose their words carefully. But there is no evidence that Mr. Howard was trying to make a racist pun or purposely use an offensive homophone. If anything, Mr. Howard was being excessively contrite in saying, 'It's an arcane word that's unfamiliar to a lot of people.' The English language is a glorious construct. Words that are correctly used cannot be barred from conversation for the simple reason that they are not shopworn." Editorial, *NYTimes*, 1/30/99, p. A26.

NINCOMPOOP

noun - a simpleton, AIRHEAD.

"It does a columnist good to confront his prejudices, so I would like to confront one of mine: I think Dan Quayle is a proven NINCOMPOOP." John Leo, *U.S. News & World Report*, 6/1/92, p. 19.

"Given the NINCOMPOOP performance of President Bush, the avariciously self-interested Congress and the lame candidacy of Democrat Bill Clinton, it is not surprising that the independent bid of Perot has received such a groundswell of support." Thomas Hardy, *Chicago Trib.*, 6/21/92, S 4, p. 4.

"[John] Adams says he is sick and tired of providing 20th-century 'NINCOMPOOPS' with somebody to feel morally superior to. Thinking to return the slur, I instruct Jefferson to tell Adams next time he sees him that I may be a NINCOMPOOP but at least I don't come from Taxachusetts." Russell Baker, *NYTimes*, 7/4/92, p. A15.

NOBLESSE OBLIGE

noun - the obligation of people of high position or status to behave generously toward others.

"First, it's [COMPASSIONATE CONSERVATISM] inegalitarian, carrying the condescending implication of charity, of inferiority and helplessness on the part of those on its receiving end. Governor Bush makes this explicit by citing as examples of compassion charities that run drug treatment programs and 'prison ministries.' There is every indication that Governor Bush, like his father, really is animated by the philosophy of NOBLESSE OBLIGE." Mickey Kaus, *NYTimes*, 6/25/99, p. A27.

NOSTRUM (OM)

noun - a favorable scheme to solve a problem, cf. SNAKE OIL and DEUX EX MACHINA.

"Clinton's politics had been inspired by the old Democratic vision of John Kennedy, but he got his real political education in the Reagan years, learning painfully just how responsive American voters could be to the patriotic and feel-good NOSTRUMS that Reagan peddled with simplistic genius." Martin Walker, The President We Deserve, Crown Publishers, 1996, p. 152.

NOT TO PUT TOO FINE A POINT ON IT

expression - not to be over delicate in stating it. As an introduction to a candid, frequently brutally truthful, remark. The point refers to the sharp end of an instrument.

"In Salt Lake City, they have scheduled a daylong hearing on 'family issues,' but have limited debate and even access to the room where the contrary opinions will be aired. NOT TO PUT TOO FINE A POINT ON IT, the issue makes many Republicans edgy." Steve Daley, *Chicago Trib.*, 5/24/92, S 4, p. 4.

"Remember Michael Dukakis and the tank? The two made for a big story in September 1988. Trying to show that he was no softie when it came to national defense, the Democratic presidential candidate got in a tank, strapped on a helmet and took a ride hoping for 'good visuals.' Dukakis ... did not cut a dashing figure in his helmet and its thick strap. NOT TO PUT TOO FINE A POINT ON IT, he looked like a GEEK." Jon Margolis, *Chicago Trib.*, 2/28/94 S 1. p. 1.

"Among [David Brock's] charges against Mrs. Clinton is this irrational passage: 'She would phone the mansion from her law office and order troopers to fetch feminine napkins from her bedroom and deliver them to her at her firm.' Even if this story were true - even if a high-powered lawyer would really send state troopers on an errand that a clerk could accomplish at the nearest drugstore - who cares? [NOT] TO PUT A FINER POINT ON IT, why does Mr. Brock care? Would he have told this story if Mrs. Clinton were fetching aspirin?" Frank Rich, *NYTimes*, 1/6/94, p. A13.

NUT (NUT CASE)

noun - a crazy, eccentric person. *adjective* - NUTTY.

"[Barry] Goldwater and his handful on the right were similarly isolated by labels like 'right-wingers,' with its ominous European sound, or dismissal in the plain American stand-up-comic style as 'right-wing NUTS.' President Eisenhower, the Republican Landslide Hero, had declared 'Moderation!' the banner that would lead them all to victory. Even a right-winger would have to be a NUT to challenge Eisenhower, wouldn't he?" Russell Baker, *NYTimes*, 11/30/93, p. A15.

"Undertaking a serious investigation of President John Kennedy's assassination is a little like conducting a sober study of unidentified flying objects. There is nothing inherently frivolous about either subject. But both fields have been dominated for so long by crackpots and NUT CASES that a sort of guilt by association attaches to each new arrival. Don't we all, on hearing that an otherwise respectable author like Gerald Posner has taken on the death of JFK (and the life of 'JFK'), wonder if the fellow has lost his marbles." Jeffrey Toobin, *Chicago Trib.*, 9/12/93, S 14, p. 3.

"Seldom can we give our president credit for finding the MOT JUSTE, but the word NUTTY does come to mind after seeing Ross Perot's performance on *60 Minutes*, doesn't it? Perot's bizarre tale about how Republican dirty tricksters were going to unleash a doctored photo of his daughter Caroline and disrupt her wedding gives some satisfaction to those of us who have been warning for months now that Perot is paranoid and much given to conspiracy theories." Molly Ivins, Nothin' But Good Times Ahead, Vintage Books, 1993, p. 157.

"John McCain will take votes from anyone: Democrats, independents, even vegetarians, as he joked last Sunday. But could he embrace the party of Ross Perot, the man Senator McCain once described as 'NUTTIER than a fruitcake'?" Richard A. Oppel, Jr., *NYTimes*, 2/26/00, p. A1.

"You can think about the tug of war between the Republicans and President Clinton over the State Department's budget in a lot of ways. I prefer to think about it like this: Out of every dollar spent by the U. S. government each year, about one penny goes to pay for our embassies and diplomats abroad, democracy support programs, denuclearizing Russia, foreign loans and foreign aid. One penny. The Republicans now want to take that penny and cut it back more…the Republicans' drive to cut the foreign operations budget by 15 percent, or $2 billion, below what Mr. Clinton is seeking (He vetoed their budget Monday) is all part of a cheap gimmick led by the House majority whip, Tom DeLay, and his merry band of right-wing NUTS, whose only guiding principle in world affairs is: 'Dumb as we wanna be.'" Thomas L. Friedman, *NYTimes*, 10/20/99, p. A31.

OOO

OBFUSCATE

verb - to made obscure, to confuse. *noun* - OBFUSCATION.

"The vice president [Bush] has raised denial, OBFUSCATION and petulance to heights not seen since the Watergate era." Thomas Hardy, *Chicago Trib.*, 1/31/88, S 4, p. 3.

"From the public humiliation of the conservative ideologue jurist Robert Bork, to the empty questioning of David Souter, to the evasions and OBFUSCATIONS of Clarence Thomas, the president [Clinton] can figure out what not to do [in choosing a Supreme Court nominee]." Anna Quindlen, *Chicago Trib.*, 4/6/93, S 1, p. 17.

"Perot has shown no use for the press and assiduously avoided it. But in a hastily convened first press conference, Perot engaged in a typical act of political damage control - OBFUSCATING, filibustering and reluctantly acknowledging that he, too, had been known to leak information." Thomas Hardy, *Chicago Trib.*, 6/28/92, S 4, p. 4.

"The exact nature of Mr. Clinton's anti-war activities has been confused by both Republican exaggeration and Democratic OBFUSCATION." Michael Kelly and David Johnston, *NYTimes*, 10/9/92, p. A13.

"Representative Barney Frank, a Massachusetts Democrat, charged that the Republicans were guilty of 'deliberate vagueness and OBFUSCATION,' because they were prepared to impeach the President [Clinton] over definitions of sex." Alison Mitchell, *NYTimes*, 12/12/98, p. A10.

"This is not a time when the mills of justice must grind slowly. Mr. Lott and his fellow senators have before them a mature case developed through months of investigation and adversarial legal argument. All that is left is for them to ignore House partisanship and [Clinton] White House OBFUSCATION and bring this sad episode to a dignified conclusion." Editorial, *NYTimes*, 1/14,99, p. A22.

"Television viewers who watched the Republican debate on Thursday night probably noticed this when Mr. [George W.] Bush, wearing an expression of apparent satisfaction with the big word he was about to unleash, promised that he would never 'obsfucate' as president of the United States. That is a good thing because the verb is 'OBFUSCATE', and this was the third time in three days that Mr. Bush seemed to mangle it. On each occasion, he paused slightly either before or after, the oratorical equivalent of a drum roll or cymbal crash. And on each occasion, it never sounded quite right. On Thursday night, it was clear why. He had the consonants mixed up, the letter 's' in the wrong place. On Friday morning, at an appearance in Rochester, N.H., he was neither obsfucating or OBFUSCATING, but he was conflating the words tariff and barriers into terriers, which he promised to knock down in the name of trade. Would retrievers and spaniels be next? Mr. Bush quickly caught himself, which he did not do when, during two previous appearances in New Hampshire this week, he referred twice to 'a post-cold world,' strangely by-passing the war. Or maybe he was just referring to global warming." Frank Bruni, *NYTimes*, 1/8/00, p. A8.

by Garry Trudeau

OLD HAT

noun - old fashioned, not of any current interest.

"Gary King, a professor of government at Harvard University, said by now the campaign is OLD HAT to voters. 'I don't think anybody seriously believes that if somebody makes one little goof in a debate that's going to change 400,000 votes,' he said. 'People aren't that stupid.' William H. Flanigan, a political scientist at the University of Minnesota, agreed, explaining that the temporary 'bumps' in the polls that Mr. Dole and Mr. Clinton got after their party's conventions were distractions that served to 'just confuse the voters' to little real effect." Richard L. Berke, *NYTimes*, 9/22/96, p. 3.

OLEAGINOUS

adjective - offensively ingratiating, SMARMY, oily; having the characteristics of a URIAH HEAP.

"If the wonderful word OLEAGINOUS didn't exist, someone would have invented it to describe [Clinton advisor] Rahm Emanuel, the White House spin artist who has set the Washington news agenda for this entire week. It was Mr. Emanuel, with downcast eyes and a noble tremor in his voice, who took to TV on Sunday to herald the cover story of the new magazine Brill's Content as a 'bombshell' with implications not only 'grave' but also 'serious.' His was a performance self-righteous enough to make one shout, 'Bring back Sidney Blumenthal!'" Frank Rich, *NYTimes*, 6/17/98, p. A31.

"But if it [the year 2000 election] becomes, more directly, a question of how best to replace Bill Clinton - if there is, finally, a reaction against the OLEAGINOUS, market-tested Presidency, with its carefully polished choreography and all those giddy gerunds - then, perhaps, there will be a campaign of more than horse-race significance, a campaign that raises essential questions about the nature of leadership and the nature of citizenship in a country so successful that politics has almost begun to seem irrelevant." Joe Klein, *New Yorker*, 6/14/99, p. 36.

OROTUND (OM)

adjective - pompous.

"But just as Mario Cuomo is the Democratic Party's Hamlet, Bill Clinton is its Polonius, a near-genius of the cloudy and OROTUND. There are bores and there are deadly bores, and there are calculated bores who put us to sleep because they need us unconscious to commit daylight robbery." Clancy Sigal, *NYTimes*, 7/23/92, p. A15.

"The vast goodwill that America generates for each new administration enfolded Clinton's inaugural day and welcomed the shortest and most succinct speech of his OROTUND career. He spoke of sacrifice and renewal, of the years of drift and the urgency of repair. It was a sound, rather than memorable speech, filled with the pride of a new generation coming of political age, and thick with devotion to the American idea." Martin Walker, The President We Deserve, Crown Publishers, 1996, p. 177.

OUT

verb - to publicly expose someone as gay.

"There seems to be general agreement among policymakers that the military shouldn't inquire about recruits' sexual orientation, and that homosexual soldiers shouldn't flaunt their sexual orientation, Clinton said. The remaining issue is whether they should be able to serve if officials learn of their homosexual status in other ways, such as being 'OUTED' by others, he said." Carol Jouzaitis and Mitchell Locin, *Chicago Trib.*, 5/28/93, S 1, p. 14.

OXYMORON

noun - combination of contradictory or incongruous words, i.e., thundering silence.

"As an unreconstructed radical, my 1960s trenchmates may expect me to zing the OXYMORONIC populist billionaire with an ideological attack from the left. But on considering the Presidential alternatives, I found myself giving Mr. Perot a left-handed compliment. Surely 1992 will go down in political history as the year when the voting public came to perceive what we 60's rads were always saying - that the enemy was the system, particularly the two soiled parties dominating the system." Warren Hinckle, *NYTimes*, 7/10/92, p. A15.

"[Princeton's Fred Greenstein] said Mr. Clinton's 'almost unnatural energy, optimism and EBULLIENCE' were combined with 'an extraordinary lack of self-discipline.' The result, he said, is that for Mr. Clinton, 'The phrase White House organization is almost an OXYMORON.'" David Broder, *International Herald Trib.*, 9/6/94, p. 3.

PPP

PABULUM (PABLUM)

noun - food or nutrient; intellectual sustenance; especially bland, insipid fare.

"The Presidential politics here was interesting chiefly in two respects: Senator John Glenn and the Rev. Jesse Jackson. Mr. Glenn is plainly getting better as a speaker. His delivery, while nothing grand, no longer puts anyone to sleep. And when he is unprepared for a question - as he is a lot of the time - he can answer with PABLUM rather than with an ill-considered answer that makes people mad, as he used to do occasionally." Adam Clymer, *NYTimes*, 7/27/83, p. A16.

"The first draft of answers to be inserted in the [President Reagan's] briefing book are easy for the briefer to obtain: Everyone in government seems eager to provide pages of suggested answers hoping to use this device to skip outside channels and make policy. Staff members at the National Security Council intercept these missives, rewriting the PABLUM from State or bureaucratese from the Pentagon, thereby asserting authority." William Safire, *Chicago Trib.*, 7/20/83, S 1, p. 15.

"[President] Clinton's major China speech last week was PABLUM. 'At the dawn of a new century, China stands at a crossroads,' he intoned. Now if only Ellen would come out for sanctions..." Maureen Dowd, *NYTimes*, 10/29/97, p. A27.

PALPABLE

adjective - capable of being touched, perceptible by touch, tangible; easily perceptible intellectually. *adverb* - PALPABLY.

"Turn, now, to politics. Consider, for example, a campaign for the Presidency. Would it be possible to imagine anything more uproariously idiotic ... In other lands, at worst, there are at least intelligible issues, coherent ideas, salient personalities. Somebody says something, and somebody replies. But what did Harding say in 1920, and what did Cox reply? Who was Harding, anyhow, and who was Cox? Here, having perfected democracy, we lift the whole combat to symbolism to transcendentalism, to metaphysics. Here we load a pair of PALPABLY tin cannon with blank cartridges charged with talcum powder, and so let fly." H. L. Mencken, The American Scene, Ed. by Huntington Cairns, Vintage Books, 1982, p. 36.

"As she looks ahead to the general election campaign, Ms. Estrich's anticipation is PALPABLE. But, with the customary cautiousness of the Dukakis organization, Ms. Estrich notes that the nomination is not yet won." Robin Toner, *NYTimes*, 5/6/88, p. 8.

"Whether Mr. Clinton can prevail is a question, since the Senate is thick with Republican thorns in the persons of Bob Dole, Phil Gramm and others. But even as Speaker Newt Gingrich took to national television for a Presidential-style address on Friday, there was a PALPABLE hope in the White House that the season, and its fortunes, would turn a bit." Todd S. Purdum, *NYTimes*, 4/10/95, p. A10.

"The President's staff and his lawyer, Robert S. Bennett, took care not to gloat in public, but their relief [on the dismissal of the Paula Jones case] was PALPABLE. Amid the final hours of the President's Africa tour, Mike McCurry, Mr. Clinton's spokesman, said that Mr. Clinton was 'pleased that he has received the vindication he has long awaited.'" Francis X. Clines, *NYTimes*, 4/5/98, p. A16.

"Leave it to psycho-biographers to ponder whether a White House psychiatrist could have helped President Clinton curb self-destructive tendencies. Or if a shrink could have alleviated President Nixon's PALPABLE paranoia, or soothed a war-haunted President Lyndon B. Johnson." David Wallis, *NYTimes*, 3/14/99, p. 4.

PANACHE (OM)

noun - flamboyant style, swaggering manner.

"Traditionally, of course, many presidential hopefuls try to establish their credentials by traveling overseas for talks with foreign leaders, though not with the PANACHE of Jackson, who is accompanied by a media entourage rivaled only by the White House press corps." Terry Atlas, *Chicago Trib.*, 7/8/84, S 5, p. 5.

"Like Ronald Reagan, however, Bill Clinton enjoyed giving a little salute to crowds during the campaign. An aide speculated that he might feel, if he stopped now, that it would seem as though he was guilty about not having served in the military. It may not be so easy to get him to stop. With the sailors, the President was clearly relishing his new PANACHE, having so much fun with that greeting that he followed it up with a second: a firm handshake." Maureen Dowd, *NYTimes*, 6/6/94, p. A4.

"'She [Hillary Rodham Clinton] has the CHUTZPAH and the grit,' he [Harold Ickes] said with the PANACHE of the WANNABE cowpoke. 'Even if she loses it will be worth the candle - for her and her supporters. The cautious side of our nature says, don't do it; the bold says, go for it. You know what? You've got to give her credit: she'll probably go for it.'" Francis X. Clines, *NYTimes*, 6/14/99, p. A14.

PANDER

verb - to gratify the desires of those whose support is being solicited; to tailor one's views to satisfy a particular audience.

"On the policy side, it was heartening that even in a conservative party, no one was fooled by Mr. [Steve] Forbes's PANDERING veer to the right on abortion between his 1996 and 2000 campaigns." Editorial. *NYTimes*, 2/10/00, p. A 30.

"Why would Mr. [George W.] Bush's campaign move so far to the right? It's the same thinking - that you can PANDER to a right-wing base and hope centrist voters suffer amnesia on Election Day - that led the G. O. P. to defeats not only in '96 but in '98." Frank Rich, *NYTimes*, 2/12/00, p. A 29.

"Let me see if I've got this right. The Republican Party is about to lose a presidential candidate who PANDERS to the far-right extremists, dislikes blacks, Jews and immigrants, rails against free markets and free trade, sees AIDS as nature's revenge on homosexuals, excoriates corporations as 'vulture capitalists' and has an unmatched talent for antagonizing people. And this is supposed to be bad for Republicans?" Steve Chapman, *Chicago Trib.*, 9/19/99, S 1, p. 23.

PANDORA'S BOX

noun - a collection of many problems and unexpected troubles.

Note:From Greek mythology. Pandora was the first woman, bestowed upon mankind as a punishment for Prometheus' theft of fire, who, by disregarding orders not to open the box, released all the troubles that beset human beings.

"The current $400 billion budget deficit promises to become Reagan's PANDORA'S BOX. Walter Mondale, in his acceptance speech before the Democratic National Convention and since, has been making it as plain as possible that Reagan will have little choice but to raise taxes next year should he be re-elected, because America is living on borrowed prime." Monroe Anderson, *Chicago Trib.*, 8/10/84, S 1, p. 23.

"...most of us devoutly hoped that Mr. [John F.] Kennedy's Houston speech, election and conduct of the Presidency had settled 'the religious issue,' that no President and no religious majority - even a self-anointed Moral Majority - would thereafter dare to challenge or attempt to coerce anyone else's religious or political standings in this pluralistic society. Mr. Reagan, in dashing those hopes, has opened a PANDORA'S BOX, releasing into the atmosphere dark elements of bigotry, disunity, incivility, hatred - that is, everything but hope." Theodore C. Sorenson, *NYTimes*, 9/11/84, p. 27.

"The cap [on discretionary spending] was the consequence of Clinton's willingness to confront the deficit. He had opened a political PANDORA'S BOX, out of which flew a host of troubles...." Sidney Blumenthal, *New Yorker*, 1/24/94, p. 37.

PANGLOSSIAN

adjective - unusually or excessively optimistic.

Note: from Dr. PANGLOSS, the supreme optimist in Voltaire's <u>Candide</u>.

"It is a portrait of a White House riven by infighting and disorganization, and an indefatigable if often indecisive President [Clinton] given to volcanic rages and sentimental spasms, a compulsive politician with a 'natural inclination toward conciliation and a PANGLOSSIAN faith in his ability to achieve what he willed.'" Michiko Kakutani, *NYTimes*, 3/12/99, p. B45.

PANTHEON (OM)

noun - a group of famous people or gods.

"Although Bill Bradley has said he will decide next month whether to run for President, several of his former longtime aides and close advisers say they believe that he has already made up his mind to seek the Democratic nomination.... Some of his advisers say that this is perhaps his last shot. After publicly flirting with the idea for a decade now, he risks being placed next to former Gov. Mario M. Cuomo in the PANTHEON of modern-day Hamlets." Jennifer Preston, *NYTimes*, 11/28/98, p. A17

"A few hours after the vote, Mr. Clinton, surrounded by Democrats, walked onto the South Lawn of the White House, his wife, Hillary, on his arm, to pre-empt calls for his resignation. The man who in better days had debated where he would stand in the PANTHEON of American Presidents said he would stay in office and vowed 'to go on from here to rise above the rancor to overcome the pain and division, to be a repairer of the breach.'" Alison Mitchell, *NYTimes*, 12/20/98, p. 1.

"The rest of the committee delegated the drafting [of the Declaration of Independence] to Adams and Jefferson. At this point one can reasonably ask why Adams did not write it himself. This was a question Adams raised with himself countless times over the ensuing years, as the significance of the Declaration grew in the popular imagination and Jefferson's authorship became his major ticket into the American PANTHEON. In his autobiography Adams recalled that he delegated the task to Jefferson for several reasons, among them his sense that his own prominence as a leader of the radical faction in Congress for the past two years would subject the draft to greater scrutiny and criticism." Joseph J. Ellis, <u>American Sphinx</u>, Knopf, 1997, p. 49.

PAPARAZZO (PL. PAPARAZZI)

noun - intrusive (in your face) news reporter or photographer.

"Cristophe complained that he was hounded by TV cameramen and PAPARAZZI, that newspapers spelled his name wrong and that everybody was wrong about him charging the president $200 for a haircut. However, he did not say how much Clinton paid." Reuters, *Chicago Trib.*, 6/21/93, S 1, p. 3.

PARADIGM

noun - example, pattern.

"Lincoln stands as a PARADIGM of the public man who was both a consummate politician and an unswerving standard-bearer of man's widest hopes and dreams." Sydney J. Harris, *Chicago Sun- Times*, 2/28/83, p. 21.

"The *kind* of campaign [in 1952] Stevenson had waged was a PARADIGM around which any candidate of the future should conjugate his own campaign." William F. Buckley, Jr., <u>The Jeweler's Eye</u>, G.P. Putnam's Sons, 1969, p. 306.

"'Mrs. Clinton is coming close to not just influencing public policy, but making public policy,' said Anna Perez, who was Barbara Bush's press secretary. If she succeeds, Ms. Perez added, Hillary Clinton 'will have designed a new PARADIGM for First Ladies.'" Gwen Ifill, *NYTimes*, 9/22/93, p. A18.

"[Hillary Clinton] has become a PARADIGM of the over-structured, over-scheduled super-mom. A recent *New Yorker* cartoon showed a woman asking a salesclerk for a jacket and adding, 'Nothing too Hillary.'" Maureen Dowd, *NYTimes* 5/18/92, p. A8.

PARALLACTIC (OM)

adjective - the difference in the perception of an object when seen from two different points.

Note: PARALLACTIC is what Westbrook Pegler used to call an out-of-town or inkhorn word.

"'I think I learned a great deal from, forgive the word, the PARALLACTIC view provided by growing up in two places [Washington and Tennessee],' he [Al Gore] says now, 'because just as having two eyes gives you depth perception, having two homes allows you to see some things that stand out in relief when viewed from two different perspectives.' Mr. Gore's father - who also favored fancy words - moved between two worlds, too, and for all his striving in Washington did not believe in leaving either Tennessee or his farm roots behind, ever, even after his career in politics ended. And he and his wife thought that working on the farm would be good for their son, whom they told friends they hoped would be president one day." Melinda Henneberger, *NYTimes*, 5/22/00, p. A16.

PARLOUS

adjective - dangerous.

"But Bush was in so much trouble that neither man had much choice. And Baker, the Houdini of politics, who never gets caught near a disaster, wouldn't be blamed if Bush lost, as he was in such PARLOUS shape when Baker took over." Elizabeth Drew, *New Yorker*, 9/7/92, p. 92.

"...the Clinton Administration today tentatively embraced a proposal to require all gun owners to be licensed.... Despite the new polls and the shooting spree in which a gunman killed five passengers on the railroad and wounded 20 others, the political equation makes sweeping changes in gun laws PARLOUS." Stephen Labaton, *NYTimes*, 12/10/93, p. A1.

"As [President] Clinton spoke, his PARLOUS situation was evident to the public. According to a new CBS News poll, 78 percent of the electorate expects Congress to have more influence over governmental affairs than he." R. W. Apple, Jr., *NYTimes*, 1/25/95, p. 1.

PARSE

verb - to fit together grammatically.

"Mr. Bush's sentences, on the other hand, often do not PARSE at all. Here, for instance, is the beginning of his reply to a question about tax cuts at a news conference a year ago, on Oct. 26, 1991: 'I think it's understandable, when you have a bad - economic numbers come in from time to time, mixed, I must happily say, with some reasonably good ones, other people get concerned. I'm concerned. But I don't want to do - take - I don't want to say to them "Well, you shouldn't come forward with proposals."'" R. W. Apple, Jr., *NYTimes*, 11/13/92, p. A9.

"Like everything else that does not PARSE in this mess, it makes no sense that Hillary Rodham Clinton, who has brought the job of First Lady into the late 20th century in every other respect, would follow a strictly restricted press diet more appropriate to Pat Nixon." Frank Rich, *NYTimes*, 3/10/94, p. A17.

PARTY ANIMAL

noun - a person who really enjoys parties and frequently over-indulges.

"As I scan the Republican horizon for 2000, all I see are frat boys - jocks and reformed PARTY ANIMALS such as George W. Bush, Dan Quayle and John McCain, plus one Southern deb [Elizabeth Dole] who definitely looks like a THROWBACK to the days of unassailable girdles and unmussable hairdos." Maureen Dowd, *NYTimes*, 4/7/99, p. A23.

by Garry Trudeau

"How then to explain the affair [with Monica Lewinsky]? Pop psychological analyses of the president have often characterized him as a man of split personalities - a good Clinton and a bad Clinton, the policy WONK and the PARTY ANIMAL." Jeffrey Toobin, <u>A Vast Conspiracy</u>, Random House, 1999, p. 91.

PARVENU (FR)

noun - a person of newly acquired wealth or power who lacks the dignity of manner associated with it.

"Oh dear. Poor commentator George Will, so shunned by the Bushies as a PARVENU, probably thought he was going to be invited to dinner parties again." Michael Kilian, *Chicago Trib.*, 2/12/95, S 5, p. 6.

PATERFAMILIAS

noun - father of the family in his capacity as head of the household.

"President Bush ran into the dangerous intersection of the personal and the political in an NBC interview broadcast Tuesday night. The staunchly anti-abortion President was presented with a hypothetical test of his 'family values': a pregnant granddaughter who came to him and insisted on having an abortion. Some who watched Mr. Bush's response, in which he said he would try to

195

dissuade her but would ultimately 'stand by my child,' saw a loving PATERFAMILIAS with strong political principles but also a heart." Robin Toner, *NYTimes*, 8/13/92, p. A1.

"But it seemed somehow telling that Mr. Clinton and his family, who own no home of their own, began their holiday with a visit to this Rocky Mountain resort and its PATERFAMILIAS, former President Gerald Ford." Douglas Jehl, *NYTimes*, 8/15/93, p. 15.

"The marriage of Julie Nixon to David Eisenhower, mingling the Nixon and Eisenhower bloodlines, was the closest Nixon came to being an Eisenhower. At last, he was PATERFAMILIAS, but he could never be Ike." Sidney Blumenthal, *New Yorker*, 8/8/94, p. 36.

"On New Year's Day of 1772 he [Thomas Jefferson] completed his self-image as an aspiring 'PATERFAMILIAS' by marrying Martha Wales Skelton, an attractive and delicate young widow whose dowry more than doubled his holdings in land and slaves." Joseph J. Ellis, <u>American Sphinx</u>, Knopf, 1997, p. 28.

PATOIS

noun - special language of an occupation or social group.

"Bill Clinton and Al Gore have developed a political act unlike any seen on a Presidential ticket before, a political tag-team show that rests on presenting the two men as equal partners in a joint venture.... They look alike (they are both of similar age and physique, although Mr. Gore is slightly younger and Mr. Clinton is slightly thicker), they walk alike (very cockily these days, being 23 points up in the polls), they even talk alike (switching from the Washington PATOIS of policy and program to the drawling cadence of country talk and back again)." Michael Kelly, *NYTimes*, 7/22/92, p. A7.

"Still, in the Ozark PATOIS he sometimes affects, Clinton has made good on an oft-stated campaign promise that he would stay on the case 'until the last dog dies.'" Steve Daley, *Chicago Trib.*, 1/23/94, S 4, p. 5.

PAUCITY

noun - scarcity, scantiness.

"...the authors said they are troubled by the administration's willingness to accommodate traditional Democratic spending programs - the president retreated on cutting subsidies to agricultural, mining and timber interests - and by the PAUCITY of public discussion of 'core values,' such as work and personal responsibility, which Clinton made a part of his campaign strategy." Steve Daley, *Chicago Trib.*, 5/25/93, S 1, p. 1.

PECCADILLO (PL. PECCADILLOES)

noun - a slight offense.

Note:Representative Hyde used "YOUTHFUL INDISCRETIONS" to describe his own sexual transgressions (see Peter Steinfels' quote below). Hyde was married and in his 40's when he carried on a four year affair with a married woman.

"President Harding's downfall was not his venality, but his geniality. He never profited from the PECCADILLOES of his friends, but he was too soft to deny them anything. If he had not been so well liked, and had not liked so many men himself, Teapot Dome would never have blemished his administration." Sydney J. Harris, <u>Strictly Personal</u>, Henry Regnery Company, 1953, p. 17.

"Over the coming weeks, agents of the Federal Bureau of Investigation will fan out around the country looking for PECCADILLOES and worse in the background of the men and women picked by President-elect Bush to run the country." Stephen Engelberg, *NYTimes*, 11/16/88, p. 14.

"Once again, an American family [the Bush family] is about to undergo a singular and daunting experience, coming under a microscope that has often turned the lives of first families into a national soap opera complete with feuds, PECCADILLOES and self-promoting relatives." Maureen Dowd, *NYTimes*, 12/12/88, p. 1.

"Last January, Mr. Hyde said his committee would need more than evidence of an illicit affair to begin impeachment proceedings. 'You don't impeach him [President Clinton] for a PECCADILLO.' Mr. Hyde said in a television interview." Jill Abramson, *NYTimes*, 7/29/98, p. A15.

"These tactical denials of traditional ethics' insistence on the power and importance of sex have become so pervasive that even a conservative like Representative Henry J. Hyde, Republican of Illinois, [in referring to the Clinton scandal] has used the word PECCADILLO to describe the President's sexual transgressions." Peter Steinfels, *NYTimes*, 8/22/98, p. A11.

"Nor was it difficult for Jefferson's fans to denounce the gossipy reports of Jefferson's principal white tormentor on this question, James Thomson Callender, a notorious alcoholic and Matt Drudge-style GADFLY of his day. Now along comes DNA testing evidence, the same leveler that exposed the sexual PECCADILLOES of President Clinton, to provide clear and convincing genetic proof that Jefferson fathered at least one child by his slave, Sally Hemings." Clarence Page, *Chicago Trib.*, 11/4/98, S 1, p. 23.

PECKERWOOD

noun - a disparaging reference to a rural white Southerner.

"Does the Reagan Supreme Court decree that the death penalty shall be limited largely to black people? Some specimen in a three-piece suit appears instantly to announce this was the dearest wish of the founding fathers. Do the Supremes decree that accused citizens can be held in prison until they can prove their innocence? Some PECKERWOOD from a right-wing think tank immediately declares this was the very scheme most cherished by Thomas Jefferson himself. As our only attorney general [Edwin Meese] observed not long ago, 'You don't have many suspects who are innocent of a crime. That's contradictory. If a person is innocent of a crime, then he is not a suspect.'" Molly Ivins, <u>Molly Ivins Can't Say That, Can She?</u>, Random House, 1991, p. 111.

PEJORATIVE

adjective - depreciatory, disparaging.

"In a year when the label 'incumbent' is akin to 'scalawag' or unprintable PEJORATIVES, voters don't appear to be distinguishing between Democratic and Republican members of Congress. The fact that they are in Congress is enough to get them in trouble with voters this year, and Bush's blanket criticisms don't help." Elaine S. Povich, *Chicago Trib.*, 8/31/92, S 1, p. 1.

PENULTIMATE

adjective - next to the last.

"Mr. Clinton made no mention of Bob Dole's late campaign speeches against a generation of affirmative action programs and in favor of immigration restrictions. But the President was clearly seeking to offer a contrasting vision on the PENULTIMATE day of the race." Alison Mitchell, *NYTimes*, 11/4/96, p. 1.

PERIPATETIC

adjective and *noun* - walking from place to place.

"'There's something going on here. People are concerned about where the country is and where it's going,' Perot, the PERIPATETIC symbol of American ANGST, said in an interview last week. His folksy pitch for government reform, deficit reduction and a balanced federal budget was received as enthusiastically at a rally Thursday night in Wichita Falls, Texas, as it had been throughout last year's campaign." Thomas Hardy, *Chicago Trib.*, 5/16/93, S 1, p. 1.

"More than a half-million copies of <u>Barbara Bush: A Memoir</u> quietly appeared in bookstores around the United States last week, reflecting Scribner's expectations that it will outdo <u>Millie's Book</u>, the 1990 best-seller dictated by the Bush family pooch to Barbara Bush (she says) when she was First Lady. Though there are few surprises, <u>A Memoir</u> is a lively and partisan recollection of 'a life of privilege' - most of it spent in George Bush's shadow - throughout the nearly 50 years of their PERIPATETIC marriage." Donnie Radcliffe, *International Herald Trib.*, 9/5/94, p. 3.

PEROTICISM (SL)

noun - simplistic solutions to major problems advanced by Ross Perot.

"But elections play out over time, and over time those down-home PEROTICISMS began to seem as predictable as smoothie political rhetoric. No matter how many charts the man hauled out, it became clear that no one could truly get rid of the deficit without even breakin' a sweat." Anna Quindlen, *Chicago Trib.*, 11/2/94, S 1, p. 21.

PEROTISM (SL)

noun - adherence to the platform, program and ideas of Ross Perot.

"The Democratic primary season is winding down, but Mr. Clinton seemed to be on anything but a victory tour as he traveled through Arkansas, Ohio and New Jersey this week. What should have been a grace period for the likely Democratic nominee, a time to polish his image and consolidate his support, has instead become a struggle to simply be heard over the roar of PEROTISM." Robin Toner, *NYTimes*, 5/28/92, p. A11.

PEROTNOID (SL)

adjective - the Ross Perot version of a paranoid person.

"A new LEXICON has taken hold of the White House: Political figures are immortalized as verbs or adjectives, says *The Washingtonian*.

"Aspin, as in 'to do an Aspin' - to take a Cabinet job, get fired and disappear from public view.'

"To Janetize is to 'defuse a GAFFE by admitting you made it.' Also see Renovate.

"An Oliver twist is a 'revisionist view of the Iran-Contra scandal, Virginia-campaign style.' A PEROTNOID person 'sees enemies, hears sucking sounds and smells rats everywhere.'

"Robbdown, as in non-adulterous massage, Virginia-campaign style." Tribune Staff, *Chicago Trib.*, 8/29/94, p. 2.

PERSNICKETY

adjective - picky, fussy, choosy.

"Here they were, paying homage to PERSNICKETY New Hampshire conservatives and smiling under a scalding sun, the hope of the G.O.P.: Bob Dole, Phil Gramm, Pat Buchanan. Bob Dornan was also there. It was the most extraordinary collection of adder-tongued talent that had ever been gathered together at a Republican repast, with the possible exception of when Richard Nixon dined alone." Maureen Dowd, *NYTimes,* 7/6/95, p. A13.

PERSONA

noun - the role, personality or front assumed by a person.

"...[George Bush] seemed compelled by some Pavlovian training - almost certainly by Ailes - to launch an attack from his repertoire of simplistic bellringers when cornered by a tough question. While that didn't destroy him in the first debate, it may have kept him from a clear-cut victory. If he doesn't resurrect the real George Bush before the next one in mid-October, he could be hurt. There already is evidence that the PERSONA invented by attack specialist Ailes is wearing thin." Editorial, *Chicago Trib.*, 9/28/88, S 1, p. 22.

"...[White House staff members] seemed to believe that the President's ideas were unfashionable, and that it was necessary to prevent him [Reagan] from following his own instincts. Though clearly devoted to him, they seemed, like his liberal enemies, to regard him as 'a sort of supreme anchorman whose public PERSONA was the most important element of the Presidency.'" Frances Fitzgerald, *New Yorker*, 1/16/89, p. 83.

"In a city where nuance, spin, imagery and propaganda are the stuff that shape the daily complexion of a campaign, Mr. Perot at times charts a more absolutist course - I'm right and they're wrong, no matter what - when it comes to the history of events that are at the core of his PERSONA as the outsider-who-knows-how-to-get-things-done candidate." *NYTimes*, 5/28/92, p. A10.

"President-elect Bill Clinton's aides today unveiled plans for his inauguration, which promises to be a festival of contrasts mirroring Mr. Clinton's own PERSONA: blue jeans and ball gowns, a soup kitchen and $125-dollar-a-plate dinners, all kicked off by - what else? - a bus trip to the White House." Thomas Friedman, *NYTimes*, 12/3/92, p. A12.

"Having used his parliamentary skills and his snarling PERSONA to assume a de facto role as head of the Republican Party, Dole is standing down his younger colleagues." Steve Daley, *Chicago Trib.*, 8/29/93, S 4, p. 5.

"During the interview, in response to questions about education and the economy, Mr. Gore displayed the kind of PERSONA - intelligent, energetic and committed to progress - that would likely serve him well if it were exhibited more often in public." Bob Herbert, *NYTimes*, 5/27/99, p. A31.

PERSONA NON GRATA (L)

adjective - an unwelcome person.

"...fellow Democrats on the Senate floor often avoid the conservative Alabamian [Sen. Richard Shelby] these days, and he's PERSONA NON GRATA at the White House. The relative isolation stems from his refusal to support President Clinton's economic plan or even to try to get the plan modified in exchange for his support." Elaine S. Povich, *Chicago Trib.*, 6/25/93, S 1, p. 8.

PETTIFOG

verb - to operate an inferior or questionable law practice; to be petty or trivial, to argue over minutiae, quibble.
noun - PETTIFOGGER.

"Exploiting court secrecy, he [President Clinton] asserts executive privilege so sweeping as to make Richard Nixon's ghost blush. By making absurd claims of unreachability that must be adjudicated by the Supreme

Court, he secretly buys years of time - and then publicly castigates the Independent Counsel for taking so long. By his PETTIFOGGING delay, he drives up the cost of the investigation - and then complains about the cost to taxpayers of prosecution." William Safire, *NYTimes*, 4/2/98, p. A29.

"The president was a Southern Democrat who'd risen from the class scorned as 'white trash.' His personal life inspired widespread snickering. The Republicans who controlled Congress detested him. They investigated every aspect of his life and then voted to impeach him. With his fate in the hands of a few moderates, he hired a claque of lawyers skilled in nitpicking and PETTIFOGGERY. The president was, of course, Andrew Johnson. The year was 1868." Peter Carlson, *Concord Monitor*, 12/30/98, p. A1.

"Finally, at the end of April, both sides [in the impeachment trial of Andrew Johnson] began to sum up their cases. The ailing Thaddeus Stevens, who spent most of the trial huddled under a blanket, rose on wobbly legs to make his final statement. The case was about Reconstruction, he said, about how the president had usurped congressional power and helped to create new Confederate governments in the South. Stevens denounced Johnson as a 'wretched man' and a 'PETTIFOGGING political trickster,' but then his strength gave out and he had to sit down and let Butler read the rest of his speech." Peter Carlson, *Concord Monitor*, 12/31/98, p. A10.

Note: According to Peter Carlson, the author of a two-part series in the *Washington Post*, reprinted in the *Concord Monitor*, Thaddeus Stevens, the aged, sickly leader of the House Republicans, after the civil war "lived in sin with his black housekeeper and didn't much care who gossiped about it."

PHILANDER

verb - to engage in many casual love affairs; to flirt.
noun - PHILANDERER.

"Like Garry Wills in 'The Kennedy Imprisonment,' Collier and Horowitz make the argument that Joe Kennedy's PHILANDERING set an example that his sons [except for Bobby] tried to follow." Steve Neal, Review of The Kennedys, An American Drama by Peter Collier and David Horowitz, *Chicago Trib.*, 6/24/84, S 14, p. 36.

"That dark and revisionist new book on three generations of Kennedys now climbing the best seller lists will be read first for its smudges of dirty linen. There is patriarch Joe Kennedy, such an insatiable PHILANDERER that his son warns female houseguests to be sure to lock their rooms at night." Joan Beck, *Chicago Trib.*, 6/27/84, S 1, p. 18.

"The Packwood investigation would do a service by calling in experts to examine this second question. Is there something in the American air that forces our Dagwoods to make themselves foolish by trying to play Don Juans? Is this what explains the compulsive PHILANDERING of so many politicians like John Kennedy, Nelson Rockefeller and Estes Kefauver, to cite only the more notorious?" Russell Baker, *NYTimes*, 11/2/93, p. A15.

"As we pass through another 'feeding frenzy' over Bill Clinton's alleged PHILANDERING, many observers inside and outside journalism will condemn the invasion of privacy, the sensationalism, the irrelevancy." Robert M. Entman, *Chicago Trib.*, 1/3/94, S 1, p. 11.

"Around October 1862, James [Garfield] had an affair with Mrs. Lucia Gilbert Calhoun. James was in New York City and still a PHILANDERER. Lucia was approximately eighteen years old. She was a young writer and reporter for the *New York Times*. Little is known about the affair except that it did occur. James told his wife, and she eventually forgave him. If the affair did take place after Garfield's marriage in 1856, this would make him the first future president known to have cheated on his wife. Although Thomas Jefferson had an affair and it's possible that George Washington did as well, in both cases they were bachelors at the time they became involved with married women." Wesley O. Hagood, <u>Presidential Sex</u>, Carol Publishing Group, 1995, pp. 53-54.

"Ellen discovered the affair [with Mary Peck], although it is not clear how she learned about her husband's PHILANDERING. Perhaps he [Woodrow Wilson] told her, or perhaps, like a subsequent president's wife, Eleanor Roosevelt, she discovered the affair on her own after reading the letters exchanged between her husband and his lover. However, unlike Eleanor, who never slept with Franklin again after her discovery of his infidelity, Ellen forgave Woodrow, and they became full marital partners again as well as lovers." Wesley O. Hagood, <u>Presidential Sex</u>, Carol Publishing Group, 1995, p. 75.

"Bill Clinton is not the first American president to have had a mistress, nor is he the first to have told a lie. His boyhood idol, John F. Kennedy, was at least Clinton's equal as a PHILANDERER, maybe his superior. And presidents as far back as John Adams (we'll leave aside the sainted George Washington) dissembled, fudged the truth - lied - when it suited their political purposes. These are, after all, human beings." Editorial, *Chicago Trib.*, 9/15/98, S 1, p. 18.

"Donna Brazile, who was just named Al Gore's new campaign manager, did not supply a terse, 'that was a long time ago in another country' response when she was asked about the night she stepped down from another Presidential campaign, Michael Dukakis's in 1988. She had agreed to resign after making some way-out-of-school comments prodding reporters to check out some rumors about Vice President George Bush. That evening, she called her mother - 'I said, "Jean," - I called my mom Jean - "I got fired." I said, "I called the Vice President a racist, a liar and a PHILANDERER."' (In fact, her comments had been limited to that third thing mentioned.)" Melinda Henneberger, *NYTimes*, 10/11/99, p. A10.

PHILIPPIC

noun - an oration or discourse full of acrimonious invectives.

"After a campaign for the White House built around a ferociously negative PHILIPPIC against Michael Dukakis, Bush needs to cut the figure of a statesman. He needs to make a fresh start. In a coincidence that no relisher of bad puns could pass by, Reagan's gift just happens to be known by the acronym START, which refers to the strategic-arms-reduction treaty that the United States and the Soviet Union have been working on at Geneva for the past few years." Jack Beatty, *Atlantic Monthly*, 2/89, p. 59.

"That meeting, and [Bill] Bennett's publicizing of it, struck a note that resonated widely throughout American politics. Quick as an overnight poll, the leading 1996 Republican Presidential contender, Senator Bob Dole, came out with an anti-Time Warner PHILIPPIC. Sudden as a shift in the summer wind, Time Warner fired its most vocal apologist for gangsta rap, Doug Morris." Michael Kelly, *New Yorker*, 7/17/95, p. 27.

PIED À TERRE (FR)

noun - a second home or temporary dwelling.

"As Hillary Rodham Clinton ponders life after 1600 Pennsylvania Avenue, Westchester County has popped up on the radar screen. And why not? It offers such amenities as leafy privacy, relative proximity to Le Cirque 2000 and, perhaps most important, something to occupy her husband: golf. . Another scenario for the Clintons would be a PIED À TERRE in Manhattan and a country place in the Bedford area, which is fast becoming Hollywood-on-the-Hudson. Golfing opportunities there are good but not great, with Waccabuc Country Club and the Bedford Golf and Tennis Club cited as having fairly challenging courses." Lisa W. Foderaro, *NYTimes*, 5/27/99, p. A27.

PLEBISCITE

noun - a vote of all the people in a state or political unit.
adjective - PLEBISCITARY.

"Perot's childlike fascination with gadgetry envisions government as a great telephone answering machine. The evident idea behind his electronic town meetings is that government is not properly responsive because the public's wishes are not well-measured. Actually, government today involves minute measurement of public appetites by servile politicians worshipful of those measurements. Such government reflects the decay of deliberative democracy into PLEBISCITARY, answering-machine democracy." George F. Will, *Chicago Sun-Times*, 5/28/92, p. 34.

PLEONASM

noun - redundancy, tautology.

"I did, however, want to hear Jesse Jackson speak. He is the only living American politician with a mastery of classical rhetoric. Assonance, alliteration, litotes, PLEONASM, parallelism, exclamation, climax and epigram - to listen to Jesse Jackson is to hear everything mankind has learned about public speaking since Demosthenes." P. J. O'Rourke, <u>Parliament of Whores</u>, Vintage Books, 1992, p. 24.

POLLYANNA

noun - an irrepressible optimist; a PANGLOSSIAN person.
Note:from the heroine of POLLYANNA, a novel by Eleanor Porter (1913).

"*Were the media fair to Reagan?* Yes and no. The media have taken a tolerant sort of there-he-goes-again attitude toward the President's simplistic ideas, POLLYANNA politics and less-than-total command of relevant facts. But this likeable-old-dodderer image has made Reagan's solid achievements seem like happy accidents or the result of good staff work. He - and the voters - deserve a clearer assessment." Joan Beck, *Chicago Trib.*, 11/7/84, S 1, p. 22.

"This same acquaintance, who describes [Hillary] Clinton as a 'pretty tough cookie,' contrasts the interpersonal styles of the two Clintons. '[Bill] is a kind of POLLYANNA, he trusts anybody, likes everyone, has a heart of gold. She's very pragmatic. She would say [of someone], "Bill, he is not your friend." People on the staff say they have heard Hillary tell Bill, "You're too much a POLLYANNA." She's the tough, pragmatic one of the two.'" Janet Cawley, *Chicago Trib. Magazine*, 5/9/93, p. 14.

POLTROON

noun - a coward.

"Well, talk about media furioso! (Or is it media furiosa?) He [Ross Perot] was roundly accused of WIMPISHNESS and POLTROONERY [for dropping out of the campaign]." Russell Baker, *NYTimes*, 9/15/92, p. A15.

"President Bush and Governor Not-Bush are getting away with the same WIMPISH POLTROONERY that incensed media persons in the Perot affair." Russell Baker, NYTimes, 9/15/92, p. A15.

POLYMATH

noun - an exceptionally learned person.

"But Al Gore doesn't need to be loved. He needs to be right. Not only is he a POLYMATH who makes the rest of us feel like slackers; he lacks the glaring flaws; no dark past, no drunken parent or dubious paternity, no private demons, no cheating at Harvard, no bad-boy brother or left-wing wife; alas, not even a Gennifer. How is this poor man to compete in the politics of Personal Biography!" Gail Sheehy, *NYTimes*, 6/2/00, p. A25.

POOBAH

noun - a person who holds a number of offices at the same time; a very important person.
Note:From the character in Gilbert and Sullivan's *Mikado* who was First Lord of the Treasury, Lord Chief Justice, Commander-in-Chief, Lord High

Admiral, Master of the Buckhounds, Groom of the Back Stairs, Archbishop of Titipu and Lord Mayor.

"Sure, [Vice President Dan] Quayle sometimes sounded pretty silly, but his remarks always resonated with at least a kernel of truth. In fact, he flattered the POOBAHS of American television by calling the culture they put on an 'elite.'" Clarence Page, *Chicago Trib.*, 11/29/92 S 4, p. 3.

"True, the Reagans, the Bushes and even (especially) the Jimmy Carters had film stars around a lot of the time. But they had them as extra celebrity guests at state dinners - a garnishment for the visiting POOBAHS. Clinton has them to the Oval Office!" Michael Kilian, *Chicago Trib.*, 6/9/93, S 7, p. 12.

POPINJAY

noun - a strutting, supercilious, pompous person.

"What ailed him [Teddy Roosevelt] was the fact that his lust for glory, when it came to a struggle, was always vastly more powerful than his lust for the eternal verities. Tempted sufficiently, he would sacrifice anything and everything to get applause. Thus the statesman was debauched by the politician and the philosopher was elbowed out of sight by the POPINJAY." H. L. Mencken, <u>A Mencken Chrestomathy</u>, Vintage Books, 1982, p. 242.

"The millions of Americans who were drawn to this moneyed POPINJAY [Ross Perot] last spring have dwindled down to a spoiled and self-important few, a bovine collection of paid and unpaid volunteers who comport themselves like 4th graders, alternatively giggling and sobbing whenever Boss Perot offers a pronunciamento." Steve Daley, *Chicago Trib.*, 10/4/92, S 4, p. 4.

POPPYCOCK

noun - nonsense, codswallop, balderdash.

"POPPYCOCK, an older term for codswallop [though not as old as the 17th Century balderdash, a silly mixture of liquids like milk and ale], comes in lots rather than loads. When told the London observer had reported that President Reagan had postponed a colonoscopy because of the 1984 election campaign, White House spokesman Larry Speakes said 'That's not true, that's POPPYCOCK, as the British would say.' So would Americans. The *Oxford English Dictionary* labels POPPYCOCK as originally United States slang." William Safire, *Chicago Trib.*, 9/4/85, S 1, p. 15.

"...Ross Perot started talking about the death of the American dream, and so many people seemed to believe the thing really was either dead or dying that it seemed unwise to make light of it. H. L. Mencken had the courage necessary to ridicule POPPYCOCK, but we modern news folk are too craven to kick a beloved old cliché, much less ridicule a billionaire trying to buy himself a Presidency." Russell Baker, *NYTimes*, 12/15/92, p. A23.

POTEMKIN (POTEMKIN VILLAGE)

noun - false front or facade.

Note:From Gregori Potemkin, a Russian political figure and member of the Court of Catherine the Great, who constructed fake villages along the route of Catherine's travels to conceal the abject poverty of the peasants. Mayor Richard J. Daley did something similar for the 1968 Democratic convention in Chicago by building fences to conceal slums on the route to the convention hall.

"Prisoners freed during Mr. Jackson's Havana visit have told how the prison facilities he visited were painted at the last minute and prisoners were given such 'luxuries' as Kool-Aid in an effort to impress him. Some convicts were even dressed in new baseball uniforms and ordered to stay on the playing field for about 70 innings until Mr. Jackson finally showed up. This was all in the grand tradition of POTEMKIN, the powerful Russian prince who impressed 18th Century Empress Catherine II on a trip through the Ukraine by erecting artificial villages to disguise the weaknesses of his administration in the Ukraine. If Mr. Jackson's proposed trip to the Soviet Union comes to pass, he ought to beware if there's an odor of fresh paint in the air." Editorial, *Chicago Trib.*, 7/9/84, S 1, p. 8.

"What if Reagan concludes, as I have, that his counterpart [Mikhail Gorbachev] really believes in his heart most of what he says, and is not just putting up a rhetorical POTEMKIN VILLAGE?" William Safire, *Chicago Trib.*, 11/27/85, S 1, p. 13.

"But there is a POTEMKIN VILLAGE quality to the [George] Bush edifice." David Broder, *Chicago Trib.*, 8/9/87, S 4, p. 3.

"Robert B. Reich, Mr. Clinton's former Labor Secretary and friend of 30 years, said on the ABC News program 'Nightline' last week: 'We have almost a virtual impeachment, a POTEMKIN President. He's going through the motions of being a President but he doesn't have very much power or authority left.'" Todd S. Purdum, *NYTimes*, 9/21/98, p. A16.

POTHER

noun - commotion, agitation, fuss; KERFUFFLE.

"The health of a President is watched very carefully, not only by the Vice-President but also by medical men detailed for the purpose by the army or navy. These medical men have high-sounding titles, and perform the duties of their office in full uniform, with swords on one side and stethoscopes on the other. The diet of their imperial patient is rigidly scrutinized. If he eats a few peanuts they make a POTHER; if he goes in for some steamed hard crabs at night, washed down by what passes in Washington for malt liquor, they complain to the newspapers." H. L. Mencken, <u>The American Scene</u>, Ed. by Huntington Cairns, Vintage Books, 1982, p. 224.

PREBUTTAL (SL)

noun - rebuttal material delivered before the speech or statement that it is meant to rebut.

"In Hartford, conclusions about the first debate were in play even before Clinton and Dole took their places on the podiums. At twenty minutes before nine, the Clinton press office distributed to the hundreds of reporters gathered in the Hartford Civic Center what was labeled 'PREBUTTAL: Dole vs. The Facts' - a six-page single-spaced memo that followed the formula 'Dole might say the following, but these are the facts.'" Ken Auletta, *New Yorker*, 11/18/96, p. 58.

PRESCIENT

adjective - having foreknowledge or foresight.

"When Tipper Gore began a campaign against violent and sexually explicit lyrics on record albums seven years ago, her crusade was widely viewed as an inappropriate call for censorship. But with the recent uproar over the lyrics of rap artists, including Sister Souljah and Ice-T, and calls from the White House for a return to family values, Mrs. Gore now looks politically PRESCIENT." Karen De Witt, *NYTimes*, 7/10/92, p. A9.

"The journalists were perhaps less than PRESCIENT in naming the major campaign development, with 46 percent citing Clinton's 'character issue' and only 17 percent citing independent Ross Perot's entrance into the campaign." Roger Flaherty, *Chicago Sun- Times*, 6/4/92, p. 28.

"In 1961, he [George W. Ball] advised President John F. Kennedy not to send 15,000 American troops to Vietnam, saying 300,000 more men would have to be dispatched later to get them out. His advice was rejected by both Kennedy and his successor, Johnson. It turned out to be eerily PRESCIENT." AP, *Arizona Daily Star*, 5/28/94, S A, p. 16.

"[Those who oppose funding for the arts] fail to appreciate what every generation of Americans has intuitively known - that the artistic imagination is critical to our civilization and our democracy. They forget the PRESCIENT words of John Adams: 'I must study politics and war that my sons may have liberty to study mathematics and philosophy. My sons ought to study mathematics and philosophy ... in order to give their children a right to study painting, poetry, music.'" Hillary Rodham Clinton, *NYTimes*, 6/21/95, p. A19.

PRETERNATURAL

adjective - exceeding what is natural; abnormal; exceptional.

"In this case, we fight against, not just PRETERNATURAL powers, but almost supernatural powers. That's almost too much for anyone to stand against - almost all alone, as I have. And then they sent in Betty Furness. And I really have never liked to campaign against women, but to send in the director of consumer protection, it seems to me, is going too far." Quote of

Senator Eugene J. McCarthy. Bill Adler, <u>The McCarthy Wit</u>, Fawcett Publications, Inc. 1969, p. 53.

"If he [Al Gore] lacks the deficits of the bad Bill Clinton, he also lacks the feel-your-pain skills of the good Clinton. Mr. Clinton's PRETERNATURAL empathy with whoever was in front of him gave him an enormous advantage in the kind of campaigning that stresses staged give-and-take with 'regular Americans.'" Editorial, *NYTimes*, 3/21/99, p. 14.

"He [President Clinton, in his MEA CULPA speech] had an almost PRETERNATURAL sense that the public agreed when he said, 'It's nobody's business but ours.' In an intuitive way, he understood what the journalists, for all their prattle about character, did not - that the American people believed there was a difference between his public and private life. Clinton didn't have a lot of company in this view, even among his own staff, but in this he was defiantly, even courageously, correct." Jeffrey Toobin, <u>A Vast Conspiracy</u>, Random House, 1999, p. 320.

PREVISION

noun - foresight.

"To the extent of his [Teddy Roosevelt's] PREVISION he was a genuine leader of the nation, and perhaps in the years to come, when his actual ideas are disentangled from the demagogic fustian in which he had to wrap them, his more honest pronunciamentoes will be given canonical honors, and he will be ranked among the prophets." H. L. Mencken, <u>A Mencken Chrestomathy</u>, Vintage Books, 1982, p. 241.

Teddy Roosevelt Exposes The Meatpackers. Artist Unknown

PRIAPIC

adjective - phallic.

Note:The etymon is Priapus, the Greek god of male generative power in classical antiquity.

"Clinton is now and probably forever our PRIAPIC President, who takes his place alongside our drunken President, Ulysses S. Grant, our napping President, Calvin Coolidge, and our treacherous President, Richard Nixon." Jacob Weisberg, *NYTimes Magazine*, 1/17/99, p. 33.

PRIG

noun - one who offends or irritates by observance of proprieties to an obnoxious degree.

"Whether those reasons for early discharge reflected hypersensitivity, PRIGGISHNESS or the hypocrisy of an ambitious young man [Ross Perot] eager to get started on his civilian career, they were not the sort that today's candidate wants made public. So he recently set forth a different reason, that presents him in a more heroic light." William Safire, *NYTimes*, 6/1/92, p. A15.

"What we have here [in Ross Perot] is a Portrait of the Young Man as a PRIG. Comparing the letter Bill Clinton wrote at age twenty-one to the letter Ross Perot wrote at twenty-five is the difference between pietistic piffle and genuine moral agony. Young Bill Clinton was clearly tortured by the war in Vietnam - not so much by the prospect of being killed as of having to kill on behalf of a corrupt regime that did not even have the support of its own people. Ross Perot, as he later admitted, did not get along with his commanding officer." Molly Ivins, <u>Nothin' But Good Times Ahead</u>, Vintage Press, 1993, p. 111.

PROCRUSTEAN

adjective - aiming or tending to produce uniformity by violent and arbitrary means; frequently appears as "PROCRUSTEAN bed."

Note:From the legendary robber PROCRUSTES, or the stretcher. "He had an iron bedstead on which he used to tie all travelers who fell into his hands. If they were shorter than the bed, he stretched their limbs to make them fit; if they were longer than the bed, he lopped off a portion." Edmund Fuller, <u>Bulfinch's Mythology</u>, Dell Publishing Co., Inc. 1959, p. 125.

"'We campaign in poetry.' he [Mario Cuomo] said at Yale in 1985, in what seem now prophetic words. 'But when we're elected we're forced to govern in prose. And when we govern - as distinguished from when we campaign - we come to understand the difference between a speech and a statute. It's here that the noble aspirations, neat promises and slogans of a campaign get bent out of recognition or even break as you try to nail them down to the PROCRUSTEAN bed of reality." Anna Quindlen, *NYTimes*, 11/12/94, p. 15.

PROTEAN

adjective - capable of assuming different forms; versatile.

Note:Derived from Proteus, a Greek sea god who could assume many different forms.

"How someone of such surpassing intellect and such PROTEAN political talents could indulge in such conduct at a time when he knew a special prosecutor was already scrutinizing his Administration and when his own re-election still hung in the balance remains the most puzzling question about William Jefferson Clinton." Todd S. Purdum, *NYTimes*, 8/18/98, p. 1.

Hank Parker

"In the Scopes trial both William Jennings Bryan and Clarence Darrow were sure that Jefferson agreed with their position on evolution. Herbert Hoover and Franklin Roosevelt both claimed him as their guide to the problems of the Great Depression. The chief chronicler of the multiple Jeffersonian legacy, Merrill Peterson, gave it the name 'PROTEAN,' which provided a respectably classical sound to what some critics described as Jefferson's disarming ideological promiscuity. He was an American's Everyman." Joseph J. Ellis, <u>American Sphinx</u>, Knopf, 1997, p. 7.

PSYCHOBABBLE (Sʟ)

noun - foolish or meaningless psychological jargon.

"Roger Stone, the Republican consultant, agreed. 'The next thing you know, Al Gore will be showing up in a tie-dyed shirt wearing crystals,' he said. William Kristol, the Vice President's chief of staff, suggested that the Democrats were not fishing for those critical blue-collar, white male votes in the right manly fashion: 'Bush and Quayle will run as macho individualists. Clinton and Gore will run on a New Age Covenant of PSYCHOBABBLE.'" *NYTimes*, 7/27/92, p. A8.

"Detractors [of Hillary Rodham Clinton] chortle over the speech's similarities to her PSYCHOBABBLING graduation speech at Wellesley in 1969 (Sample: 'We are, all of us, exploring a world that none of us understands and attempting to create within that uncertainty...'). But, quite frankly, I don't find Hillary Clinton's ramblings any more unsettling than Ronald Reagan's mental cruise down Highway 101 during his second 1984 debate with Walter Mondale." Clarence Page, *Chicago Trib.*, 5/26/93, S 1, p. 27.

"In an era when politics has become overloaded with PSYCHOBABBLE about meaningful exchanges, encounters and shared pain, the image of the 83-year-old former president and movie star [Ronald Reagan] sitting in Bel Aire playing 'Git Along Little Doggie' or 'Streets of Laredo' [on the harmonica], seemed, well, just right somehow. If Bill Clinton is a saxophone sort, Ronald Reagan is surely a harmonica man. The presidents who could play the harmonica, with varying degrees of skill, were Lincoln, Teddy Roosevelt, Coolidge and Eisenhower." New York Times News Service, *Chicago Trib.*, 4/3/94, S 1, p. 7.

"Vice President Al Gore emerges from Earth in the Balance (Plume), his 1992 book about the environment, as the QUINTESSENTIAL A-student who has belatedly discovered New Age PSCHOBABBLE. Like his speeches, his book veers between detailed policy assessments (predictably illustrated with lots of charts and graphs) and high-decibel outbursts of passion, between energetically researched historical disquisitions and loony asides about 'inner ecology' and 'spiritual TRIANGULATION'..." Michiko Kakutani, *NYTimes*, 11/22/99, p. A 24.

PUISSANT

adjective - powerful. *noun* - PUISSANCE.

"But out where the grass grows high, and the horned cattle dream away the lazy afternoons, and men still fear the powers and principalities of the air - out there between the corn-rows he [William Jennings Bryan] held his own PUISSANCE to the end." H. L. Mencken, The Vintage Mencken, Vintage Books, 1956, p. 162.

PUSH POLLING

noun - negative campaigning in the guise of poll taking.

"Gov. George W. Bush of Texas has expressed outrage at the accusation from the McCain camp that his campaign is involved in the controversial political technique known as PUSH POLLING, in which workers, posing as pollsters, spread negative charges about a candidate. Mr. Bush has threatened to fire any campaign staff member involved with PUSH POLLS." Don Van Natta Jr., *NYTimes*, 2/15/00, p. A20.

"John McCain's complaint about the polling tactics used by George W. Bush's campaign strikes a nerve. It's hard to figure what people dislike more: telephone solicitors who interrupt their dinner or politicians who act like sheep. The PUSH POLL controversy implicates both. This started when a woman at a McCain event in South Carolina told the senator how dismayed she was by a telephone call taken by her teenage son. It was a pollster who, according to the woman, denigrated McCain by asking questions that made him out to be a liar, cheater and fraud. Her son, she said, is a McCain fan and was crestfallen at the tone and substance of the call. Bush denied his campaign had anything to do with the call." Editorial, *Chicago Trib.*, 2/15/00. S 1, p. 14.

"Al Franken was devastated that the McCain people wouldn't go with his PUSH-POLL idea for the Michigan primary. He wanted voters to be hit with the following call: 'We're an independent polling company conducting a survey for Tuesday's primary. If you knew that while John McCain was hanging by his thumbs in a North Vietnamese prison, George W. Bush was throwing a keg party at a Yale secret society that didn't allow Catholics to date Jews, would you be more or less likely to vote for Bush.'" Frank Rich, *NYTimes*, 2/26/00, p. A31.

PUSILLANIMOUS

adjective - cowardly, marked by contemptible timidity.
noun - PUSILLANIMITY.

"What makes these contradictions so nagging is Ronald Reagan's public PERSONA. He sailed into office as the Strong Leader, flailing his predecessor for being so PUSILLANIMOUS about Iran. He cast himself as the Model Executive, smart enough to hire the best and let them run things. Now, in his own Iran crisis, he has gone passive, reduced to pleading ignorance as a defense and imploring former aides to bail him out." Editorial, *NYTimes*, 12/24/86, p. 26.

"In the Nixon years, he [Pat Buchanan] was the coiner of such phrases as 'instant analysis' and 'the new Federalism' and emerged from Watergate not only unbesmirched but strengthened. Pat was also the brains behind many of the alliterative barbs of Spiro Agnew ('PUSILLANIMOUS Pussyfooters' and 'vicars of vacillation' were Buchanan's; 'NATTERING NABOBS of negativism' was mine) and he survived the fall of that nolo-contendering clayfoot." William Safire, *NYTimes*, 1/19/87, p. 17.

"'The PUSILLANIMOUS idea that we had friends in England worth keeping terms with, still haunted the minds of many,' he [Jefferson] recalled, and therefore 'those passages which conveyed censures on the people of England were struck out [of the Declaration of Independence], lest they should give them offence.'" Joseph J. Ellis, <u>American Sphinx</u>, Knopf, 1997, p. 53.

PUSSYFOOT

verb - (1) to walk stealthily; (2) to be noncommittal.
noun - PUSSYFOOTER.

"In particular, he devotes himself to a merciless study of what, after all, must remain the deceased Moses's [President Woodrow Wilson's] chief contribution to both history and beautiful letters, *viz.* his biography of Washington. This incredible work is an almost inexhaustible mine of bad writing, faulty generalizing, childish PUSSYFOOTING, ludicrous posturing, and naive stupidity." H. L. Mencken, The Vintage Mencken, Vintage Books, 1956, p. 117.

"Even the biggest Republican enchilada is getting itchy over the Bush Administration's PUSSYFOOT performance. Ronald Reagan took time off from his memoirs last week to let it be known that he was concerned about his successor's 'excessively cautious approach to nuclear arms reductions negotiations with the Soviets,' among other things." Tom Wicker, *NYTimes*, 5/9/89, p. 31.

QQQ

QUAYLE

verb - to ridicule or make a laughing stock of someone, i.e. what the media did to Vice President Dan Quayle after his "Murphy Brown" and "pototo(e)" incidents.

"'At the root of this is what happened to Dan Quayle,' said P. J. O'Rourke, the humorist and foreign desk chief for *Rolling Stone* magazine. 'He got laughed off the national political radar screen. This is a preemptive strike. Politicians are trying to vaccinate themselves against getting QUAYLED.'" Jennifer Senior, *NYTimes*, 3/7/94, p. B4.

QUICKSILVER

adjective - MERCURIAL, characterized by unpredictable, rapidly changing, moods.

"The White House is a strange place. Politicians who move in often seem to lose track of how the public feels. But that was not supposed to happen to Bill Clinton and his band of MTV-bred advisers with their QUICKSILVER reflexes." Thomas Friedman, *NYTimes*, 5/24/93, p. A1.

"Al is the Good Son, the early-achieving scion from Harvard and Tennessee who always thought he would be President. (So did his parents.) George is the Prodigal Son, the late-blooming scion from Yale and Texas who never thought he would be President. (Neither did his parents.)

"As the robotic, plodding Mr. Gore tried to loosen up, the loose, QUICKSILVER Mr. Bush tries to stay robotically on message." Maureen Dowd, *NYTimes*, 6/16/99, p. A31.

QUINTESSENCE

noun - the essence or embodiment of a thing in its purest form.

"One is Martin Van Buren, the QUINTESSENCE of the kind of man you'd buy a car from. The most praiseworthy thing ever said of him was 'he rows to his goal with muffled oars.' Lincoln was known as 'Honest Abe.' Van Buren was called 'the Sly Red Fox of Kinderhook,' 'the Little Magician' and 'the Flying Dutchman.' Throughout his long, devious career, he managed to be on both sides of every public issue that came before him." Michael Kilian, "Would Lincoln hawk a Datsun?", Chicago Trib., 2/22/83, S 1, p. 12.

"Jefferson was, then, a QUINTESSENTIAL Whig, but the Whig values were so appealing because they blended so nicely with his own QUINTESSENTIALLY Jeffersonian character." Joseph J. Ellis, American Sphinx, Knopf, 1997, p. 43.

"Clinton's proposals are not particularly far-reaching; many are either small-scale items or repackaged versions of old programs. What many find interesting, though, is Clinton's sudden interest in appearing to be a champion of the poor after fighting so hard for so long to appear a centrist leader of the middle class.

"Theories abound as to why the QUINTESSENTIAL New Democrat has been sounding more like an Old Democrat: Clinton is reaching for a legacy. Or Clinton is trying to energize the Democratic base for the 2000 elections." Naftali Bendavid, *Chicago Trib.*, 8/17/99, S 1, p. 14.

QUI VIVE (FR)

noun - alert, vigilant; most commonly used in the phrase "on the QUI VIVE."

"To be a liberal in the Reagan era - not to mention being a lefty, pinko comsyp - strikes most of us as damned hard cheese. Duty requires the earnest liberal to spend most of his time on the QUI VIVE for jackbooted fascism, in a state of profound depression over the advance of the military-industrial complex, and down in the dumps over the incurable NINCOMPOOPERY of a people addicted to 'The Newlywed Game.'" Molly Ivins, Molly Ivins Can't Say That, Can She?, Random House, 1991, p. 83.

RRR

RAGTAG

adjective - ragged, unkempt, motley.

"Inspiring many young people, as George McGovern did in 1972, to join his RAGTAG band of volunteers, Gary Hart put together a fairly effective organization for the Feb. 20 Iowa caucuses, in which he finished second, and a potent one in New Hampshire, where he broke through with his first victory last week." David Axelrod, *Chicago Trib.*, 3/7/84, S 1, p. 5.

"Worse yet, the RAGTAG [George Bush] Presidential motorcade got stuck on the way home in Beltway traffic, forced to wait in a half-mile backup at a construction site along with the common folk." Maureen Dowd, *NYTimes*, 10/9/90, p. A1.

Frank J. Young "Teddy, you have traveled this road once too often."

"Taft believed that Roosevelt had picked up many votes from Wilson of the 'labor, socialistic, discontented, RAGTAG and bobtail variety,' but he concluded that hundreds of thousands of Republicans, afraid of wasting their votes had supported Wilson in order to escape the danger of Roosevelt." Donald F. Anderson, <u>William Howard Taft</u>, Cornell Univ. Press, 1973, p. 199.

RAINMAKER (OM)

noun - a person who is very effective; in the legal world, a lawyer who is adept at getting clients.

"But the man [Vernon E. Jordan] running Mr. Clinton's transition is about as inside as anyone can get. 'He's a RAINMAKER,' said Charles Lewis, executive director of the Center for Public Integrity, a non-profit research group. 'He trades on his stature and he SCHMOOZES all over town.'" Richard L. Berke, *NYTimes*, 11/13/92, p. A10.

"Daley, 45, took a substantial cut in pay when [President] Clinton appointed him as a special counselor. Partners at Mayer, Brown & Platt are paid an estimated $200,000 to $450,000 a year.... The White House ethic standards are also meaningless, says Lewis of the Center for Public Integrity. 'When you're a RAINMAKER in the firm and you know everybody, you don't have to lobby,' Lewis said. 'Everyone knows that Bill Daley's firm is that firm. There are ways for them to cash in and for them to benefit without him ever picking up the phone.'" Michael Arndt, *Chicago Trib.*, 11/24/93, S 1 p. 15.

RAMBOISM (SL)

noun - aggressive use of force to solve problems.
Note:From the movie "Rambo."

"Indeed, one New York literary agent who preferred to remain anonymous hopes that Mr. Regan, the White House chief of staff, turns out to be wrong about a meeting between the President and Colonel North, the National

Security Council aid who was dismissed for his role in his arms sales and diversion of profits to Nicaraguan rebels. 'It would make a tremendous movie scene with the President and this sort of RAMBO sitting by the fire in the Oval Office,' the agent said excitedly." Maureen Dowd, *NYTimes*, 12/19/86, p. 16.

"The Reagan proposal for $100 million in aid to the contra forces in Central America is frightening and reprehensible.... President Reagan argues that the U.S. must show its machismo in Central America to scare the Russians. This misguided RAMBOISM is doomed to failure because it ignores the internal realities of Central America." Richard W. Slatta, Chicago Trib., 3/13/86, S 1, p. 23.

RAMBUNCTIOUS

adjective - rowdy, boisterous, loud, unruly, uncontrollable.

"The first time that George W. Bush was arrested, he had just stolen a Christmas wreath. Mr. Bush, then a 20-year-old junior at Yale, was head of a notoriously RAMBUNCTIOUS fraternity, and with the Christmas holidays approaching, he and some of his buddies had declared themselves the 'decorating committee.' ... It was not the perfect crime. Mr. Bush later recalled that he and his friends had perhaps had a few beers and were loud and boisterous. In addition, a police car was approaching. The police arrested Mr. Bush and charged him with disorderly conduct. Eventually the charges were dropped, but the episode underscored Mr. Bush's path through the uproar of the late 1960's: at a time when many university students risked arrest for their vociferous political protests, Mr. Bush broke the law not out of principle but for a prank... In short, while some students took to the barricades, Mr. Bush took to the bar." Nicholas D. Kristof, *NYTimes*, 6/19/00, p. A1.

RAPSCALLION

noun - scamp, rascal.

"'It is not that Mr. Bush and Mr. Dukakis are RAPSCALLIONS,' said the *Economist*. 'What they are not, it seems, is presidential.'" R. C. Longworth, *Chicago Trib.*, 11/2/88, S 1, p. 5.

"'I think his [George W. Bush's] political philosophy comes completely from the philosophy of the independent oil man,' said Joe O'Neill, a fellow RAPSCALLION in childhood." Nicholas D. Kristof, *NYTimes*. 5/21/00, p. 1.

RARA AVIS (L)

noun - a rarity, an exceptional person; literally, a rare bird.

"Bob Dole is a rare bird [RARA AVIS] among modern politicians. Most with the help of hired troupes of packagers, strategists and pollsters, make themselves more attractive to the public at large than they are to insiders who know them well and understand their weaknesses as well as strengths. With Mr. Dole, it is the other way around." R. W. Apple Jr., *NYTimes*, 9/26/96, p. 1.

RATIOCINATION

noun - reasoning.

"The selection of J. Danforth Quayle for the veep nomination drove the Republicans to new heights of RATIOCINATION. The ineffable Clements said, 'Texas is probably the greatest quail-hunting area in the United States, so we can relate to Mr. Quayle. You find them in the bush. That's where Mr. Quayle is: he's in the bush with Bush.'" Molly Ivins, <u>Molly Ivins Can't Say That, Can She?</u>, Random House, 1991, p. 191.

RED MEAT (OM)

adjective - a harsh, vitriolic attacking speech.

"His audience was an unusual one for such a RED-MEAT speech - a luncheon of electronic industry executives at the Hotel del Coronado here, which is one of Mr. Clinton's favorite hotels in southern California - and they sat in silence as Mr. Dole, unsmiling as he pounded the lectern for effect, delivered what was unquestionably the harshest speech of this general election campaign." Adam Nagourney, *NYTimes*, 10/16/96, p. A13.

"A fiery former Vice President Dan Quayle, dispensing rhetorical RED MEAT Friday to conservative activists, ridiculed President Clinton and Vice President Al Gore as 'New Age socialists,' vowing that in his own presidential campaign he would never 'back down' from his core beliefs." Michael Tackett, *Chicago Trib.*, 1/23/99, S 1, p. 3.

"Patrick Buchanan dumped the Republican Party Monday, announcing his departure with RED-MEAT rhetoric about 'hollow' and 'malleable' candidates in the established parties and concluding with a doomsday prediction that the 2000 election is 'the last chance to save our republic before she disappears into a godless new world order.'" Editorial, *Chicago Trib.*, 10/26/99, S 1, p. 20.

"Mr. [Donald] Trump was apparently informed that Mr. Buchanan's book argues that Hitler was not a threat to any vital American interests after 1940. So the developer whipped off an indignant fax, in which he misspelled 'Adolf.' But no matter. Pat Buchanan, the master of the RED-MEAT quote, was left complaining on TV that his position had been misinterpreted. Even in retreat, he didn't sound really enthusiastic about our role in whipping the Nazis. ('Hitler declared war on the United States. We had no alternative but to fight him.')." Gail Collins, *NYTimes*, 9/21/99, p. A31.

"Back in 1992, the Anti-Defamation League charged him [Pat Buchanan] with 'a 30-year record of intolerance unmatched by any other mainstream political figure' and 'a disregard or hostility toward those not like him and a consequent displeasure with the exercise of freedom by these others.' Buchanan has toned down his RED-MEAT rhetoric since then, but not by much." Clarence Page, *Chicago Trib.*, 9/8/99, S1, p.19.

RELIGIOSITY

noun - intense, public and sentimental observance or display of religion.

Note: Harvard Law Professor Alan Dershowitz has referred to the candidates running for president in 2000 as "running for bishop rather than President" because of the intensity of their professions of religious faith. Frank Rich writes that Governor George W. Bush "has long spoken of how faith helped him end his youthful hell-raising at age 40"and that Al Gore announced to a group of religion reporters that "the purpose of life is to glorify God." In their campaigns, Senator John McCain and former Senator Bill Bradley have treated their religious beliefs as a private matter.

"There isn't a single candidate for President in 2000 who can top Bill Clinton in RELIGIOSITY. He has been the P. T. Barnum of public displays of faith, from the '92 campaign, in which he campaigned in full preaching mode in black churches, to his Monica MEA CULPA of a year ago this week, when he worked in allusions to both the New Testament and the Yom Kippur liturgy while confessing his sins at an annual Washington prayer breakfast." Frank Rich, *NYTimes*, 9/11/99, p. A25.

"As Jonathan Rauch has argued in National Journal, 'The more genuinely devout the President, the less likely he is to fuss about God', such as Jimmy Carter, who ended his speeches with 'Thank you very much' rather than the usual God-bless. Mr. Carter also proved that RELIGIOSITY, even when genuine, is no predictor of a great Presidency." Frank Rich, *NYTimes*, 9/11/99, p. A25.

RETROMINGENT

adjective - characterized by urinating backwards.

Note: Molly Ivins is wrong in saying cows are the only mammals that are RETROMINGENT. Other mammals include cats and especially large members of the cat family, lions and tigers, and elephants.

"Bush's finest day back in the 1984 campaign started in Minnesota when he had to get up at 6 A.M. and milk a cow in order to demonstrate his concern for the plight of the American farmer.... Either Bush had forgotten how to milk, or that cow was a Democrat. He couldn't get a drop out of her. Bush also forgot that cows are RETROMINGENT, a word one seldom gets to use. Cows are the only mammals that pee backwards. That's why one should never walk behind them, even though they don't kick." Molly Ivins, <u>Molly Ivins Can't Say That, Can She?</u>, Random House, 1991, p. 118.

RODOMONTADE (RHODOMONTADE)

adjective and *noun* - bragging speech, vain boasting or bluster, BRAGGADOCIO, gasconade.

"His [Abraham Lincoln's] early speeches were mere empty fireworks - the hollow RHODOMONTADES of the era. But in middle life he purged his style of ornament and it became almost baldly simple - and it is for that simplicity that he is remembered today. The Gettysburg speech is at once the shortest and the most famous oration in American history." H. L. Mencken, <u>The Vintage Mencken</u>, Vintage Books, 1956, p. 79.

ROIL

verb - to disturb violently, to stir up.
adjective - ROILING.

"After days of ROILING party strife over Patrick J. Buchanan, Gov. George W. Bush of Texas today asked the renegade Republican to stick with the party, saying 'I'm going to need every vote I can get among Republicans to win the election.'" Alison Mitchell, *NYTimes*, 9/25/99, p. A1.

ROMAN À CLEF

noun - a novel in which real persons are disguised.
Note: An example of a ROMAN À CLEF is John Ehrlichman's <u>The Company</u> based on the Nixon Watergate scandal.

"Unkindest ROMAN À CLEF: Patti Davis' <u>Home Front</u> that did an amateur knife job on the First Parents [Reagans]." Joan Beck, *Chicago Trib.*, 1/1/87, S 1, p. 23.

"After a day of trying to minimize damage from the Iran-Contra scandal, coming home to 'By the way, Patti's started another ROMAN À CLEF and Ron Jr. is modeling bathing suits in *GO* magazine' is probably not relaxing." Anna Quindlen, *NYTimes*, 3/11/87, pp. 21, 22.

"From the time Mary Todd Lincoln was suspected of being a Confederate spy to the time Billy Carter introduced 'Billy Beer' to the time Patti Davis wrote an astringent ROMAN A CLEF about growing up in the Reagan family, Presidents have had problems curbing their rebellious, jealous, greedy or mischievous kinfolk." Maureen Dowd, *NYTimes*, 12/12/88, p. 1.

ROORBACK

noun - a defamatory falsehood published for political effect.
Note:In the 1844 presidential election a reference to <u>ROORBACK's Tour Through the Western and Southern States</u> was made to discredit candidate James K. Polk. The book, by a fictitious Baron Von ROORBACK, was later exposed as apocryphal.
"Nor is the typical American journalist's credulity confined to such CANARDS and ROORBACKS from far places. He is often victimized just as easily at home, despite his lofty belief that he is superior to the wiles of press agents. The plain fact is that most of the stuff he prints now emanates from press agents, and that his machinery for scrutinizing it is lamentably defective." H. L. Mencken, <u>The American Scene</u>, Ed. by Huntington Cairns, Vintage Books, 1982, p. 249.

ROOT CANAL (OM) (SL)

adjective - painful.

"At a meeting of young Republicans in July [1985], Mr. Dole remarked with barbed humor that 'Kemp wants a business deduction for hair spray.' Speaking to the same group, Mr. Kemp came back with the retort: 'In a recent fire, Bob Dole's library burned down. Both books were lost. And he hadn't even finished coloring one of them.' A few months ago, a longtime adviser to Mr. Dole, trying to explain how the former Senator thinks, singled out Mr. Kemp as a politician he found particularly irksome. 'He can't figure out how you can get to be Jack Kemp,' the adviser said. In Mr. Dole's view, he said, Mr. Kemp is 'non-deserving.'... For his part, Mr. Kemp often was publicly disdainful of what he called Mr. Dole's 'ROOT-CANAL' approach to economics. And he openly blamed Mr. Dole and his fellow deficit hawks for keeping Republicans in the minority." Elizabeth Kolbert, *NYTimes*, 9/29/96, p. 18.

ROUNDHEELS

noun - a pushover, usually in a sexual connotation.

"Making [the Criminal Division of the Department of Justice] the scapegoat for the failure to protect America's deepest nuclear secrets is typical of the Clinton-Reno refusal to accept responsibility for endangering national security. Reno has appointed her personal Whitewash Brigade of favorite ROUNDHEELS. This enables her to rebuff Congress and the press for months with the usual 'I cannot comment because an inquiry is ongoing.'" William Safire, *NYTimes*, 5/10/99, p. A27.

RUBE GOLDBERG

adjective and *noun* - a complex way of performing a simple function, based on the involved cartoons of Rube Goldberg.

"...[President] Clinton emphasized his roots as the son of a nurse from a rural region of the country and his wife's longtime interest in children's health. And he described his effort as a personal battle to restructure a health care system that he said 'RUBE GOLDBERG in his wildest dreams could not have designed.'" Gwen Ifill, *NYTimes*, 10/29/93, p. A9.

"What the Clintons needed [in drawing up the health care reform bill] was a drawing by Eero Saarinen. What the experts gave them was a blueprint by RUBE GOLDBERG." Russell Baker, *NYTimes*, 2/5/94, p. 15.

"Amazingly, Tuesday was the second anniversary of *NYTimes* article that broke the Whitewater mess - as Whitewatergate is known to those of us who have not yet convicted the President [Clinton]. But it was just last week that the 16-year-old collision of a failed land deal and a failed S.&L., a story comprehensible only with RUBE GOLDBERGESQUE flow charts, became a national craze." Frank Rich, *NYTimes*, 3/10/94, p. A17.

RUST BELT

noun - a geographic area, such as the Lake States, where heavy industry is declining and factories and steel mills are being shut down.

"Still, Mr. Clinton scoffed at the latest polls with the comment, 'We came to fight until November.' He set off from New York at once in pursuit of crucial RUST BELT votes, foregoing a vacation like the one the former Gov. Michael S. Dukakis of Massachusetts took after his nomination in 1988." R. W. Apple, Jr., *NYTimes*, 7/18/92, p. A1.

SSS

SACERDOTAL

adjective - priestly.

"It is an unwritten part of the presidential job to act, on occasions of great national sentiment, as medicine man, monarch, and minister to the hapless flock. Ronald Reagan sealed his own grip on the presidency as mourner-in-chief after disaster befell the *Challenger* space shuttle. Clinton became presidential, perhaps for the first time, when he fulfilled his SACERDOTAL duty at the day of national mourning in Oklahoma. That was the mystical explanation for the return of the Comeback Kid." Martin Walker, The President We Deserve, Crown Publishers, 1996, p. 338.

SALAD DAYS

noun - (1) a time of youthful inexperience; (2) an early flourishing period or heyday.

"Even now, virtually none of the President's senior aides share that assessment [carrying Texas], despite recent polls showing Mr. Clinton running neck and neck here with Bob Dole, or slightly ahead. But the President, born in Arkansas, retains a sentimental attachment to his old neighboring state, dating to his SALAD DAYS as the George McGovern campaign coordinator here in 1972." Todd S. Purdum, *NYTimes*, 9/28/96, p. 11.

SAVAGE

verb - to criticize harshly.

"Even today, when in general [George] Bush seemed so commanding, he teetered on the brink of excess by calling himself and Senator Quayle a pair of 'pit bulls' ready to SAVAGE the opposition." R. W. Apple, Jr., *NYTimes*, 8/18/88, p. 14.

"The attention [Alexander] Haig has received has been in connection with his harsh attacks on the GOP front-runner, Vice President George Bush, whom he has SAVAGED in debates and in speeches as a do-nothing vice president." Philip Lentz, *Chicago Trib.*, 1/22/88. S 1, p. 1.

"Why the SAVAGING of Bill Clinton? Some of it is his own fault for being less than straightforward. Some is condescension toward a Southerner, as was true with Jimmy Carter. Some is resentment of the independence and intelligence of Mrs. Clinton. But much is ideological: the anger of the right that a centrist Democrat is in the White House." Anthony Lewis, *NYTimes*, 5/2/94, p. A15.

"President Clinton can hardly expect political support from the conservative Mr. Murdoch. But he signed into law the bill giving Mr. Murdoch the tax break. Why? Was he afraid that the Murdoch press would SAVAGE him even more cruelly if he vetoed it?" Anthony Lewis, *NYTimes*, 5/8/95, p. A13.

"'I think it's important for us and the Republican Party to understand that our candidate is going to have to weather a SAVAGING attack if Al Gore is the nominee,' Mr. Bush said. 'The idea of me pointing out a major difference certainly is not SAVAGING. It is a difference of opinion, and I'm going to continue to talk about differences of opinion.' When asked what approach he would take in the debate with Mr. McCain on Tuesday night, he said, 'I'll be short of SAVAGERY.' " Frank Bruni and B. Drummond Ayres Jr., *NYTimes*, 2/15/00, p. A20.

SAW

noun - an old familiar saying, maxim or proverb.

"Mr. [Ross] Perot says his goal is the opposite, to open the process up via a campaign built on volunteers, a system of electronic town meetings and a President who eschews ceremonials. The Vox Poppa. He says folks are concerned about his principles, not his positions. This reminds me of the old SAW about the tree falling in the forest: if principles exist apart from issues, can you really hear them?" Anna Quindlen, *NYTimes*, 6/3/92, p. A15.

"Jeez, just because Jim Wright is in trouble, now they're saying everybody in Texas politics is a crook. David Broder wrote a column saying Jim Wright is just a product of his environment, and everybody knows Lyndon Johnson was outrageous, and now they've taken to quoting the old SAW about how an honest man in the Texas Legislature is one who stays bought. Our name is mud." Molly Ivins, Molly Ivins Can't Say That, Can She?, Random House, 1991, p. 58.

"The problem is not simply the old actors' SAW about the inevitability of being upstaged if you do a scene with a kid or a dog. Reagan's book [*An American Life*] is so clogged with patently untrue fantasies that some reviewers have suggested as a more appropriate title *An American Lie*." Calvin Trillin, Too Soon to Tell, Warner Books, 1995, p. 62.

"As a Presidential candidate, Buchanan has sometimes appeared to be a tribune of the populist left. He began his Presidential campaign this year championing the cause of West Virginia's endangered steelworkers. But this book ['A Republic, Not an Empire'] is the work of a right-wing crank. It is full of the old SAWS of the American right. He describes the Soviet spy Alger Hiss as an 'FDR confidant.' He extols America First, which opposed United States intervention in World War II, without acknowledging the anti-Semitism of its most famous spokesman, Charles Lindberg. He warns that without stemming the flood of immigrants, 'America will cease to be a First World nation by 2040' - a statement clearly equating capability and national origin." John B. Judis, Review of <u>A Republic Not an Empire</u> by Patrick J Buchanan, *NYTimes*, 10/24/99, p. 16.

SCAMP

noun - playful, a rascal, mischief-maker

"...Mr. McCain, a senator from Arizona, is the rebellious son who still upholds his family's tradition of military service; the insolent SCAMP who goes to Vietnam in search of adventure and learns a new 'seriousness of purpose' during a harrowing five and a half years as a prisoner of war." Michiko Kakutani, *NYTimes*, 11/22/99, p. A 24.

"The people of Illinois still hold a warm spot for President Clinton, bad-boy behavior and all, but in most cases it's a lot closer to their wallets than their hearts. They want to keep the Clinton era's economic mojo, with its expanded wealth, steamy-hot stock market and low unemployment. But the thought of naming buildings after such a public SCAMP is viewed as almost unthinkable to many voters. Only among African-American voters is there support for naming federal buildings or schools after Clinton, a reflection of the strong backing Clinton has always had among African-American Democrats." Charles M. Madigan, *Chicago Trib.*, 11/10/99, S1, p. 1.

"Bill Clinton's bipartisan legacy is this: Given the choice between SCOLDS, and SCAMPS, the country opts for SCAMPS." Frank Rich, *NYTimes*, 8/28/99, p. A25.

SCHISM

noun - a separation, division or split.

"Mr. Buchanan's flirtation with the Reform Party has caused a SCHISM among Republicans over how he should be dealt with, with some vilifying him as being far outside the party mainstream and others trying to keep him and his followers in the fold." Alison Mitchell, *NYTimes*, 9/25/99, p. A10.

SCHMOOZ (SCHMOOZE) (Y)

noun and *verb* - informal chat, heart-to-heart talk.

"[George] Bush's nice disposition and fondness for SCHMOOZING make for excellent congressional relations." Ken Adelman, *Chicago Trib.*, 3/12/88, S 1, p. 9.

"Four years ago Quayle sometimes appeared intimidated by the press and sometimes openly hostile - his handlers kept him isolated from reporters on his campaign plane. Now he is Mr. Affability, chatting and SCHMOOZING with reporters and sometimes even inviting the media to join him in his forward cabin on Air Force II." Janet Cawley, *Chicago Trib.*, 9/20/92, S 1, p. 9.

"President Clinton, who has been at war with the press for much of his term, is reaching out to the enemy camp. For the past two weeks, Clinton has been holding a series of private, off-the-record SCHMOOZE sessions with selected journalists, in some cases soliciting advice about his troubled presidency. He has usually been holding court on a secluded White House patio, serving iced tea and cookies, and talking candidly about his problems with the media and Congress." Howard Kurtz, *Wash. Post*, 8/26/94, p. D1.

SCREED

noun - a long discourse or diatribe.

"Now, suddenly, a new enemy has appeared, and it is none other than the president's wife, Hillary Rodham Clinton. Although the first lady's position on fluoride has yet to be released, fundamentalists are convinced that Hillary is a worthy successor to communists and gays. Consider, for instance, Jerry Falwell's recent SCREED against the Clintons, both Bill and Hillary. 'Now our 42nd president and his "Mother Superior," Hillary, and all those around him have determined under God that we're going to change the rules,' Falwell cried. 'We're not going to be a nation under God anymore.'" Randall Balmer, *Chicago Trib.*, 4/21/93, S 1, p. 27.

"Ronald Reagan, for instance, never went to the mat for the hundreds of reorganization proposals offered in 1984 by his commission headed by J. Peter Grace, the chairman of W.R. Grace & Company. Democrats in Congress saw the Grace Commission's work as a conservative SCREED to dismantle social programs, and, absent nurturing by Mr. Reagan, most of the recommendations died on the vine." David E. Rosenbaum, *NYTimes*, 9/8/93, p. A14.

"It's not against the law. Nor is it unprecedented: Mr. Gingrich showed us a list of books by legislators, including Vice President Gore's ill-selling SCREED on the environment, written more as a springboard for publicity than for profit. If Al can earn thousands, why not Newt millions?" William Safire, *NYTimes*, 1/2/95, p. 17.

"In the lines drawn by The Wall Street Journal, which has published four thick books of anti-Clinton SCREEDS since '92, the goal is that Mr. Starr, 'a hymn-singing son of a fundamentalist minister,' succeed in 'prosecuting the entire culture that gave birth to what Bill Clinton represents.'" Frank Rich, *NYTimes*, 12/16/98, p. A31.

"We analyzed Steve Forbes's beauty makeover (acid peels *and* hair straightening?). We marveled at the sparrow-like Gary Bauer comparing himself to the eagle-like Ronald Reagan. We admired the Howard Beal style of the mad and angry Alan Keyes, who ends his SCREEDS by stalking off the stage. We pondered the enduring question about Dan Quayle: *Why?*

"The truth is, we didn't care about the boys. We wanted the girl. Elizabeth Dole got off to her usual Little Miss Perfect start. When all the candidates lined up for a group photo, she pounced on her mark with a head-of-her-Harvard-law-school-class smile, leaving the boys to fumble in her coiffed wake." Maureen Dowd, *NYTimes*, 5/5/99, p. A31.

"When Mr. Bush gave a speech that seemed to stand up bravely to his party's hard right by spanking Robert Bork, it turned out that what many saw as a damning reference to Mr. Bork's best-selling SCREED, 'Slouching Towards Gomorrah,' was inadvertent. 'He may not even have realized he was referring to a book,' cracked Mr. Bork of Mr. Bush." Frank Rich, *NYTimes*, 10/23/99, p. A27.

SCRUMPTIOUS

adjective - excellent.

"Using other quotations that she attributed to Mr. Clinton, Ms. Matalin then referred indirectly to Mr. Clinton's struggle to keep his weight down. She wrote: 'You feel like a "one-man landfill?" (Bill Clinton on "This Week," 2/16/92) No, Willie, it's not those Wendy's burgers or Dunkin' Donuts or even those SCRUMPTIOUS home-baked cookies. It's that Alka-Seltzer feeling you get when you're the leader of the "garbage load" (Clinton, AP, 7/31/92) party.'" Andrew Rosenthal, *NYTimes*, 8/3/92, p. A10.

SEASON TICKET-HOLDER (OM)

noun - a donor of very large political contributions ($250,000 in the case of the 1996 Republican National Committee).

"At the same time, donations from high-ticket givers has increased as well. Membership in 'Team 100,' individuals who have given more than $100,000 to the party a year, remains steady at around 300, said Mr. Leach. But another tier has been added: SEASON TICKET-HOLDERS, donors who have given $250,000 or more and do not want to be solicited again during the Presidential campaign. Most SEASON TICKET-HOLDERS are corporations, Mr. Leach [finance chairman of the Republican National Committee] said." Leslie Wayne, *NYTimes*, 10/25/96, p. A10

SEGUE

verb - to continue without pause, to blend into the next item without interruption (usually used in connection with a musical performance).

"On other matters, Reagan said there is 'reason for concern' that schools go too far in sex education. 'The worry about separating church and state has SEGUED over to sex education, so that it is where it is being taught; there is a total avoidance of any moral connotation with regard to sex,' he said. 'And to teach sex, as a purely physical function without taking into consideration the moral precepts that are involved - I think that should be of concern to those in charge of education.'" *Chicago Trib.*, 6/7/84, S 1, p. 18.

"At some points [Dan Quayle] looked awkward, waiting too long to answer questions or avoiding the questions he was asked by using tortured transitions to find some way to SEGUE into campaign trail BLATHER." Charles M. Madigan, *Chicago Trib.*, 10/6/88, S 1, p. 10.

"When Mr. Clinton was elected, it seemed reasonable to assume that he would stop campaigning. Instead, he has done something unique for a President-elect. He has SEGUED from the last race into the next one. The emerging style of his presidency is the style of the endless campaign." Michael Kelly, *NYTimes*, 10/21/92, p. A1.

"[President] Clinton SEGUED from his comments about the bombing into a renewed defense of direct Federal loans for college education in the face of Republican proposals to scale them back, and a renewed attack on Republican tax-cut proposals as favoring the rich at the expense of the middle class." Todd S. Purdum, *NYTimes*, 4/25/95, p. A9.

"For example [in the Nixon tapes], there is a March 1971 meeting involving Nixon, top aide H.R. Haldeman and Treasury Secretary John Connally, which had been called ostensibly to discuss a variety of economic matters facing the administration.

"Apparently unknown to Connally, Nixon and Haldeman also planned to use the meeting to persuade him to replace Vice President Spiro Agnew when Nixon ran for re-election in 1972. Thus, at the end of their economic discussion, the two men SEGUED into a discussion of the vice president." James Warren, *Chicago Trib.*, 3/18/99, S 1, p. 5.

SEMINAL (OM)

adjective - creative, original.

"A prominent Democrat of a younger generation, Senator Christopher J. Dodd of Connecticut, said he was 'totally convinced' that Mr. Jackson recognized that his candidacy was 'the SEMINAL event of the year' and that the Chicago clergyman would therefore do his utmost to advance the cause of the Democratic ticket in November, whether he is one of the nominees or not." R. W. Apple, Jr., *NYTimes*, 4/29/88, p. 8.

"Washington, Jan. 22 - As top Republican Party officials met here in an unusually low-key session that reflected the party's recent setbacks, President Reagan was preparing a State of the Union Message that one adviser said today could be a 'SEMINAL event' in Mr. Reagan's struggle to regain his political footing." Phil Gailey, *NYTimes*, 1/23/87, p. 8.

SERAGLIO

noun - harem; a brothel.

"While Republicans insist that the Clinton trial is not about sex, Senator Moynihan has magic-marked and gladly reads aloud [Alexander] Hamilton's near satirical, now PRESCIENT reference [in the Federalist Papers] to warnings that Americans studying their Presidents might some day have 'to blush at the unveiled mysteries of a future SERAGLIO.'" Francis X. Clines, *NYTimes*, 1/14/99, p. A13.

"Bill, the State Department is a SERAGLIO from which the beauties have all been kidnapped, leaving behind a drove of squeaking eunuchs with nothing to do. Mr. [Franklin Delano] Roosevelt and Mr. Hopkins between them preempt most of the foreign policy; General Donovan's outfit is moving in on the rest; and the castratos at State impotently continue to pass papers around which might as well be toilet tissue." Herman Wouk, <u>War and Remembrance,</u> Pocket Books, 1978, p. 882.

SERMONETTE

noun - a short sermon.

"President Reagan, rallying Republicans to fight what he called Democratic 'SERMONETTES about fairness and compassion,' offered another hint of his candidacy for re-election Friday." News Story, *Kansas City Times*, 9/24/83, p. A-5.

SHENANIGAN

noun - a devious or tricky practice or course of conduct; usually used in the plural.

"He [Ronald Reagan] also served notice that he would lobby for 'politically neutral' redrawing of congressional districts after the 1990 census. 'Keep it fair,' he warned, or they may find the Gipper on their statehouse steps calling attention to their SHENANIGANS.'" Bruce Buursma, *Chicago Trib.*, 2/7/89, S 1, p. 11.

"Clinton's problem today is that his alleged perjury concerns a subject that most people understand - extramarital sex. Weinberger's alleged perjury was rooted in a far more consequential high-level conspiracy to subvert Congress and the Constitution, but he had the good fortune that comparatively few people understood the subject - multinational arms deals interwoven with hostage negotiations and Third World civil wars. Bush handed down Weinberger's pardon 12 days before the trial that stood to reveal the extent of Bush's own complicity in the SHENANIGANS. Talk about obstructing justice and abusing power!" Eric Zorn, *Chicago Trib.*, 12/15/98, S 2, p. 1.

"[George W.] Bush did not play it very well. He talked freely of his personal triumphs, such as having replaced wild drinking and partying with religious values at age 40. He also has declared, while castigating Oval Office sexual SHENANIGANS, that he has remained faithful to his wife." Clarence Page, *Chicago Trib.*, 8/22/99, S 1, p. 17.

SHIBBOLETH

noun - favorite phrase of a party or sect; slogan, catchword.

"'I find him [President Reagan] a pleasant PERSONA and enjoy relations on a purely personal basis,' said Mr. Wright, a Texas Democrat. 'But the minute the subject gets on to anything of substance, he clams up and wants to recite the SHIBBOLETHS that form his ideological matrix.'" *NYTimes*, 11/15/87, p. 16.

SILK-STOCKING

adjective - socially prominent, affluent.

"Except for a few snarls from Sen. Dole, true election fervor [in the Illinois primary] was limited to the outpouring of minority hope for Rev. Jackson and the adulation for Ronald Reagan piled on the shoulders of Vice President Bush by SILKSTOCKING Republicans." Editorial, *Chicago Trib.*, 3/16/88, S 1, p. 20.

SISYPHEAN

adjective - an endeavor requiring continuous, hard but unproductive labor; suggestive of the labors of Sisyphus.
Note:From Sisyphus, a cruel king of Corinth whose punishment in Hades was to roll up a hill a huge stone which constantly rolled down again.

"With his dedication to dealing simultaneously with the deficit and public investment, Clinton had committed himself to solving an untested political equation. In his effort to answer it, he was nearly torn apart. The struggle for solvency threatened to reduce Clinton to a SISYPHEAN figure. As his power wobbled, his authority to control the very meaning of his Presidency was almost lost." Sidney Blumenthal, *New Yorker*, 1/24/94, p. 34.

"If Hillary [Clinton] wins a senate seat, she'll immediately be cast by liberals and feminists as 'Madame President.' Emma Thompson, without the accent. It would require a SISYPHEAN effort, though." Maureen Dowd, *NYTimes*, 10/24/99, p. 15.

SKIRT CHASER

noun - a WOMANIZER, one who chases after women.

"Mosbacher said he gave more credence to Gennifer Flowers' story that she had had an affair with Clinton than to the recent report that Bush as vice president had an affair with Jennifer Fitzgerald. Also Sunday, U.S. Treasurer Catalina Villalpando called Clinton and the Democrats' newly named liaison to Hispanic voters, former San Antonio Mayor Henry Cisneros, 'two SKIRT-CHASERS.'" Mitchell Locin, *Chicago Trib.*, 8/18/92, S 1, p. 10.

"[Former U.S. Treasurer Catalina] Villalpando caused controversy at the Republican convention in 1992 by calling Bill Clinton and former San Antonio Mayor Henry Cisneros, the current U.S. housing secretary 'SKIRT

CHASERS.' Bush staffers forced her to apologize." Reuters, *Chicago Trib.*, 2/18/94, S 1, p. 7.

"Danielle Crittenden, editor of The Women's Quarterly, a conservative publication, said of the silent women, 'It's embarrassing to them, that this first feminist President [Clinton] - the great respecter of intelligent, strong women, who appointed Madeleine K. Albright and Ruth Bader Ginsburg - it's embarrassing if their hero turns out to be just another SKIRT CHASER.'" Katharine Q. Seelye, *NYTimes*, 2/2/98, p. A18.

"There is something startling about the vocabulary that women who have supported President Clinton now use in conversations about him: phrases like SKIRT CHASER and laughingstock, nouns like idiot and jerk, adjectives like FECKLESS, sleazy, self-indulgent, gross." Janny Scott, *NYTimes*, 8/28/98, p. A14.

SKULDUGGERY

noun - underhanded behavior, deception, trickery, hugger-mugger.

"In yet another attack on Perot by a member of the Bush administration, Martinez told the U.S. Conference of Mayors that Perot 'advocates reckless, Wild West covert operations and apparently regards the Bill of Rights as an antique inconvenience. 'This nation didn't win a hard-won victory in the Cold War only to surrender its constitutional liberties to a secretive computer salesman with a penchant for SKULDUGGERY,' Martinez said. Perot's anti-drug proposals show little regard for civil rights, he said." *Chicago Trib.* wires, *Chicago Trib.*, 6/24/92, S 1, p. 10.

"It was a tale of Texan proportions, complete with epic name-calling, massive lobbying and political SKULDUGGERY. It was Ross Perot's foray into the turbulent world of education reform - and it offers a rare chance to examine how he operates in a political arena." Susan Chira, *NYTimes*, 6/29/92, p. A1.

"For weeks and months, there have been allegations of irregularities, even SKULDUGGERY, in an Arkansas real estate deal involving Bill Clinton and his wife 15 years ago. But to most Americans, it seemed like much ado about not very much, and the whole thing took place long ago and far away." R. W. Apple, Jr., *NYTimes*, 3/25/94, p. A8.

SMALL POTATOES

noun - a person or situation which is of small or trivial importance.

"Compared to Richard Nixon and Watergate, Clinton and Monicagate is SMALL POTATOES. Still, potatoes are potatoes. The president has disgraced himself, debased the dignity of his office and wounded his party's political future." Clarence Page, *Chicago Trib.*, 8/19/98, S 1, p. 23.

SMARMY

adjective - unctuously flattering, sycophantically TOADYING.

Note:George Will, the conservative columnist and confidant of Nancy Reagan, once called George Bush a SMARMY lapdog because he felt that Bush was TOADYING to the Republican party's right wing.

"San Francisco - the Annual Hookers Convention here was a SMARMY affair in a seedy auditorium, and guess who was there? The President's son! Yes, Mr. and Mrs. America, young Ronald Reagan strolled into the Tuesday night event to research the lament of the prostitute as part of his Democratic Convention coverage duties for Playboy magazine." Sneed & Lavin, Inc., *Chicago Trib.*, 7/19/84, S 1, p. 28.

"That's Nixon's greatest gift. He never quits. Several years ago *Newsweek* gave him a comeback cover. Now *Time* has followed suit. His rehabilitation is as fiercely contested as the 1960 election, but does it matter? Only those who have no threshold for industrial-strength SMARMINESS may demand a recount." Mary McGrory, *Rocky Mountain News*, 4/8/90, p. 71.

SMART CARD (SL)

noun - an identification card with a magnetic strip which carries a computer chip capable of holding extensive information.

"A Centerpiece of President Clinton's health-care plan, a Health Security card for all Americans, carries with it astonishing technological possibilities and alarming privacy concerns.... To ally fears, the Clinton plan emphasized that the Health Security card will not be a 'SMART CARD,' meaning one that carries a computer chip capable of holding extensive medical records. Rather, the card will have a less-sophisticated magnetic strip on the back containing limited administrative information.... But witnesses told the Senate hearing it might be just a matter of time before the system adopted SMART CARDS, which can provide more than 100 times the information of the proposed Health Security card." Michael Tackett, *Chicago Trib.*, 10/28/93, S 1, p. 1.

SMIDGEN

noun - a very small amount, a tad.

"Speaking with clean clarity, Senator John McCain has become the only Republican Presidential candidate to accept and pass a political and moral challenge that faces them all. He said exactly where Patrick Buchanan belonged in the Republican Party: out... Maybe Senator McCain's clarity and Buchanan's mental ugliness will bring a SMIDGEON of moral courage to Bush, Dole & Co., maybe." A. M. Rosenthal, *NYTimes*, 9/24/99, p. A27.

SNAKE OIL

noun - a liquid falsely claimed to have medicinal value; by extension, any false claim.

"Jesse Jackson accused his Democratic presidential rivals Monday of 'selling the American public SNAKE OIL' by advocating higher defense budgets and increased social spending, while Gary Hart called for major tax reforms on the day income taxes were due." News Story, *Chicago Trib.*, 4/17/84, S 1, p. 5.

"The charm of Ronald Reagan fronted for the SNAKE-OIL salesmen of the New Right. They invented Reaganomics: the notion that the government could cut taxes drastically, increase defense spending enormously and then spend its way out of the deficit." Anthony Lewis, *NYTimes*, 10/22/87, p. 23.

"[Republican George Bush and Democrat Michael Dukakis] tried to whip up for the media a clownish portrait of the other guy as a political SNAKE-OIL salesman of questionable honor and good sense." Editorial, *Chicago Trib.*, 9/18/88, S 4, p. 2.

"And who can resist the paranoiac symmetry of Mr. Perot's vision of American government? Fellow citizens, he says, we are battling a conspiracy so vast we may never know its true dimension, a conspiracy so insidious that each of you may have enlisted without knowing it. Every half-century or so, the festival of democracy coughs up a new bottler of this venerable SNAKE OIL. It makes us drunk for a while, but it is not addictive, and the hangover is usually mild in comparison with the fun we had." Editorial, *NYTimes*, 1/14/93, p. A16.

"[Senator Charles Robb] called the former Marine colonel [Oliver L. North] a 'document-shredding, Constitution-trashing, Commander in Chief-bashing, Congress-thrashing, uniform-shaming, Ayatollah-loving, arms-dealing, criminal-protecting, resume-enhancing, Noriega-coddling, Social Security threatening, public school denigrating, Swiss banking law breaking, letter-faking, self-serving, election-losing, SNAKE-OIL salesman who can't tell the difference between the truth and a lie.'" Michael Janofsky, *NYTimes*, 11/8/94, p. A11.

"For coarse burlesque-house comedy it will be hard to improve on President Clinton playing the dim-witted young dynamo who wakes up to find that once again somebody has put chewing gum in his hair. The ham-fisted performance by the Senate's Republican leader, Trent Lott, is also choice. Trying to play the statesman while killing campaign finance reform, he came across like a touring tent-show villain who sells SNAKE OIL to the rubes during intermission." Russell Baker, *NYTimes*, 10/14/97, p. A19.

"Henry Hyde and his House prosecution team are trying to sell the Senate and the country on the notion that summoning Monica Lewinsky, Betty Currie and other witnesses will magically seal the case against Bill Clinton. This is impeachment SNAKE OIL." Editorial, *NYTimes*, 1/16/99, p. A30.

SNICKERSNEE

noun - a large knife.

"To find a match for it [Woodrow Wilson's biography of George Washington], one must try to imagine a biography of the Duke of Wellington by his barber. Well, Hale spreads it out on his operating table, sharpens his SNICKERSNEE upon his bootleg, and proceeds to so harsh an anatomizing that it nearly makes me sympathize with the author." H. L. Mencken, The Vintage Mencken, Vintage Books, 1956, pp. 117-118.

SNOLLYGOSTER (OM)

noun - an unprincipled political job seeker.

Note:President Harry S. Truman defined the word incorrectly as a "man born out of wedlock." He was corrected by newspaper reporters who, relying on H. L. Mencken, said the word meant an unprincipled political jobseeker. In The American Language, Mencken refers to the period of 1812 to 1861 as one of "uncouth neologisms" and includes SNOLLYGOSTER among such words.

"A SNOLLYGOSTER, apparently confined to the South, was a political jobseeker who wants office, regardless of party, platform or principles, and who, whenever he wins, gets there by sheer force of monumental talknophical assumacy." H. L. Mencken, The American Language: Supplement I, Knopf, 1961, p. 241.

"That's a power a President has - to bring back old words, as Harry Truman did with SNOLLYGOSTER - a linguistic power that Reagan will soon discover." William Safire, *Chicago Trib.*, 12/1/80, p. 20.

"Almost 100 years ago (Aug. 17, 1896) *The Georgia Cracker* had this to say: 'A SNOLLYGOSTER is a man who is ambitious for office regardless of party, platform or principles, and if he gets there at all he does so by monumental talk.' Gee, now who does this remind us of today?" Letters to Editor, Robert J. Bagby, *Chicago Trib.*, 7/2/92, S 1, p. 18.

SNOOKER

verb - to confuse, cheat or hoodwink.

"[President John F.] Kennedy let himself be SNOOKERED by the military and the intelligence community in the disastrous Bay of Pigs episode but he played both well in his brilliant handling of the Cuban missile crisis." Germond/Witcover, *Chicago Trib.*, 11/26/83, S 1, p. 9.

"[Secretary of State James A. Baker 3d], smarting at suggestions that he had been SNOOKERED in his talks last week with the Soviets, used a White House briefing about the coming summit conference to try to smother a brushfire of criticism from conservative columnists and the Republican right that he was too generous with President Mikhail S. Gorbachev." Thomas Friedman, *NYTimes*, 5/24/90, p. A8.

SOBRIQUET

noun - nickname; MONIKER.

"Indeed, [Hillary Rodham] Clinton virtually will have to immerse herself in the political equivalent of Clorox to eradicate the stubborn stain of 'carpetbagger,' a SOBRIQUET frequently hurled at her last week here." Lisa Anderson, *Chicago Trib.*, 8/2/99, S 1, p. 8.

"In their spirited primary battle, George W. Bush uses the SOBRIQUET 'the Chairman' to tar John McCain as a Washington insider." Stephen Labaton, *NYTimes*, 2/18/00, p. A1.

SOCCER MOM

noun - a mother, frequently suburban, who spends a lot of time driving her children around to school and other activities, including sports events such as soccer.

"In her own controlled way, Mrs. Dole made a bold move at the G.O.P. dinner in the 'Live Free or Die' state. She called for stiffer regulation of guns, observing, 'I don't think you need an AK-47 to defend your family.' Incredibly, one man booed her when she urged gun safety locks to protect children.

"In the aftermath of Littleton, when other Republicans have taken cheap shots at Hollywood, Mrs. Dole was the only one in the mediocre mob who had the courage to stand up to the N.R.A., saying special interests should not dictate policy.

"Of course, you can be sure when Mrs. Dole's pollster, Linda DiVall, publicly praised her guts, that the candidate's stand was also smart politics. She is pitching her 'Let's make history' candidacy to middle-of-the-road SOCCER MOMS who are turned off by Charlton Heston's assertion that 'we cannot let tragedy lay waste to the most rare and hard won human right in history.'" Maureen Dowd, *NYTimes,* 5/5/99, p. A31.

"Al and W. are in a DONNYBROOK to see who will win the beauteous Erin. Both candidates are trying, with the language they use and the issues they choose, to court waitress moms and SOCCER MOMS. Mr. Bush (who's promising to 'cultivate the gardens of good will' among children) and Mr. Gore (who's booking himself on Lifetime, the network for women) are scaling back on the sports and war metaphors and focusing on children, schools and the future." Maureen Dowd, *NYTimes*, 4/5/00, p. A31.

SOIREE

noun - an evening party or reception.

"As I, Madame Radcliffe and other social correspondents have recently noted in the public print, the down-home, just us Yale Law School bumpkins slaving away for the common man Clintons have treated the State Dinner with the same contempt that the Paris Mob viewed the SOIREES thrown by Louis XVI and Marie Antoinette." Michael Kilian, *Chicago Trib.*, 6/30/93, S 7, p. 4.

SOLIPSISTIC

adjective - self-indulgent; extreme concern for one's own feelings.

"Perhaps the most original, unexpected ploy [in choosing a vice-presidential running mate] was Clinton's SOLIPSISTIC choice of Gore in 1992: a fellow Southerner, a fellow baby boomer, a fellow moderate - this flew against the prevailing wisdom that a Vice-President should balance the ticket (by coming from another part of the country or wing of the party or from a different generation from the President)." Joe Klein, *The New Yorker*, 7/3/00, p. 31.

SOPORIFIC

adjective - sleep inducing, causing lethargy.

"Bob Dole, the Republican nominee, has been reinvigorated [by an outcry about campaign contributions, some of them illegal, from wealthy foreigners] after weeks of SOPORIFIC campaigning." R. W. Apple, Jr., *NYTimes*, 11/2/96, p. 8.

SORCERER'S APPRENTICE

noun - someone in training to be a sorcerer or magician.

"Stockman may be the true fiscal and economic genius the country has been waiting for. He may be no more than the SORCERER'S APPRENTICE. Time may tell. It may not tell. Time is capricious. But the record of past efforts at total control of the Federal Budget argues against the success Stockman projects for his program and efforts." Eugene J. McCarthy, *Culpeper News*, 3/5/81.

"Calls from reporters about the prosecutors flooded into Starr's offices, and not just about their job histories, either. Journalists dredged up rumors about drug use, sexual orientation, divorces, and school records, which the stunned prosecutors tried to shoot down as best they could. As Blumenthal later described his role, he was like the SORCERER'S APPRENTICE.

"All he meant to do was raise a few questions about some controversial cases on the public record, and he couldn't help it if those legitimate issues spiraled into something much more vicious and personal. He was, he explained, very sad about what happened to the prosecutors." Jeffrey Toobin, A Vast Conspiracy, Random House, 1999, p. 280.

SOTTO VOCE

noun - under one's breath; very softly.

"As he [Lyndon Johnson] strolled through the House Dining Room at lunchtime acting if he were some visiting celebrity, nodding to left and right, 'head huddling' with one man or another, or as he sat at a table, talking too loudly, other Congressmen muttered under their breaths. Albert Thomas of Houston would sit staring at Johnson, snarling SOTTO VOCE: 'Listen to that sonofabitch talking about himself.'" Robert A. Caro, The Years of Lyndon Johnson: The Path to Power, Knopf, 1982, p. 533.

SPIN (OM) (Sʟ)

noun - interpretation or desired meaning, esp. with respect to a political statement or speech.

"I'm not sure what he [Pat Robertson] means, but New Hampshire wasn't important to him. 'Yeah, that's not what he said before he got there. He said he was going to really kick butt. Then he didn't kick any, so he says that's okay because he didn't have to.' That is what the pundits now call 'SPIN.' The candidates put different SPINS on how they do. 'Yeah, they even try to SPIN us. And that's why Simon blew it. He should have been jumping up and down holding up one finger and saying he was No. 1 because he finished third instead of fourth.'" Mike Royko, *Chicago Trib.*, 2/19/88, S 1, p. 3.

"'What he [Dukakis] has to do,' said one Democratic strategist who did not want to be named, 'is put a SPIN on the issue stuff that hits on character.'" Jon Margolis, *Chicago Trib.*, 9/11/88, S 1, p. 4.

"The night after the debate a Bush aide had what he described as a 'Fellini-esque dream.' 'There was a darkened room with track lighting and kind of wisps of light,' he said. 'The room was jammed with people SPINNING round and round and all saying, "We won, he never laid a glove on us."'" Dorothy Collin, *Chicago Trib.*, 10/5/88, S 1, p. 5.

"Ross Perot, whose flirtation with an independent Presidential candidacy has shaken the political establishment of both parties, likes to boast that he has no handlers, no 'SPIN doctors' and, most important, no speech writers." *NYTimes*, 7/9/92, p. A8.

"Thomas Hoving, the former director of the Metropolitan Museum of Art, was one of the few prominent Perot supporters who admitted to feeling 'duped.' Mr. Hoving described Mr. Perot as 'a tiny, SPIN-merchant Wizard of Oz.' He then amended those words as 'too good' for the former candidate." Alessandra Stanley, *NYTimes*, 7/27/92, p. A14.

"And for independent voters, Mr. [Bill] Bradley offers a populist, Perotlike critique of Mr. Clinton and Mr. Gore's leadership styles, asserting that politics today is 'obsessed with the mechanics of winning, which is polling, fund-raising and SPINNING.'" James Dao, *NYTimes*, 9/13/99, p. A14

SPOILER

noun - a candidate for political office with little chance of winning, but capable of taking votes away from other candidates.

"Facing ignominious defeat by Republicans in New Hampshire - a state whose primary he carried last time out - Pat Buchanan is now out to wreak vengeance as a SPOILER. He can taste the 13 million taxpayer dollars available to the Reform Party. A liberal former Democratic governor, hands clasped, tells me fervently, 'Thank God for Pat Buchanan - he could elect Al Gore.'" William Safire, *NYTimes*, 9/16/99, p. A29.

"So now Democrats root for the NATIVIST Buchanan to get the Reform [Party] nomination just as Republicans root for the liberal Warren Beatty. Neither major party would allow those would be SPOILERS to be part of the Presidential TV debates; the Reform Party would be doomed to represent the resentful fringes of left or right." William Safire, *NYTimes*, 9/16/99, p. A29.

SQUISHY

adjective - soft and yielding; by extension, in the political sense, too accommodating and compromising on principles.

"Senator John McCain of Arizona has called for a change in the party platform to reach out to people who support abortion. And Lamar Alexander, the former governor of Tennessee, has said he will accept a running mate who backs abortion rights.

"Such positions have jolted some conservatives and sharply divided the Presidential field, with several of the more ideological candidates, including Gary Bauer, Steve Forbes and Senator Robert C. Smith of New Hampshire, portraying their rivals as too SQUISHY." Richard L. Berke, *NYTimes*, 6/21/99, p. A13.

"The [George W.] Bush move to the SQUISHY center is seen most clearly in his embrace of big-government, Washington-knows-best NOSTROMS on education." Gary L. Bauer, *NYTimes*, 10/7/99, p. A31.

"Mr. Buchanan, dogged over the years by accusations of anti-Semitism, contended in a recent television interview that the Harvard criticism (that 'non-Jewish whites get the shaft' at Harvard compared to Jews and Asians) was intended 'tongue in cheek.' But Mr. Krauthammer quickly wrote that there was not a hint of irony in the complaint's angry wording in behalf of 'white Christians.' He accused the supposedly candid Mr. Buchanan of going 'impish and SQUISHY' in his TV persona." Francis X. Clines, *NYTimes*, 10/2/99, p. A8.

"Yet [Kenneth] Starr, like Bush himself, never convinced the hard-core right that he was one of them. In 1991, he lost out on an appointment to the Supreme Court because conservatives in the Justice Department branded him a 'SQUISH' - an unreliable conservative. (The seat went to Clarence Thomas instead.)" Jeffrey Toobin, <u>A Vast Conspiracy</u>, Random House, 1999, p. 76.

STEMWINDER (OM)

noun - a forceful, often long and emotional, rousing speech.

"As every schoolchild used to know, and a few octogenarians still do, Lincoln's [Gettysburg Address] was preceded by a two-hour STEMWINDER delivered, the newspapers said, by a former politician and diplomat named Edward Everett." Russell Baker, *Chicago Trib.*, 4/22/88, S 1, p. 23.

"Studds felt [Senator Eugene] McCarthy had a large advantage over [President] Johnson's men in style as well as substance: 'Our senator and governor [were] real STEMWINDERS and fist pounders - and lousy speakers to boot,' he said. That made McCarthy 'a very appealing change of pace for the people of New Hampshire.'" Charles Kaiser, <u>1968 in America,</u> Weidenfeld & Nicolson, 1988, p. 88.

"As President Bush likes to say, this is a weird election year, and now comes the latest surprise: after 10 torpid months, Mr. Bush has suddenly reawakened as a fist-shaking, STEMWINDING Presidential candidate." Michael Wines, *NYTimes*, 10/22/92, p. A1.

"Mr. Clinton often winds his STEMWINDERS down with a land-of-opportunity aphorism, this one in a Seattle speech: 'If you want to be an American, what you have to do is believe in the Declaration of Independence, the Bill of Rights and the Constitution and show up and behave yourself and do right, and you're part of our country.'" Michael Wines, *NYTimes*, 10/9/96, p. C18.

STONEWALL

verb - to avoid answering a charge or question, to be evasive, obstructive.

"Manchester, NH - For days, Jesse Jackson had been STONEWALLING it in a manner reminiscent of Richard Nixon." Steve Neal, *Chicago Trib.*, 3/1/84, S 1, p. 23.

"Facts, of course, are what the Democratic Senators were demanding in their meeting with Clinton yesterday. Mr. Clinton has clearly underestimated how seriously other political professionals take being lied to eyeball to eyeball. Senator Barbara Mikulski said it was important that 'the President not engage in any more STONEWALLING.' Even Mike McCurry, who has so loyally preserved that wall, seemed grumpy today at the misleading work he has done for Mr. Clinton. Asked why the Senators had referred so specifically to the STONEWALL, Mr. McCurry said, 'They probably referred to our inability to provide straightforward answers for eight months now.'" Editorial, *NYTimes*, 9/11/98, p. A26)

"Peggy Noonan, who last year inveighed against a President [Clinton] for prizing winning over telling the truth, has now called upon Mr.[George W.] Bush to STONEWALL and expressed latent nostalgia for 'the old tolerance' of 'normal failings.' According to the new relativism she posited in *The Wall Street Journal*, a sexual fling may be O.K. too, as long as it can be deemed a romantic 'love affair' and doesn't involve a 'sick manipulator being serviced in the hallway.'" Frank Rich, *NYTimes*, 8/28/99, p.A25.

DR. STRANGELOVE

noun - a mad scientist obsessed with the idea of nuclear destruction.
adjective - STRANGELOVIAN.
Note:From the movie "Dr. Strangelove" with the title role being played by Peter Sellers.

"Over the past four years publishing contentious books about Bill Clinton - most of them highly unfavorable - has become something of a cottage industry. Although a few ... have been fair minded, the bulk read either as tabloid partisan potshots or as investigative tracts on Whitewater. As Leslie H. Gelb put it in a column in the *New York Times*, 'My colleagues and I, like journalistic DR. STRANGELOVES, are ready to nuke Mr. Clinton at the slightest provocation.'" Douglas Brinkley, *NYTimes Book Review,* 9/22/96, p. 14.

STRETCHER (OM) (SL)

noun - falsehood.

"The writers find that [Michael] Dukakis has mostly been true to his reformer ideals, though with a few STRETCHERS, as Huckleberry Finn would say." *Chicago Trib. Sunday Magazine,* 3/6/88, S 14, p. 3.

"It's not easy to find the point at which the acceptable STRETCHER becomes a flat-out WHOPPER, or when emphasizing the positive goes so far it becomes a hopeless distortion of reality. In [George W.] Bush's case, largely because of the weakness of his office, the hardest task is to find any footprints at all. He has walked most lightly on the political life of the state. And where one can find his mark on a bill or a policy, it often turns our to have been more strongly shaped by others." Molly Ivins and Lou Dubose, <u>Shrub, The Short but Happy Political Life of George W. Bush</u>, Introduction, p. XIV.

STUDLY (SL)

adjective - having the characteristics of a stud or attractive male.

"In high school, the girls thought George [Bush] was pretty STUDLY because he was tall and athletic and, of course, rich." *Chicago Trib.,* 9/22/92, S 7, p. 1.

"First the Vice President, to warm up his image, planted the notion that he and Tipper were the models for Oliver Barrett IV and Jenny Cavilleri [in "Love Story"]. But Mr. Segal reined him in, making it clear that Tommy Lee Jones was the model for the sensitive, STUDLY part of the character, while Al [Gore] got the neurotic father-fixated part, and Tipper got zip." Maureen Dowd, *NYTimes,* 12/17/97, p. A19.

"'We certainly didn't talk about world affairs,' recalls Mr. [George W.] Bush's girlfriend in those [Andover high school] years, Debbie Taylor, with whom he danced the twist, played tennis and listened to the Crystals' song 'He's a Rebel.' 'I thought he was kind of STUDLY,' Ms. Taylor recalled, laughing." Nicholas D. Kristof, *NYTimes,* 6/10/00, p. A10.

STUMBLEBUM

noun - a clumsy, incompetent person.

"Vice President Dan Quayle may be no Jack Kennedy, but he was no STUMBLEBUM either in the second of the 1992 campaign debates last night." R. W. Apple, Jr., *NYTimes*, 10/14/92, p. A1.

"But the part about Mr. Bush's being weaker depends, beyond the numbers, on some pretty facile arguments. They go this way: that the primaries hurt Mr. Bush by opening divisions in the Republican Party, tying him to its right wing, denting his shiny image and exposing him, in the word of one Gore enthusiast, as an uninformed and inarticulate 'STUMBLEBUM." Adam Clymer, *NYTimes*, 3/17/00, p. A16.

STURM UND DRANG (GER)

noun - turmoil; literally, storm and stress.

"Reno will appear Wednesday before the House Judiciary Committee to defend her handling of the fundraising investigation, especially her slowness to request an independent counsel. Republicans will emphasize that then Atty. Gen. Edwin Meese quickly sought an independent counsel in the Iran-Contra matter, in contrast to what they see as foot-dragging by Reno. Democrats will try to embarrass Republicans by showing that many of them have made numerous fundraising phone calls from their offices, despite excoriating Clinton and Gore for doing the same thing. Despite all the political STURM UND DRANG, most observers predict that the fundraising flap will have little staying power." Naftali Bendavid, *Chicago Trib.*, 10/15/97, S 1, p. 19.

"Bill Clinton has been an exhausting President. He requires too much work and stirs up too much STURM UND DRANG. After Mr. Clinton leaves, everyone will surely be in the mood for a little peace and quiet." Maureen Dowd, *NYTimes*, 11/25/98, p. A27.

SUCCUBUS

noun - a demon which assumes female form to have intercourse with men.

"As a feminist close in age to Monica S. Lewinsky, I would like to offer a response to the White House scandal. The issue is not whether or not President Clinton is a WOMANIZER: if someone cheats on a partner, it does not make him or her a sexist pig. To me, the feminist issue is one of the new media's and the public's portrayal of Ms. Lewinsky. Portrayals of Ms. Lewinsky as a vulnerable, innocent young thing are sexist, to be sure. Portrayals of her as a psychologically unbalanced, obsessive SUCCUBUS are also wrong. (How many of us could stand the test of having every inch or our lives examined and judged?)" Meg Daly, Letters to the Editor, *NYTimes*, 2/2/98, p. A24.

SUPERANNUATED

adjective - disqualified by advanced age.

"Dewey took the position that the Roosevelt administration was SUPERANNUATED. In his acceptance address, his main point was that the Democrats had 'grown old in office,' had become 'tired and quarrelsome,' and that 'wrongdoing, bungling and confusion' prevailed in the 'vital matters of taxation, price control, rationing, labor relations, manpower...'" Paul F. Boller, Jr., Presidential Campaigns, Oxford Univ. Press, 1996, p.260.

SWELL

noun - a person of high social standing.

"The Clintons have been holding State Dinners for weeks - four in one week - on the sneak! The only difference is that no actual head of state has been invited to them, and the guest lists have been kept to 40, instead of the full blown 100. Also, because they are technically private occasions (though funded by taxpayer dollars), no social correspondent has been allowed to cover them. Thus, America has been spared the sight of a glittery Hillary carrying on like a la-dee-dah lady, and Bill all spiffed up like a SWELL, exchanging bon mots with the Washington, national and international elite." Michael Kilian, *Chicago Trib.*, 6/30/93, S 7, p. 4.

"The local ladies and SWELLS thought that, after four years of George and Barbara Bush's country club, Biff and Muffy, well-mannered dullness, capital life would again be a wonderful frolic. That there would be parties, parties, parties. That having Democrats around would be FUN! That it would be like when, yes, the *Kennedys* ran the town. Well, the sad, dreary, depressing truth of it is that the Clintons have been about as much 'fun' as an Episcopal funeral. They make the Bushes seem like Scott and Zelda Fitzgerald." Michael Kilian, *Chicago Trib.*, 6/9/93, S 7, p. 4.

"There are many steps in this tax minuet. One of the most amusing is the Republican attempt to box President Clinton into dancing to Republican music. If the Senate can be persuaded to go along with the House's generous tax boons for SWELLS, it might provide a Presidential veto so the Republicans could denounce him as an accursed taxer." Russell Baker, *NYTimes*, 4/8/95, p. 17.

SYNECDOCHE

noun - a figure of speech by which a part of something is referred to instead of a reference to the whole, or the whole for a part, or the name of a material for the thing made (i.e. new threads for a new suit).

"He [Ronald Reagan] is the great American SYNECDOCHE, not only a part of our past but a large part of our multiple pasts. That is what makes many of the questions asked about him so pointless. Is he bright, shallow, complex, simple, instinctively shrewd, plain dumb? He is all these things and more. SYNECDOCHE is just the Greek word for a 'sampling,' and we all take different samples from the rich store of associations that have accumulated around the Reagan career and PERSONA." Garry Wills, Excerpt from Reagan's America, Reprinted in *NYTimes*, 1/5/87, p. 10.

"William Safire (column, Dec. 10) says it is 'SYNECDOCHE' that President Clinton be impeached for lying about a sexual affair - a stand-in offense for the many other unsubstantiated, unproved or now-discredited allegations against the President.... If that's SYNECDOCHE in action we'd all better watch out. Speeding, jaywalking, your next PECCADILLO - any one of them, by Mr. Safire's standard, could be prosecuted big time if someone alleges you committed even bigger crimes somewhere, sometime, somehow." Nicholas Christopher, Letter to Editor, *NYTimes*, 12/11/98, p. A30.

SYNTAX

noun - the rules of grammar.

"Whatever one thought of the substance of what he said - and there was plenty of room for argument, because he stated his view bluntly in some cases - the man from Little Rock [Bill Clinton] left not the slightest doubt that the White House will get its SYNTAX tightened when he moves in on Jan. 20." R. W. Apple, Jr., *NYTimes*, 11/13/92, p. A1.

"For the most part, Mr. [George W.] Bush eschews the mangled SYNTAX of his father, sticking to simple platitudes and clichés, but he, too, has a way with the bizarre image. In one chapter, he writes that he pursued the purchase of the Texas Rangers baseball team 'like a pit bull on the pant leg of opportunity'; in another, he writes that a 'gap of hope threatens the very fabric of America.'" Michiko Kakutani, *NYTimes*, 11/22/99, p. A 24.

TTT

TABULA RASA

noun - the mind in its blank state before being affected by experiences or impressions.

"The [Senator John] Glenn advisers also say that their research indicates one major problem for Glenn: no one knows much about him other than the fact that he was an astronaut (many think he walked on the moon). One adviser said, 'The crucial thing for us is to go out there and fill the TABULA RASA about him.'" Elizabeth Drew, *New Yorker*, 11/21/83, p. 184.

"'The early lead was an illusion,' Siegel said. 'The American people didn't know very much about Michael Dukakis. [Bush's] job was to fill in the TABULA RASA in a way appealing to the 20 percent persuadable in a general election. He allowed Lee Atwater to fill it in with pollution.' Atwater is one of Bush's senior strategists, one known for aggressive politics, and he and his colleagues proceeded to fill in Dukakis' TABULA RASA with a picture of a man outside the political mainstream." Jon Margolis, *Chicago Trib.*, 11/10/88, S 1, p. 21.

"There has never been a better time for a candidate like him [Ross Perot]. Start to talk about his lack of qualifications, and the short shadows cast by his opponents make the words die on your lips. He is a TABULA RASA for a nation that feels no one else has given it so much as a pen. This makes him an instructive, maybe useful part of this process. I just can't see how it makes him a good President." Anna Quindlen, *NYTimes*, 6/3/92, p. A15.

"In 2000, the Ashcroft-Bauer-Forbes right will go up against the McCain-Alexander middle, and George W. Bush, for now a telegenic TABULA RASA who is all things to all people, will have to define himself far more clearly, one way or the other, if he chooses to stand in the crossfire." Frank Rich, *NYTimes*, 11/11/98, p. A31.

TALKING HEAD

noun - pretentious talker, esp. a participant in a television talk show (normally only head and shoulders are visible).

"'We are living in our new house, built on our famous tiny lot, and it is perfect for us,' the 69-year-old [former President] Bush recently wrote in a letter faxed to a reporter. He declined a request for an interview because, he explained, 'I have not wanted to appear as one more carping TALKING HEAD, nor has Barbara.'" Sam Howe Verhovek, *NYTimes*, 1/5/94, p. A6.

TATTERDEMALION

adjective and *noun* - bedraggled, disreputable, dilapidated.

"What moved him [William Jennings Bryan], at bottom, was simply hatred of the city men who had laughed at him so long, and brought him at last to so TATTERDEMALION an estate. He lusted for revenge upon them. He yearned to lead the anthropoid rabble against them, to punish them for their execution upon him by attacking the very vitals of their civilization. He went far beyond the bounds of any merely religious frenzy, however, inordinate." H. L. Mencken, The American Scene, Ed. by Huntington Cairns, Vintage Books, 1982, p. 230.

TCHOTCHKE (Y) (OM)

noun - a person's favorite small articles or doodads.

Note: Like many Yiddish words there are various meanings and many spellings for TCHOTCHKE (TSATSKE, CHOTCHKE, etc.).

"The Clintons continue to break creative new ground in family dysfunction. Will they live together in Chappaqua? Why did she refer to her New York address as 'my house'? Is something more cataclysmic than a commuter arrangement in the offing? And what else, precisely, is she packing? If she roots around in that closet of Arkansas TCHOTCHKES, maybe she'll find the complete set of Rose Law Firm billing records." Maureen Dowd, *NYTimes*, 12/8/99, p. 31.

TEFLON

adjective and *noun* - trademark for synthetic resins used for coating cooking utensils to prevent sticking.

"Ronald Reagan is reputed to be a 'TEFLON President' with a knack for shedding accusations against him. Herbert Hoover was just the opposite. Every charge, whether true or false, stuck to him like a feather to hot tar." John Herbers, *NYTimes*, 6/11/84, Review of <u>An Uncommon Man</u> by Richard Norton Smith, p. 21.

"Rep. Patricia Schroeder of Colorado refers to him as the TEFLON president. Nothing seems to stick to Reagan. Schroeder and the rest of the Democratic establishment find that both perplexing and troubling. They see many of their traditional supporters faulting most of Reagan's particular policies, yet expressing support for the man and his presidency.... Reagan's TEFLON coating is not indestructible, but it is thick and slick." Dwight R. Lee and Robert S. Elgin, *Chicago Trib.*, 9/7/84, S 1, p. 27.

"President TEFLON has done it again. He has vetoed a work program for America's job-hungry youth and two health proposals that would have benefited older citizens. And, if his extraordinary luck continues, it won't cost him a thing.... His continues to be, in Rep. Patricia Schroeder's apt phrase, a 'TEFLON presidency,' to which nothing seems to stick: not wrongheaded policies, not meanness, not factual distortion, not out-to-lunch inattention to his job, not even what, if told by anyone else, would be just plain lies. He manages to remain, incredibly, America's nice guy." William Raspberry, *Chicago Trib.*, 11/5/84, S 1, p. 19.

"Don't mess with Bill Clinton. How the president of the United States became TEFLON Bill instead of Velcro Bill, given the obvious level of misbehavior, is another story. But there is no doubt as his presidency moves toward its end that even armies of special prosecutors with Superglue tubes in hand couldn't make anything stick.

"This drives his enemies on the domestic scene, inside and outside of politics, some of whom hate him, crazy." Charles M. Madigan, *Chicago Trib.*, 6/13/99, S 2, p. 1.

TENDENTIOUS

adjective - showing a special prejudice, bias or purpose.

"By the TENDENTIOUS criteria used by the Bush campaign, Bush has raised taxes more often in four years than Clinton has in 12." George F. Will, *Chicago Sun-Times*, 8/28/92, p. 27.

TENTERHOOKS (ON)

noun - in a state of distress, tension or uneasiness. Usually preceded by "on."

"To a large degree, Mr. Clinton's immediate prospects [to avoid impeachment] depend on whether he can hold the Democrats. The Democratic House whip, David Bonior, and the Senate minority leader, Tom Daschle, have not bolted. But their expressions of loyalty could hardly be more conditional. Their responses, like the silence of the First Lady, underscore the reality that this Presidency is on TENTERHOOKS." Editorial, *NYTimes*, 9/11/98, p. A26)

TERRA INCOGNITO

noun - unexplored land, region or subject.

"With the primaries behind them, strategists in both parties are surveying the TERRA INCOGNITA of a three-way race that could redraw the electoral map and test the assumptions of a generation of Presidential campaigns. Ross Perot's surge in opinion polls could very easily subside, but it is already causing a fundamental rethinking of strategy in both major parties." Robin Toner, *NYTimes*, 6/4/92, p. A11.

THERMO-MASOCHISM (SL)

noun - dressing inappropriately for the weather so that a person is either uncomfortably cold or hot.

"Hatless, gloveless and coatless in a New Hampshire tradition of THERMO-MASOCHISM, on a noonday of overcast that threatened snow, Mr. Hart wore a blue pin-striped suit and a blue tie bearing the Presidential eagle." *NYTimes*, 12/16/87, p. 14.

"For the first time this season, the weather in New Hampshire has gotten extremely cold. That enables us to determine how many of the contenders plan to follow the old tradition [of THERMO-MASOCHISM], pioneered by John Kennedy, and demonstrate their toughness by dressing as if it's springtime in Los Angeles, even though the temperature is hovering around zero. 'The report was that Kennedy had long underwear on, but he denied it,' says Michael York, the state librarian." Gail Collins, *NYTimes*, 12/3/99, p. A29.

Note: Gail Collins, in her December 3, 1999 column in the *New York Times*, states that William Henry Harrison, reacting to criticism that he was too old to be President, started giving very long speeches and the longest of all at his inauguration in a cold rain. Harrison's THERMO-MASOCHISM resulted in his death a month later of pneumonia.

THROTTLEBOTTOM

noun - an ineffective, ridiculous person.

"Television comedians have turned Mr. Quayle into a favorite butt of their jokes, treating him as a real-life Alexander P. THROTTLEBOTTOM, the little-heeded Vice President in the 1930's musical 'Of Thee I Sing.' Wherever politicians or journalists or others make speeches, they find that any mention of Mr. Quayle's name, even with strongly partisan Republican audiences, often produces an outburst of titters." R. W. Apple, Jr., *NYTimes*, 9/27/89, p. 10.

THROWBACK

noun - a reversion to a former type; an atavism.

"Reagan's is a melodramatic, heroic prose that other politicians would blush to use, but he gets away with it, because in his case it is authentic. He is a THROWBACK figure out of the fifties, a time when problems seemed simpler and American's military might was unchallenged." Elizabeth Drew, *New Yorker*, 2/20/84, p. 131.

TMPWA (SL)

noun - the most powerful woman in America (i.e. the First Lady).

"Rooted to the spot that had proved so well situated, I awaited Hillary Clinton. Along came TMPWA ['the most powerful woman in America'] herself, who quickly took up the Clintonian theme of appreciation for counseling: 'You gave me some good advice early in the campaign. I took it.'" William Safire, *NYTimes*, 12/14/92, p. A11.

"'More than a first lady,' is the MANTRA of her first senate ad. If she [Hillary Clinton] is more, doesn't that make all the others, including her idol Eleanor, mere? The ad is a little astounding because it finally blurts out what we suspected Hillary felt all along: that she was entitled to more, that being the most powerful woman in American [TMPWA] politics for eight years was not enough." Maureen Dowd, *NYTimes*, 5/7/00, p. 21.

TOADY

noun and *verb* - a sycophant, a lickspittle.

"The newly constituted U.S. Civil Rights Commission has lost no time is distancing itself from the old orthodoxy. It has gone on the attack against all racial quotas, ruled out inquiry into the effect administration budget cutbacks have had on black colleges and taken official UMBRAGE at former Vice President Walter Mondale, who attacked its members as administration TOADIES." Editorial, *Chicago Trib.*, 1/23/84, S 1, p. 14.

"Deaver's book - with all its TOADYING and last-minute cuts to avoid offence - makes clear that Nancy Reagan effectively manipulated the President and his staff to achieve what she thought was best." William Safire, *Chicago Trib.*, 1/27/88, S 1, p. 15.

"Trudeau, creator of Doonesbury, probably has done more than anyone else to imprint on the public mind the caricature of Bush as WIMP - the elitist preppie TOADYING to his patrons and torturing the English language, a man so lacking in character and backbone that he seems a disembodied voice." David Broder, *Chicago Trib.*, 8/21/88, S 4, p. 3.

"Quick to note a vogue in TOADYING, the *New Republic* offered a Quayle Revisionism Award, only to have readers write in suggesting the prize be given to the *New Republic*'s own senior editor, Morton Kondracke, for saying Dan Quayle was 'well-informed, intelligent, candid and engaging.'" P. J. O'Rourke, Parliament of Whores, Vintage Books, 1992, p. 39.

"'He has to walk a fine line, the nature of which is pretty clear,' said Stuart Rothenberg, a political analyst in Washington. 'Bill Clinton has been Al Gore's No. 1 benefactor. He is also the No. 1 reason Al Gore is the heavy favorite to become the party nominee for President. So he needs to remain loyal to the President but at the same time maintain a separate identity to avoid the appearance he is Bill Clinton's TOADY.'" Michael Janofsky, *NYTimes*, 8/26/98, p. A12.

"The overtures [to Perot by Dole] were seized on by talk-radio programs eager for fresh material in a less-than-dramatic campaign season. Rush Limbaugh mocked the Dole campaign on his national radio program, saying that Mr. Dole should know from 'Politics 101' that he should not have let word of the trip leak out. Turi Ryder, who has a liberal talk show in Los Angeles, devoted most of her afternoon program to ridiculing Mr. Dole, accusing him of TOADYING to Mr. Perot, and telling her listeners, 'Can't we think of some other way for Bob Dole to win this election than by turning himself into a quivering bowl of rice pudding?'" Richard L. Berke, *NYTimes*, 10/25/96, p. A10

TONY

adjective - high-toned, aristocratic, stylish.

"When a fatigued and frazzled President Clinton vacationed in August, he jetted to Martha's Vineyard for TONY dinners with printed menus, photo opportunities with the sailing Kennedys and ritual golf with celebrities." Michael Tackett and William Gaines, *Chicago Trib.*, 12/19/93, S 1, p. 1.

"...the big draw for the Republican faithful here at the TONY Design Center of the Americas and elsewhere across the state in the last two days was less Jeb Bush, the party's candidate for governor, than Jeb Bush's parents, former President George Bush and his wife, Barbara." Karen DeWitt, *NYTimes*, 10/12/94, p. A14.

TOO CLEVER BY HALF

expression - to be overly clever.

"Both [Lincoln and Franklin Roosevelt] were denounced as unprincipled for failing to move as fast or as consistently as their more ideologically inclined contemporaries would have liked. 'Lincoln was a sad man because he couldn't get it all at once,' Roosevelt told a friend. 'Nobody can.' In the interest of getting all they could, both Roosevelt and Lincoln were often accused of being TOO CLEVER BY HALF." Geoffrey C. Ward, *NYTimes*, 5/2/97, p. A19.

"We take no particular delight in saying it, but the Bill Clinton depicted in the Starr report is neither surprising nor unfamiliar. Whether the issue has been evading the draft, smoking marijuana, Gennifer Flowers or Paula Jones, Clinton has always been TOO CLEVER BY HALF in explaining embarrassments or personal lapses." Editorial, *Chicago Trib.*, 9/15/98, S 1, p. 18.

"Most people are willing to forgive youthful mistakes. In the case of the roguish Clinton, they have forgiven some adult mistakes. What people should not have to endure is another president who believes he can con them with carefully PARSED answers intended to evade or mislead. That is the most troubling aspect of the last week, that George W. Bush has run the risk of sounding Clintonesque.

"Now, Clinton has made a career out of being TOO CLEVER BY HALF; Bush, to his credit, has not. Bush could go a long way toward restoring public faith in its leaders by offering simple, declarative answers in this campaign, even when the questions are distasteful." Editorial, *Chicago Trib.*, 8/22/99, S 1, p. 16.

TOTEM

noun - an object serving as an emblem of a family or clan; any venerated symbol or emblem.

"By now, most Americans are tired of hearing the slogan that was posted in President-elect Clinton's Little Rock campaign headquarters. 'It's the economy, stupid!' had already become a famous phrase, a TOTEM of single-minded political shrewdness, a rabbit's foot of words that will be evoked in local and national elections well into the next century." Eugene Kennedy, *Chicago Trib.*, 11/30/92, S 1, p. 15.

"If there was any tension between the two men [President Bush and former President Reagan], neither wanted to show it. Bush - though he's dismantling some HALLMARK policies and TOTEMS marking the Reagan era - insists he is carrying on in Reagan's conservative tradition." Timothy J. McNulty, *Chicago Trib.*, 4/27/89, S 1, p. 5.

TOUR DE FORCE (Fr)

noun - a feat of skill or strength.

"Yet the attack [by Newt Gingrich], so violated the traditional comity of the House that then Speaker Tip O'Neill 'lost his cool' (in Gregorsky's words) and a few days later - in a full session of Congress - accused Gingrich of 'the lowest thing I've ever seen in my 32 years in Congress.' Representative Trent Lott demanded that O'Neill's words be stricken from the record, and the presiding congressional officer ruled in his favor. Gingrich's TOUR DE FORCE made all the network news shows that night - and a star was born. 'I am now a famous person,' Newt crowed to the press." Gail Sheehy, *Vanity Fair*, 9/95, p. 221.

TRIANGULATION (OM)

noun - the political strategy of a candidate or office holder of opposing or questioning the positions on issues taken by his own Party as well as the positions of the other Party.

Note: The term "TRIANGULATION" is attributed to political consultant Dick Morris as the name of the strategy which he advised Clinton to follow.

"The other, subtle weapon in Mr. McCain's political arsenal is that, in a brilliant coup of TRIANGULATION, he is as much the un-Kenneth Starr/un-Henry Hyde as he is the un-Clinton. He's the first major G.O.P. presidential candidate in years who is not running as a pious moral SCOLD in hock to the religious right." Frank Rich, *NYTimes*, 2/12/00, p. A 29.

"For weeks now, Mr. Bush has been distancing himself from issues for which conservatives have long fought. Ripping a page out of Dick Morris's playbook, he is pursuing a poll-driven strategy of TRIANGULATION. He is distancing himself from conservatives in the Republican Party and running as a WOBBLY moderate under the banner of 'compassion'" Gary L. Bauer, *NYTimes*, 10/7/99, p. A31.

"But that may be harder to do if Mr. [George W.] Bush, who has criticized fellow Republicans twice in the span of a week, continues to take a page from Mr. Clinton, who defined himself as a 'New Democrat' by standing far apart from Congressional Democrats. Mr. Clinton's political strategist, Dick Morris, called it 'TRIANGULATION' because Mr. Clinton tried to stand equally distant from Republicans and Democrats." Alison Mitchell, *NYTimes*, 10/7/99, p. A1.

"'What Clinton has done by TRIANGULATION has taken the spirit out of the Democratic Party,' Representative Lindsey Graham, Republican of South Carolina, said today, making clear his own irritation with Mr. [George W.] Bush. 'That's not the model to govern well.'" Alison Mitchell, *NYTimes*, 10/7/99, p. A1.

"But the amusement [of Democrats at George W. Bush's criticism of the Republican house] was tempered for some by the memory of how Mr. Clinton's definition of himself as a New Democrat led to his election and re-election. 'Remember the end result,' said Representative Sam Gejdenson, a Connecticut Democrat. 'The last guy who TRIANGULATED won.'" Alison Mitchell, *NYTimes*, 10/7/99, p. A24.

TROGLODYTE

noun - a cave dweller, a hermit; a reactionary person.

"...it probably won't be long before we see Robert Dole courting the Republican TROGLODYTE right by promising to punch Mikhail Gorbachev in the snoot if the Russian Navy doesn't quit bumping our ships." Russell Baker, *NYTimes*, 2/17/88, p. 31.

TROPHY WIFE (SL)

noun - a second (or third) wife of a very prominent and successful businessman, politician or celebrity, acquired as a reward or prize for such success, usually tall, young, thin and beautiful.

"By all accounts, including those of his enemies, [Bill] Bennett works hard at practicing the virtues he preaches: he is a faithful husband to his wife of thirteen years.... When Bob Dole or Phil Gramm or Pete Wilson or Newt Gingrich declaims on the subject of family values - the social cost of divorce and illegitimacy, and the suffering caused by men who abandon their families - their words are undermined by the fact that each of them is on his second wife. Bennett, on the other hand, is comfortable denouncing not only walk-out husbands and fathers of the inner city but also those of his own class - successful middle-aged white men gone in search of TROPHY WIVES." Michael Kelly, *New Yorker,* 7/17/95, p. 27.

"To clothe their quest for a cosmetic scoop with high-toned purpose, gossip writers say that Mr. Dole should fess up to 'demystify' male face lifts, just as he helped demystify prostate operations be talking about his during the '96 campaign. But for me the issue isn't *whether* he had plastic surgery. (Even his oldest friends don't believe his lame line about looking so different because he lost 12 pounds and had a couple of moles taken off.) The issue is *why* he did it. And that's the beauty part. Bob Dole did it because he really, really wants to be First Lady. Even as mean and adder-tongued as he can be at times, Mr. Dole would certainly be one of the nicest First Ladies we've had in recent memory. He never really seemed comfortable trying to be president. But when he talks about playing Denis Thatcher to Liddy's Iron Magnolia, he sounds as if he means it. TROPHY WIFE shtick suits the Kansan's subversive black humor." Maureen Dowd, *NYTimes,* 11/12/97, p. A23.

TUMBREL

noun - a cart carrying condemned persons to the place of execution.

"There is a fatalistic splendor to Bob Dole's campaign. It isn't even really a campaign anymore. It's something more interesting, more absurd, more dark, an inarticulate slouching around cornfields in Ohio and half-empty gyms in Missouri, boldly courting bad luck, bad timing and bad metaphors, inexorably sound-biting itself toward doom... Republicans wonder why Mr. Dole is so serene in the TUMBREL. Why on earth did he want the nomination? Was it just for the sake of getting it, or keeping other people from having it?" Maureen Dowd, *NYTimes,* 9/26/96, p. A19.

TURNCOAT

noun - traitor; one who switches sides.

"Gramm's tenacity and treasure chest may yet propel him to the White House, but he could also suffer the fate of his fellow Texas TURNCOAT, the late John B. Connally, who spent $11 million in 1980. Connally finished sixth with 1.5 percent of the New Hampshire vote, ahead of Dole, who won fewer than 600 votes." *Boston Globe,* 2/21/95, p. 12.

In addition, Mr. Gore is fiddling with his stump speech. He is trying to tell voters more about himself, and to make a personal connection to inspire local

Democrats across the country to work on his behalf. This also includes casting his opponent for the nomination, Bill Bradley, as a TURNCOAT for leaving the Senate after the Republicans had assumed control of it and briefly considering a run for the Presidency as an independent." Katharine Q. Seelye, *NYTimes*, 10/7/99, p. A25.

TWINK (TWINKIE) (SL)

noun - a NERD, a GOODY TWO-SHOES, someone out of step with his generation.

"But baby boomers weren't going to vote for baby boomers. We *know* us. We're nuts. We don't want anyone in our generation anywhere near the ICBM launch codes, he might start channeling Idi Amin. Plus Quayle was a TWINK. He got all the way through the sixties without dying from an overdose, being institutionalized by his parents or getting arrested for nude violation of the Mann Act on a motorcycle. At least he was a draft dodger - although Dan timidly joined the National Guard instead of bravely going to his physical in panty hose." P. J. O'Rourke, <u>Parliament of Whores</u>, Vintage Books, 1992, p. 29.

TWIT

noun - a bothersome or annoying person, a NERD.

"Calling George Bush shallow is like calling a dwarf short.... Even though he vacillates constantly, he is not a hopeless TWIT, a total TWINKIE, or a damn fool. That's a misimpression based on the fact that, as *Newsweek* magazine once put it, 'At least once a day he achieves a level of transcendent DORKINESS.' Bush merely has TWIT tendencies." Molly Ivins, <u>Molly Ivins Can't Say That, Can She?</u>, Random House, 1991, p. 149.

TWOFER (SL)

noun - a person representing two different minority groups who is picked to fill an office, i.e. a black woman, a Jewish woman.

"Former Representative Shirley Chisholm says all the candidates for the Democratic Presidential nomination have approached her about joining them as a Vice-Presidential candidate. 'It could come down at the convention to a battle between a black or a woman for Vice president,' said Miss Chisholm, 59 years old, at a news conference here Saturday. 'I could possibly be considered because I meet both criteria - a "TWOFER."'" *NYTimes*, 3/5/84, p. 13.

TYRO

noun - novice.

"Other Presidents have bridled at being treated as TYROS. John F. Kennedy was said to have been ashen-faced after a meeting in Vienna in which Nikita S. Khrushchev wagged his finger at the young, untested President; by contrast, when Francois Mitterrand sternly lectured Bill Clinton at a lunch in Washington last year about sanctions on various countries, Mr. Clinton nodded obligingly." Maureen Dowd, *NYTimes*, 6/7/94, p. A4.

UUU

UBIQUITOUS

adjective - being everywhere at the same time, omnipresent.

"UBIQUITOUS as ever, he [Ross Perot] routinely pops up on TV chat shows, from 'Today' to 'The Tonight Show,' and on May 30 will air his third 30-minute, nationally televised program." Thomas Hardy, *Chicago Trib.*, 5/16/93, S 1, p. 1.

UMBRAGE

noun - offense, resentment.

"Only one of the evening's developments seemed to surprise this nerveless political exegete. That was when Rev. Pat Robertson displayed unclerical UMBRAGE through his smile because Tom Brokaw called him a 'television evangelist.'" Tom Wicker, *NYTimes*, 2/11/88, p. 25.

"Governor Clinton took UMBRAGE at the implication that he did not think for himself. 'I'm the only person up here who hasn't been part of Washington in any way for the past 20 years,' he said, asserting that what he says has not been cooked up by someone else." Robin Toner, *NYTimes*, 10/16/92, p. A11.

UNFLAPPABLE

adjective - poised, confidant, assured.

"Add the word 'UNFLAPPABLE' to the list of words one might use to describe First Lady Hillary Rodham Clinton. Consider that for nearly five minutes Mrs. Clinton sat expressionless on stage at Hersey High School while a few feet from her 418 graduating seniors flailed their arms in a raucous dance, some threw a fellow student repeatedly into the air, and others sprayed white string from aerosol cans in all directions. The celebration, prior to the first lady's commencement address, clearly was an unnerving moment for most school officials who joined Mrs. Clinton on stage during the graduation ceremony. Teachers could be seen wiping their brow or stealing a glance at the first lady to see how she reacted to the HIGH JINKS." Ray Quintanilla, *Chicago Trib.*, 6/5/95, S 2, p. 3.

URIAH HEEP

noun - a clerk in <u>David Copperfield</u> by Charles Dickens who posed as an humble person but was really very ambitious and unscrupulous; a fawning, TOADYING, unscrupulous and overly ambitious person.

"Watching Lyndon Johnson fawn over the children's father when he was present, knowing all the time that Johnson was sleeping with their mother when he was absent; watching Johnson praise the older man to his face, knowing all the time that behind his back he was taking from him the woman he loved; seeing how unshakably deferential, how utterly humble, he was in playing upon Marsh's affections, this observer, a lover of Charles Dickens, was reminded forcefully of a character in David Copperfield - a character who, she felt, lacked only a Southern drawl to be Lyndon Johnson in the flesh. 'Every time I looked at Lyndon,' she says, 'I saw a URIAH HEEP from Texas.'" Robert A. Caro, The Years of Lyndon Johnson: The Path to Power, Knopf, 1982, p. 489.

"And consider Bob Dole, URIAH HEEP as undertaker. We now get to watch some of the finest minds of our time, not to mention some of the most expensive, try to convince us that Bob Dole is warm and fuzzy. The man whose response to the State of the Union address brought to mind the words, 'Somewhere in Transylvania, there is an empty grave...' Cute, cuddly-like-a-teddy-bear Dole. You notice they've already trained him to smile more, poor man. It's so awful." Molly Ivins, You Got to Dance With Them What Brung You, Random House, 1998, p. 122.

UXORIOUS

adjective - doting on, irrationally fond of, or affectionately over submissive toward one's wife.

"He [Michael Dukakis] might not generate as much passion as Jesse Jackson in his speech at the convention, but he continued to win points as the most UXORIOUS politician since Ronald Reagan." Maureen Dowd, *NYTimes*, 7/21/88, p. 11.

VVV

VACUOUS

adjective - lacking content, empty, stupid.

"Perhaps even more damaging - because of what it says about his judgment - is Bush's selection of the VACUOUS Sen. Dan Quayle as his running mate." Editorial, *Milwaukee Journ.*, 10/23/88.

"Mary Frances Berry, one of the three people Mr. Reagan dismissed from the Civil Rights Commission, called the President's remarks 'VACUOUS.'" *NYTimes*, 1/14/89, p. 7.

"He [Donald Trump] refers to W. as the anointed 'son of the President who should have finished the war' and says he looks 'VACUOUS.' He thinks Bill Bradley is 'not exactly Cary Grant.' Al Gore has made 'dreadful mistakes,' including alpha girl....'I think the only difference between me and the other candidates,' he summed up, 'is that I'm more honest and my women are more beautiful.'" Maureen Dowd, *NYTimes*, 11/17/99, p. A29.

"The antidote to Mr. Bush's VACUITY and Mr. Gore's playacting is not necessarily more authenticity; Mr. Trump, after all, is nothing if not authentic - authentically fatuous - and Mr. Ventura can turn authenticity into shtick, at which point it becomes authentic boorishness." Frank Rich, *NYTimes*, 10/23/99, p. A27.

"My principal complaint with [George H. W.] Bush however was that I thought he was the most VACUOUS man to occupy the Oval Office in my time in Washington....Indeed he took his responsibilities to the American people so lightly that he chose Dan Quayle for vice president, twice. He had so little respect for the institutions of our democracy that he handed a lifetime appointment to the Supreme Court to Clarence Thomas just to make a point about race." Jack Germond, Fat Man In A Middle Seat, Random House, 1999. P. 239.

VAPID

adjective - dull, insipid.

"Nor is there any way that Bill Clinton, or any poll-driven successor, will tackle the tough issues before us. Anybody who was expecting the 'real' Clinton to stand up and assert himself after the '96 campaign has been sorely disappointed. Clinton's warm and fuzzy State of the Union message was a pure product of consumer research, full of VAPID symbolism about the importance of education but nearly devoid of references to the painful choices that lay ahead on entitlement spending and deficit reduction." John McCarron, *Chicago Trib.*, 2/17/97, S 1, p. 17.

"On television, Ms. Noonan said, she described the President's speech as 'marked by a kind of airy and old-fashioned oratory.' On the telephone hours later, she described it as 'VAPID, VAPID, VAPID,' and added, 'It was the worst Inaugural Address of our lifetime, and I think the only controversy will be between those who say it was completely and utterly BANAL and those who say, 'Well, not completely and utterly.' " Todd S. Purdum, *NYTimes*, 1/21/97, p. A12.

VET (BR) (OM)

verb - to check or evaluate.

"The dilemma is this: If the Bush staff failed to VET the potential running mate aggressively on this issue, it was incompetent, and Mr. Bush asks us to let him bring that band of bunglers into the White House; on the other hand, if the Bush staff did ask the tough questions the way reporters were expected to, and Mr. Quayle mislead them, then the running mate was duplicitous or incredibly naive - and not the sort best suited to be one heartbeat from the Presidency." William Safire, *NYTimes*, 8/22/88, p. 19.

"Though Wood had done nothing unlawful - she had hired a nanny who was an illegal alien at a time when it was still legal to do so - her failure to provide the President's VETTERS with the details ahead of time persuaded them that she was ill equipped to navigate the political minefields of Cabinet service. With Wood's withdrawal, charges of ineptitude against Clinton mounted." Sidney Blumenthal, *New Yorker*, 3/8/93, p. 43.

"The Democratic Convention in New York should be a livelier forum for a Veepstakes. ... Bob Kerrey of Nebraska was media-VETTED in the primaries, and can energize the old Gary Hart reformers." William Safire, *NYTimes*, 5/14/92, p. A15.

VIAGRA ELITE (SL)

noun - people who can afford to buy Viagra (at $10 a pill) or can get it through their insurance plan.

Note: A coinage as arresting as GUCCI COMMUNISM. How can you not try to work it into the conversation at the next party?

"Bob and Elizabeth Dole may have told us more than we wanted to know about their sex lives. But I'm glad they did. The 74-year-old former presidential candidate revealed last week on CNN's 'Larry King Live' that he was in a group that tested the new anti-impotency drug Viagra. As casually and candidly as he might sound recommending a golf club for a chip shot, he pronounced it to be 'a great drug.' His 61-year-old wife, president of the American Red Cross, agreed with a smile in New York City on Sunday, 'It's a great drug, OK?'... I am delighted the Doles have come out in their own way, as a happy Viagra couple. With their help, Viagra has potential not only as a life-enhancing drug, but also a life-saving medical benefit. Which raises my concern about a potential new class in American society: the VIAGRA ELITE. They are the folks who can afford to buy Viagra or have it provided for them by their health plans. The rest fall into a Viagra-less underclass. If you are poor your ability to buy Viagra under Medicaid can vary wildly from state to state, since federal officials have left Medicaid drug coverage up to the individual states." Clarence Page, *Chicago Trib.*, 5/13/98, S 1, p. 21.

VOODOO ECONOMICS

noun - false, unsound economic theory

Note: VOODOO ECONOMICS was the term used by George H. W. Bush to disparage Ronald Reagan when they were contesting for the Republican presidential nomination in 1980. Reagan was arguing that he could decrease taxes, increase military spending and balance the budget all at the same time. Bush said this was impossible and called it VOODOO ECONOMICS. However he eagerly sought and gladly accepted the position of vice-presidential candidate to run with Reagan.

"[John McCain] alone has positioned himself to deflect the inevitable Gore attack that a Republican president will throw the monkey wrench of

VOODOO ECONOMICS into a booming economy." Frank Rich, *NYTimes*, 2/12/00, p. A 29.

WWW

WAFFLE

verb - to vacillate.

"The religious right showed [in the Iowa straw poll] some strength in Iowa, though not nearly as much as in years past. But Republicans who are trying to move slightly away from the right wing remain respectful - witness Mrs. Dole's WAFFLING when asked whether she believed in the theory of evolution. Politics is interesting because it is unpredictable, and this season just became a little more so. For now, it is worth remembering that there are real divisions in the Republican Party, and they are a little clearer today than they were before the voting in Iowa." Editorial, *NYTimes*, 8/17/99, p. A18.

WALPURGIS NIGHT

noun - the eve of May day on which witches ride; by extension a nightmarish event or situation.

"Newt Gingrich is the Republican who makes Democrats think of WALPURGIS NIGHT. With everyone talking about Gingrich's 'first hundred days,' you might think he is the new Franklin Roosevelt risen out of Georgia to rebuild a stricken nation." Russell Baker, *NYTimes*, 11/19/94, p. 15.

WANNABE (SL)

noun - a person who wants to be a particular kind of person or hold a particular job.

"It's 1996. Presidential primaries have been abolished. So has the Electoral College. Gone are formal televised debates between the candidates and tough but boring Q&A's on Sunday morning news shows.... The time has come for the November sweeps. In the special Hollywood set before network cameras, each candidate perches in collapsible chairs 20 feet above vats of Gerber's baby food, awaiting the voters' decision. At home, Mr. and Mrs. America and everyone in between go to their interactive TV sets and punch the appropriate buttons. The numbers are tallied. One by one each of the presidential WANNABES, spring-latched chair seats is released and, in a cataclysm of fireworks, derisive rap music and a crescendo of canned audience laughter, they fall into the PABLUM, leaving only one to be crowned president. The people have spoken." Editorial by the *San Francisco Examiner*, quoted in the *Chicago Trib.*, 6/19/92, S 1, p. 23.

"Offering a sample of the influence he could wield should he enter the Presidential primaries as a Republican, as some in the party fear, Mr. Perot told his supporters that his crowd 'sent a signal to every Presidential WANNABEE for 1996.'" Richard L. Berke, *NYTimes*, 10/25/93, p. A11.

"We *wanted* a lo-cal, polyunsaturated, salt-free election slate. Otherwise we wouldn't have been out on the lawn rolling in every stinky detail of the candidates' lives. We didn't even try to get the presidential WANNABES to tell us what they meant or what they'd do. Instead, we spent election year peeking down Donna Rice's bathing suit, poking Bob Dole's war wound, trying to get Jesse Jackson to say 'hymie' again, trading locker-room stories about Jack Kemp and waiting for Kitty Dukakis to explode. Every person in American has done or said *something* that would keep him or her from being president." P. J. O'Rourke, Parliament of Whores, Vintage Books, 1992, p. 32.

"Within eight days, however, the Dole ascendancy came and went. Bush and his New Hampshire savior, then Gov. John Sununu, hung a 'Senator Straddle' label on the Kansan, and another White House WANNABE, Pierre S. du Pont of the Delaware du Ponts, waved an anti-tax petition at Dole in a GOP debate." Steve Daley, *Chicago Trib.*, 8/29/93, S 4, p. 5.

WASTREL

noun - a spendthrift or wasteful person.

"[Budget director Leon Panetta] abhorred Reagan's deficits; to him, Reagan was a WASTREL. During the 1992 campaign, Panetta had openly criticized Clinton for not taking deficits seriously enough, and in the summer he had presented a program to wipe them out within five years." Sidney Blumenthal, *New Yorker*, 3/8/93, p. 43.

WELTANSCHAUUNG (GER)

noun - world view, a comprehensive conception of the world.

"'Nothing is more contemptible,' Joseph Alsop told me when I took up this line of work, 'than a columnist without a WELTANSCHAUUNG.'... Judging from the President's interviews (with little help from a muddy speech in Milwaukee read for him last week by Vice President Gore) the Clinton-Talbott WELTANSCHAUUNG includes a view of a new Russia whose foreign policy can be shaped benignly by evidence of Western trust." William Safire, *NYTimes*, 1/10/94, p. A11.

WHIPPERSNAPPER

noun - an insignificant and pretentious person.

"His [Lyndon Johnson's] reply to the charge that he was too young subtly reminded the audience where Shelton stood on the Court issue: 'I'd rather be called a young WHIPPERSNAPPER than an old reactionary,' he said." Robert A. Caro, The Years of Lyndon Johnson: The Path to Power, Knopf, 1982, p. 432.

WHITE HAT

noun - a good person or role model. The use of "black hat" for a bad person is more common.

"The press, more than a few of whom early on appeared to be looking feverishly for a strong oak limb over which to hang the noose, has earned public scorn and enabled Clinton, the Marcel Marceau of Pennsylvania Avenue, to portray himself as a victim. In the matter of public trust and confidence, Independent Counsel Ken Starr is running on empty. In this tawdry epic, there are no WHITE HATS and just one beret." Mark Shields, *St. Petersburg Times*, 2/23/98, p. 10A.

WHITE SHOE

adjective - socially elite. cf. TONY.

"It [Jeb Bush's campaign message] is not the WHITE-SHOE Chamber of Commerce conservatism of his father [former President George Bush] but, he says, a response to the moral relativism - and moral decay - of the times. 'I look at systems like welfare and the education of our children and I see 30-year-old pilot programs that don't work,' Bush said in an interview." Steve Daley, *Chicago Trib.*, 9/7/94, p. 1.

"No one took him [George H. W. Bush] seriously, but he didn't seem to be a bad guy. He was just another WHITE-SHOE Republican going from one appointive job to another and probably dreaming of a place on the national ticket." Jack Germond, <u>Fat Man In A Middle Seat</u>, Random House, 1999, p. 240.

WHOPPER (OM)

noun - an extravagant lie. cf. STRETCHER.

"But Susan Estrich, the Dukakis campaign manager, issued a statement saying, 'George Bush went to lunch today and served up another plate of WHOPPERS.' Among the 'WHOPPERS' she cited was his statement that Mr. Dukakis doubled taxes on businesses in Massachusetts that employ fewer than 35 people. 'George was flat wrong,' she said." Allan R. Gold, *NYTimes*, 9/20/88, p. 10.

"In 1980 Ronald Reagan told us the biggest WHOPPER of them all. The wonder is that anybody believed him. In his warm and agreeable way, he told us that he would increase military spending, reduce taxes and at the same time, miraculously, he would demolish the deficit and balance the budget. Mr. Reagan was wildly popular. It was as if Santa Claus had been elected President." Bob Herbert, *NYTimes*, 9/22/93, p. A21.

"'Of all the WHOPPERS George Bush tried to get away with in his speech last night, the biggest one wasn't even about me,' Mr. Clinton said. 'It came at the end, when this President compared himself to Harry Truman. Harry Truman had a sign on his desk in the Oval Office that said, "The buck stops here." If George Bush had a sign on his desk, it would say, "Don't blame me. I'm just the President."'" Gwen Ifell, *NYTimes*, 8/22/92, p. 8.

"Do you believe that the president of the United States was completely honest on July 1, 1991, when, in announcing the nomination of conservative, African-American Judge Clarence Thomas to the Supreme Court, he told the public that Thomas was 'the best man for the job on the merits' and that 'the fact that he is black and a minority has nothing to do with this.'? Were not these words of George Bush about a relatively inexperienced federal judge and longtime bureaucrat with an undistinguished reputation in serious legal circles a first-degree WHOPPER?" Eric Zorn, *Chicago Trib.*, 10/6/98, S 2, p. 1.

"Bush's problem is not a lack of intelligence or (as some have suggested) an excess of the tranquilizer Halcion. At bottom, his problem is a simple lack of anything to say. That's why he babbles. That's why he contradicts himself. That's why he tells you how you should perceive what he's saying, instead of just saying it. That's why he tells transparent WHOPPERS." Michael Kinsley, Introduction to Jonathan Bines, <u>Bushisms</u>, Workman Publishing Company, 1992.

WIGGY

adjective - crazy, insane, NUTS.

"Reached at an airport in South Carolina, Mr. [John] McCain was clearly hurt that people who had watched his 17-year career in the House and Senate were suddenly calling him WIGGY. But he knows that the prospect that he would be president - with a promise to upend the table of special-interest goodies - drives Washington WIGGY. 'I'm having trouble hearing you, Maureen,' he says mischievously. 'Those voices in my head. STOP THOSE VOICES!'" Maureen Dowd, *NYTimes*, 11/21/99, p. 15

"It was a disturbing image, with elements of Nixon, Lear and 'Caddyshack.' The most gregarious of Presidents was playing golf solo. 'The White House press office,' the A.P. story concluded, 'refused to release his score.' Is the president getting WIGGY in the final days? Will he start talking to the portraits in the White House?" Maureen Dowd, *NYTimes*, 10/20/99, p. A31.

WIMP (SL)

noun - an ineffective, weak, unaggressive person.

"Bush shouted 'Shut up and sit down!' at the families of missing servicemen. He did say 'please' and the protesters who had heckled him apologized later. But whether Bush actually lost his temper or was just trying to prove he's not a WIMP, the whole world saw him being tacky." Ellen Debenport, *Chicago Trib.*, 8/2/92, S 4, p. 3.

"Bush and Sununu are in danger of returning America to the Reagan and Watt era. A key test of whether there is any substance to Bush's claim to be an environmentalist will be in the debate heating up on reauthorization of the Clean Air Act. This is no time for Bush to WIMP-out." Harry C. Blaney III, *Chicago Trib.*, 2/14/90, S 1, p. 15.

"I'm worried about My Man George [Bush] because in Washington, the city where everyone says what everyone else says, everyone is saying the guy is a WIMP. Or, as George puts it, they're calling him 'the *W* word - and it doesn't stand for *wussy*. Trouble is, when a lot of people start calling Bush a WIMP, he tends to go into some kind of a snit to prove his standing in what he once memorably referred to as 'the manhood thing.'" Molly Ivins, <u>Molly Ivins Can't Say That, Can She?</u>, Random House, 1991, p. 142.

"George W. Bush fighting the WIMP factor? That rings a bell. 'I hate to say it, but I think Bush's problem is that he's WIMPY,' confided Barbara Looney, a retired gift wrapper at Macy's who lives in North Augusta, S.C. 'He just seems to dilly-dally.' Her friend Lois Marable, a fellow retiree in a black velour sweatsuit and beaded slippers, agreed: 'I do not like the way he looks on television. He looks like a WIMP.'" Maureen Dowd, *NYTimes*, 2/16/00, p. A29.

WINDBAG

noun - a talkative person; a GASBAG.

"'[Henry Hyde] did not bother with questions,' noted the [*New Republic*] in September 1987. 'He did not even pretend to be much interested in finding the truth. He was on the side of the president, loyalty, motherhood, the Marines, tomorrow, the Contras, the American people, the past, the Founding Fathers, the flag, the sun, the moon, the stars at night, and Henry Hyde. He's never hidden his WINDBAG under a bushel…'" Dennis Bernstein and Leslie Kean, *Henry Hyde's Moral Universe*, Common Courage, 1999, p. 139.

WITCHES' BREW

noun - a dangerous and disgusting concoction.

"President Clinton's counsel in the Senate impeachment trial referred to a 'WITCHES' BREW' concocted by U.S. Rep. Henry Hyde and the other House managers to try to establish the president's guilt. I was curious as to what a WITCHES' BREW was so I consulted the shades of H.L. Mencken and Jonathan Swift. The recipe for a WITCHES' BREW calls for a BROBDINGNAGIAN portion of HUBRIS, a DOLLOP of guile, a MODICUM of sanctimony, a HUMONGOUS portion of hypocrisy and generous helpings of Puritanism and prurience,. The MISHMOSH should be half-baked for an interminable period of time. It should be stirred, not too vigorously, by a URIAH HEEP DOPPELGÄNGER with the initials H.H. to get the full flavor." John E. Clay, Letters to the Editor, *Wilmette Life*, 2/4/99, p. 7.

WOBBLY

adverb - hesitating, vacillating.
adjective - inclined to hesitate or vacillate.

"George Bush, the leader of the alliance, made the decision: to do nothing [in Bosnia]. Why he was so craven remains a mystery. He had just come out of the Persian Gulf war a hero, the man who said Iraq's aggression 'will not stand' and acted on that vow. The fall of Prime Minister Margaret Thatcher may well have made the difference. She had goaded him to action against Iraq, telling him: 'Don't go all WOBBLY on us, George.' Her successor, John Major, had jelly in his spine." Anthony Lewis, *NYTimes*, 12/2/94, p. A15.

"Strap on the electrodes and rev up the car battery. It's time for President Clinton to administer another jolt of shock therapy to Britain's Prime Minister, John Major. He's gone WOBBLY again on Northern Ireland." Thomas L. Friedman, *NYTimes*, 7/12/95.

"I say press for a vote to legitimize the President's decision. Take the half-loaf he is forced to offer. By rallying behind Clinton now, we get into position to stiffen his spine if he goes WOBBLY, or push him upward when escalation is required." William Safire, *NYTimes*, 2/19/98, p. A21.

"Where is Maggie Thatcher when we need her? Shortly after Iraq invaded Kuwait, she met with President Bush and told him, 'This is no time to go WOBBLY.' There is no one around to tell that to Bill Clinton. And WOBBLY he went. Saddam Hussein once again plays the pull-America's-chain game and Clinton meekly permits a return to the status quo ante." Charles Krauthammer, *Chicago Trib.*, 11/23/98, S 1, p. 15.

WOMANIZER

noun - a man who excessively and illicitly pursues women. cf. SKIRT CHASER.

"Of his alleged WOMANIZING, Kennedy wryly observed [in the television portrayal by Mike Farrell] that through American history, the White House 'has not exactly been a monastery.' 'For women, power has always been the greatest aphrodisiac. After I visited Ireland, I was told 375 women had confessed going to bed with me.'" Kenneth R. Clark, *Chicago Trib.*, 6/9/84, S 2, p. 14.

"It's been pretty well documented that John F. Kennedy was a dedicated bedroom athlete before and after his election. And I'm sure historians can point to other presidents who went in for the same form of recreation. One might even make a case that if a president must have an occasional diversion, WOMANIZING is less time-consuming and demanding than many others." Mike Royko, *Chicago Trib.*, 5/4/87, S 1, p. 3.

"Mr. [Wendell] Willkie, who lived in Manhattan, was a courageous, powerful personality. He was admired for integrity, independence and for the Horatio Alger character of a career that had brought him wealth, fame and influence. He was also a 'WOMANIZER.'" William. J. vanden Heuvel, *NYTimes*, 12/19/87, p. 17.

"Former Sen. Gary Hart gave another bizarre twist to this most unusual presidential campaign Tuesday when he suddenly re-entered the race he was forced to leave last May because of charges of WOMANIZING." Philip Lentz, *Chicago Trib.*, 12/16/87, S 1, p. 1.

"By any measure, [Nicholas Longworth's] morals left much to be desired, and the wonder is that the prudish [Theodore Roosevelt] - whose morals were straight out of a Victorian primer - consented to the marriage. Most likely TR, who did not allow even the mildest sexual jokes or innuendoes to be made in his presence, was the only politician in town who hadn't heard the stories about Nick's WOMANIZING." Carol Felsenthal, <u>Alice Roosevelt Longworth</u>, G.P. Putnam's Sons, 1988, p. 97.

"At age fifty-one George Washington wrote, 'When once the woman has tempted us and we have tasted the forbidden fruit, there is no such thing as checking our appetites, whatever the consequences may be.' When he mentioned the forbidden fruit, was he talking about sex or simply the type of passion that can develop between a man and a woman but can never be legitimately fulfilled? Although a few historians believe that George Washington was a WOMANIZER and some of his friends called him the 'Stallion of the Potomac,' there is little evidence that this was the case." Wesley O. Hagood, <u>Presidential Sex</u>, Carol Publishing Group, 1995, p. 1.

"In that same memoir ['Nixon Off the Record'], Ms. Crowley quotes Nixon as saying rather wistfully: 'The charges of WOMANIZING against Clinton are of course true. It could be a serious liability. But then again, it wasn't for Kennedy.' The tragedy of Richard Nixon is that he never appreciated that JFK turned WOMANIZING into that asset we call 'Kennedyesque,' even when it happens in Little Rock. Nixon's last best hope for a Camelot aura may be if someone spreads the rumor that he and Bebe Rebozo were not alone in their oceanfront villa in Key Biscayne." Frank Rich, *NYTimes*, 11/15/97, p. A23.

"WASHINGTON, Aug. 1 - Hillary Rodham Clinton says in a new magazine interview that she thought her husband had overcome his WOMANIZING 10 years ago but that deep scars from abuse he suffered as a child had led to his infidelity and that he had not sufficiently examined those problems to conquer them." News Story, *NYTimes*, 8/2/99, p. A10.

WONK

noun - a serious student, a grind, a swot.

"One gleeful Republican campaign official suggests that it is less her sex than her demeanor, noting that Mrs. Clinton is 'a hall monitor' type whose drive and earnestness are off-putting: 'She doesn't complement Clinton because she appears to be another liberal policy WONK. It doesn't seem like a family - more like a merger.'" Maureen Dowd, *NYTimes* 5/18/92, p. A8.

"...Democratic strategists believe Clinton's reputation as a 'policy WONK' pairs well with Gore's expertise on the environment and new technologies to attract suburban voters, who also may welcome the ticket's abortion-rights position." Mitchell Locin, *Chicago Trib.*, 7/10/92, S 1, p. 4.

"There is a lot of work to be done in getting back to sensible English. Sad to say, we media folks haven't been much help with our own weakness for trendy, faddish expression. An 'ICON' used to be a sacred image; now, endlessly, it can be anything from a catalog to a basketball player. And get used to 'WONK,' as in 'Clinton policy WONK,' even though the people who use it aren't exactly sure what it means." Editorial, *Chicago Trib.*, 2/17/93, S 1, p. 12.

"Patient [the Presidency of Bill Clinton] also suffers from acute WONKINESS (scientific term *policius ad nauseam*), otherwise known as 'agenda clash' or 'Creeping Carterism,' after a similar condition suffered by an earlier patient." Clarence Page, *Chicago Trib.*, 5/16/93, Sec 4, p. 3.

"But like her or not, [Hillary Rodham] Clinton has proved that the first lady can be more than a White House ornament. Eleanor Roosevelt, whom she admires, played a significant role on the national and international stage in her day, but a policy WONK she wasn't.

"In the harrowing last couple of years, even Hillary Clinton's detractors have given her credit for the strength and dignity with which she handled a most personal and public crisis, the Monica Lewinsky affair. Sure, some said she should have walked out on her PHILANDERING husband. But she knew what she was doing, for her family and for her future.

"In New York, she's not a 'Stand by Your Man' woman anymore. She has a new theme song: 'It's My Turn.'" Editorial, *Chicago Trib.*, 7/9/99, S 1, p. 22.

"'A two-hour marathon,' Mr. McCain said dismissively, promising reporters that should he be elected President he would keep the ritual address to Congress to a crisp 15 minutes. 'I think what you should do is give a vision for America,' he said, 'not give a laundry list that looks like a Chinese menu with one from column A and one from column B. I know he likes that,' he said, 'because he's a policy WONK.' Mr. McCain by contrast is not a policy WONK, at least when it comes to domestic issues." Alison Mitchell, *NYTimes*, 2/9/00. p. 1.

WORDSMITH (Sl)

noun - an expert in the use of words; a person who uses an extensive vocabulary, a word MAVEN.

"One of the reasons [Adlai] Stevenson gained popular acclaim for his eloquence was that he had better ghostwriters than anyone since U.S. Grant persuaded Mark Twain to write the old soldier's Civil War memoirs. Of all Stevenson's gifted WORDSMITHS, [John Bartlow] Martin was consistently described by associates as the most versatile." Steve Neal, *Chicago Trib.*, 1/8/87, S 1, p. 23.

"President Reagan has decided to take three of his skilled WORDSMITHS with him next week for his meeting with Mikhail S. Gorbachev. Never before has Mr. Reagan taken so many speechwriters with him anywhere." James F. Clarity and Warren Weaver, Jr., *NYTimes*, 11/14/85, p. 14.

"...Ted Sorensen, Kennedy's talented speechwriter/ adviser, is now a part-time, traveling WORDSMITH for Dukakis." David Broder, *Chicago Trib.*, 10/7/88, S 1, p. 29.

"It is undignified for Presidents and candidates to surrender their bodies and minds to cosmeticians, barbers, clothing designers, market analysts, tooth-cappers, hair-dyers, artificial mechanics and hired WORDSMITHS in order to pass for star-quality television performers. Yet anyone who balked at submitting to these comic indignities would be laughed out of politics as a man of the dead and mercifully gone past." Russell Baker, *NYTimes*, 6/9/92, p. A13.

"Woodrow Wilson, who won that [1912] year's presidential election, was an equally agile WORDSMITH, Davis noted." Ron Grossman, *Chicago Trib.*, 9/22/92, S 5, p. 2.

"Snap judgments in such matters are notoriously unreliable, but after Mr. Clinton finished his 22 minutes in the chill midday sun today, a sampling of reaction from his audience on the Mall and professional, though largely partisan, WORDSMITHS elsewhere indicated that he had fallen somewhere short of the outfield wall." Todd S. Purdum, *NYTimes*, 1/21/97, p. A12.

"Mr. Conrad followed up. Did Mr. Gore know that, according to a Senate Republican report, more than 103 White House coffees had helped raise more than $26.4 million? And given that report, would it not be fair to describe the coffees as 'a fund-raising tool?' 'I hesitate to WORDSMITH it,' Mr. Gore replied. 'I would not call them fund-raising tools.'" James Dao, *NYTimes*, 6/28/00, p. A21.

WOWSER

noun - (1) an obtrusively puritanical person, a killjoy or BLUENOSE; (2) an incredible, ridiculous statement, situation or proposition.

Note:H. L. Mencken was much taken with, and tried to popularize, the first meaning of WOWSER.

"...Clinton's new, improved plan to allow gays in the military - which, in a logic only the White Rabbit could follow, states that the military must admit gays, provided the recruits do not declare themselves or behave as gays. Under this WOWSER, it is permissible for a gay service person to spend his or her leave marching in gay-rights parades or shopping for Truman Capote pinup posters. But, if a drill sergeant consequently were to suggest service person is gay, it is not permissible for said service person to reply in the affirmative." Michael Kilian, *Chicago Trib.*, 7/28/93, S 5, p. 3.

"The biggest WOWSER, though, is M. Larry Lawrence, the San Diego real estate wheeler-dealer and hotel mogul who tossed 75 grand the Democratic Party's way in time for Bill's president campaign and who Bill and Hillary would now like to be our next ambassador to Switzerland." Michael Kilian, *Chicago Trib.*, 12/8/93, S 5, p. 3.

WUNDERKIND (GER)

noun - a child prodigy.

"While this will be McGovern's third presidential campaign [counting his late-starting 1968 effort]. Stassen is running for the seventh time. Back in 1938, at the age of 31, he became the youngest governor in American history. During the next decade, he was the nation's political WUNDERKIND - a World War II naval hero, author of the United Nations charter, and, in 1948, almost the GOP presidential nominee." Steve Neal, *Chicago Trib.*, 9/15/83, S 1, p. 19.

"A black political WUNDERKIND runs for the Democratic nomination in hopes of winning black delegate support and getting concessions from the eventual nominee. The scenario is familiar, but the name is not Jesse Jackson. That strategy was tried 16 years ago by Julian Bond of Georgia, civil rights activist and the first black ever presented for vice president at a national convention." Michael Hirsley, *Chicago Trib.*, 8/13/84, S 1, p. 4.

"Mr. Stephanopoulos, in fact, works for noted WUNDERKINDER. Mr. Clinton's running mate, Sen. Al Gore of Tennessee, went to Congress at 28, and Mr. Clinton was elected to his first term as Governor at 32." Gwen Ifill, *NYTimes*, 9/1/92, p. A11.

"For 10 days the comic strip 'Doonesbury' has been portraying the president [Clinton] as a waffle. Straight-cornered, not soggy from syrup, the waffle chats with a well-dressed aid who appears to be Joshua Steiner, the Treasury Department WUNDERKIND who disavowed his damaging diary about the Whitewater affair." James Barron, *International Herald Trib.*, 9/2/94, p. 20.

XXX

XENOPHOBIC

adjective - fearful of foreign influences.

"Perot overrode his advisers once again in their desire to start the campaign in mid-August and to hold more campaign rallies before Reform Party loyalists and friendly groups. (His choice for Vice President, Pat Choate, a maverick political economist whose controversial book 'Agents of Influence' was seen by many as XENOPHOBIC, will have the role of attending more traditional campaign rallies.)" Elaine Sciolino, *NYTimes Magazine*, 9/22/96, p. 84.

"But like so many populists of a century ago, Mr. Buchanan has not stuck to economic arguments alone. He fuses his class antagonisms with cultural and social grievances. He rails against abortion, homosexuality, illegitimacy, immigration, sexual license, moral decay and godlessness. Some commentators, including conservatives, have accused him of XENOPHOBIA and anti-Semitism." Alan Brinkley, *NYTimes*, 9/16/99, p. A29.

YYY

YAHOO

noun - a crude person, a HIND, a barbarian.
Note:From the YAHOOS in Jonathan Swift's *Gulliver's Travels*.

"If Mr. Reagan wishes to carry on like one of H.L. Mencken's snake-fondling YAHOOS in a country better known for worshiping rock singer Michael Jackson, he is not being unconstitutional, he is merely being dumb." Michael Kilian, *Chicago Trib.*, 9/11/84, S 1, p. 14.

"The Bush camp tried to portray Hillary Clinton as a wild-eyed radical feminist who will order her husband to emancipate children as his first executive order. The Democrats try to suggest that an extremist fringe in the GOP has locked Bush in a closet and won't let him out until he declares war on single mothers. (Come on. Nobody detests the worst of the extremist YAHOOS, Patrick Buchanan, more than Bush does)." Editorial, *Chicago Trib.*, 8/22/92, S 1, p. 20.

"Lord knows that George Bush, Ronald Reagan and every other administration going back to Andrew Jackson loaded up our foreign missions with all manner of boobs, YAHOOS and other party faithful. But despite his brave promise to 'reinvent government,' Arkansas Bill's ambassadorial boob quotient is running pretty high as well." Michael Kilian, *Chicago Trib.*, 12/8/93, S 5, p. 3.

"[George] Bush is also presumably above Nixon's YAHOO anti-Semitism, although he has consistently been a promoter of Fred Malek, the White House aide who was instructed by Nixon, on a previously released tape, to gather up the names of Jews who worked in the Bureau of Labor Statistics, presumably for the purpose of purging the members of the Jewish conspiracy that Nixon fantasized was responsible for some unwelcome quarterly numbers." Calvin Trillin, Too Soon to Tell, Warner Books, 1995, p. 88.

YELLOW-DOG

adjective - cowardly, despicable. cf. BOLL WEEVIL.

"Though [former Attorney General Griffin B.] Bell says he is a lifelong Democrat, he wrote a newspaper opinion piece supporting the re-election of President George Bush last year. He rejected suggestions that he might be a traitor. 'I am not a YELLOW-DOG Democrat,' he explained." Timothy Egan, *NYTimes*, 7/29/93, p. A7.

"But in 10 days, for the first time in his life, Mr. Tenenbaum will cast a vote in a Republican presidential primary here. And like thousands of other

Democrats and independents across South Carolina and the country who are transforming this year's presidential race, he will give that vote to Senator John McCain. 'It's not an easy thing for a YELLOW-DOG Democrat like me to do,' said Mr. Tenenbaum, vice-president of a large steel company in Columbia, the state capital. 'And I don't even agree with everything he stands for.'" David Firestone, *NYTimes*, 2/10/00, p. 1.

YIN-YANG

noun - the feminine, dark, negative influence (YIN) interacting with the masculine, bright, positive influence (YANG).

"It is commonplace for us to think about the president and his wife in YIN-YANG terms. Nancy was said to be Edgar Bergen to her husband's Charlie McCarthy, and Rosalynn was Ruth Gordon to Jimmy's Garson Kanin. I suppose Betty was Lucy to Gerald Ford's Ricky Ricardo. Barbara Bush is Jiminy Cricket to the president's Pinocchio. True or not, this is her image." Anna Quindlen, *Chicago Trib.*, 5/15/90, S 1, p. 15.

"'The president [Clinton] is both monarch and prime minister. They are the YIN AND YANG of the office. There is a special tension between them. The requirements of one undercut the other. If you are a tough politician, it is hard to be like Queen Elizabeth." William Neikirk, *Chicago Trib.*, 4/28/95, S 1, p. 16.

YOUTHFUL INDISCRETION (SL)

noun - a euphemism for improper or immoral behavior.

Note: This was the term used by Congressman Henry Hyde in referring to a long-term adulterous relationship which he had with a married woman when he was also married and in his forties. His comment when the affair became public during the Clinton impeachment proceedings was that "I thought that the statute of limitations had long since run on those YOUTHFUL INDISCRETIONS." Hyde was taken to task by many, including the *Chicago Tribune* in an editorial, on the ground that these "indiscretions" were hardly youthful.

"Mr. [Henry] Hyde, displaying the same linguistic flair that led him to describe an adulterous affair in his 40's as a 'YOUTHFUL INDISCRETION,' believes that the entertainment industry 'gets away, literally, with murder.' He promoted his scheme to stamp out media homicide in a Washington Post op-ed essay this week that approvingly quoted the recent moral pronouncements of the very President [Clinton] he had vilified as the Antichrist." Frank Rich, *NYTimes*, 6/19/99, p. A27.

"And the 52-year-old Governor [George W. Bush] - who has admitted to YOUTHFUL INDISCRETIONS and wildness about which he has declined to elaborate, except to say that they are behind him and he is now a faithful husband and family man - said he had no fears that opponents would unearth skeletons from his past to derail a campaign.

"Had there been skeletons that would have destroyed a candidacy, you'd have found them in 1994 or 1998,' Mr. Bush said, referring to his first and second campaigns for governor." Rick Lyman, The *NYTimes*, 3/3/99, p. A14.

"...Callender had correctly accused Jefferson of making unsolicited advances toward Elizabeth Walker, a married woman, when he was a young bachelor in 1768. Jefferson acknowledged the truth of this YOUTHFUL INDISCRETION in 1805, made a public apology to her husband, John Walker, but claimed it was the only charge 'founded on truth among all their allegations against me.'" Joseph J. Ellis, <u>American Sphinx</u>, Knopf, 1997, p. 303.

"It is clear to Cherie Hancock [the married woman with whom Hyde had a long-term affair] and her family members that knew the couple well that Henry Hyde, now having more fully developed his 'dark, murky side,' lied in his public statement about the type of relationship this was when *Salon* exposed it in 1998. First of all, the characterization 'YOUTHFUL INDISCRETION' is obviously not applicable to a long-term, serious and romantic relationship in which Hyde took vacations with members of his partner's family. And he was not particularly youthful, being forty-five years old and an accomplished state representative by the time the relationship ended. That's just five years younger than Clinton was at the time of his liaison with Lewinsky.

"Cherie Hancock was disgusted with the cowardice of his explanation. 'It's a lie. Of course it's a lie,' she says. 'The word "indiscretion" is an insult. There is absolutely no question that he was lying to the public in that statement.' Her family member also says Hyde lied about the nature of the relationship. 'Seven or eight years? Some YOUTHFUL INDISCRETION.'" Dennis Bernstein and Leslie Kean, *Henry Hyde's Moral Universe*, Common Courage, 1999, pp. 63-64.

"[George W.] Bush has made it clear that when it comes to YOUTHFUL INDISCRETIONS, he belongs to the Henry Hyde school of aging: He was a youth until he was forty." Molly Ivins and Lou Dubose, <u>Shrub, The Short But Happy Political Life of George W. Bush</u>, Random House, 2000, p. 82.

YUPPY

noun - young urban professional.

"Probably more important, Senator Hart, who managed George McGovern's campaign in 1972, attracted the young. The hippies and yippies of yesteryear, with their headbands and sandals, are what Hart campaigners now call "YUPPIES" - young urban professionals, in their corduroy sports coats and Frye boots. They volunteered for him, worked for him and voted for him. Half his total came from people under 30. New Hampshire's growing population of YUPPIES (Young Urban Professionals) made a natural constituency: exit polls later showed that Hart won the under-40 vote by almost 3 to 1." *Time*, 3/12/84, p. 23.

"The New Hampshire results underlined Mondale's generation-gap problems. His only plurality came from voters over 50. Hart froze out the front runner by mobilizing "The Big Chill" vote, which his campaign calls YUPPIES - young urban professionals." *Newsweek*, 3/12/84, p. 24.

"Republicans are hoping for the best: that Tipper Gore's relentless wholesome style will clash with Hillary Clinton's 'YUPPIE wife from hell' image and cause a noisier battle than the one expected between Al Gore and Dan Quayle. 'We're looking forward to the debate in this campaign,' said William Kristol, Vice President Dan Quayle's chief of staff. 'That is, the debate between Tipper and Hillary.' Democrats, of course, are hoping for the opposite: that Tipper Gore's more traditional stay-at-home approach to child-raising will complement Mrs. Clinton's Supermom PERSONA and represent the full range of options available to modern women." Maureen Dowd and Frank Rich, *NYTimes*, 7/14/92, p. A9.

BIBLIOGRAPHY

NEWSPAPERS

Albuquerque Journal
Arizona Daily Star
Boston Globe
Chicago Sun-Times
Chicago Tribune
Concord (NH) *Monitor*
Culpeper(VA) *News*
*International Herald Tribun*e
Kansas City Star
Kansas City Times
Miami Herald
Milwaukee Journal
New York Times
Philadelphia Daily News
Rocky Mountain News
Sarasota Herald Tribune
San Francisco Chronicle
St. Louis Post Dispatch
St. Petersburg Times
USA Today
Washington Post
Wilmette [Illinois] *Life*

MAGAZINES

Atlantic Monthly
Harper's
New Republic
New York Review of Books
New York Times Book Review
New York Times Magazine
New Yorker
Newsweek
Time
U.S. News & World Report
Vanity Fair

BOOKS

Adler, Bill, <u>The McCarthy Wit</u>, Fawcett Publication, Inc., 1969
Anderson, Donald F., <u>William Howard Taft</u>, Cornell University Press, 1973
<u>Bartlett's Quotations</u>, 15th Edition

Bernstein , Dennis and Kean, Leslie, <u>Henry Hyde's Moral Universe</u>, Common Courage, 1999

Bines, Jonathan, <u>Bushisms</u>, Workman Publishing Company, 1992

Boller, Paul F. Jr., <u>Presidential Campaigns</u>, Oxford University Press, 1996

Brock, David, <u>The Seduction of Hillary Rodham</u>, Free Press, 1996

Buchanan, Patrick J., <u>A Republic Not an Empire</u>, Regnery, 1999

Buckley, William F. Jr., <u>The Jeweler's Eye</u>, G.P. Putnam's Sons, 1969

Byrd, Max <u>Jefferson, A Novel,</u> Bantam, 1993

Caro, Robert A., <u>The Years of Lyndon Johnson: The Path to Power,</u> Knopf, 1982

DeVries, Peter, <u>The Glory of the Hummingbird</u>, Popular Library, 1976

Donald, David, <u>Lincoln's Herndon</u>, Knopf, 1948

Ellis, Joseph J., <u>American Sphinx</u>, Knopf, 1997

Felsenthal, Carol, <u>Alice Roosevelt Longworth,</u> G.P. Putnam's Sons, 1988

Fuller, Edmund, <u>Bulfinch's Mythology</u>, Dell Publishing Co., Inc. 1959

Germond, Jack, <u>Fat Man In A Middle Seat</u>, Random House, 1999

Goodwin , Doris Kearns, <u>No Ordinary Time: Franklin and Eleanor Roosevelt: The Home Front in World War II</u>, Simon & Shuster 1994

Hagood, Wesley O., <u>Presidential Sex</u>, Carol Publishing Group, 1995

Hanna, Edward, Hicks, Henry & Koppel, Ted, <u>The Wit and Wisdom of Adlai Stevenson</u>, Hawthorn Books, 1965

Harris, Sydney J., <u>Strictly Personal</u>, Henry Regnery Company, 1953

Hersh, Seymour, <u>The Dark Side of Camelot</u>, Little Brown, 1997

Ivins, Molly & Dubose, Lou, <u>Shrub, The Short But Happy Political Life of George W. Bush</u>, Random House, 2000

Ivins, Molly, <u>Nothin' but Good Times Ahead</u>, Vintage Books, 1993

Ivins, Molly, <u>Molly Ivins Can't Say That, Can She?</u>, Random House, 1991

Ivins, Molly, <u>You Got to Dance With Them What Brung You</u>, Random House, 1998

Kaiser, Charles, <u>1968 in America,</u> Weidenfeld & Nicolson, 1988

McCarthy, Eugene J., <u>No Fault Politics: Modern Presidents, the Press, and Reformers,</u> Random House, 1998

McCarthy, Eugene J., <u>Required Reading,</u> Harcourt Brace Jovanovich, 1988

McCarthy, Eugene J., <u>Selected Poems,</u> Lone Oak Press, 1997

McCarthy, Eugene J., <u>Up 'Til Now</u>, Harcourt Brace Jovanovich, 1987

Maraniss, David, <u>First in His Class: The Biography of Bill Clinton</u>, Simon & Schuster, 1995

Mencken, H. L., <u>American Language: Supplement I</u>, Knopf, 1961

Mencken, H. L., <u>American Scene</u>, Ed. by Huntington Cairns, Vintage Books, 1982

Mencken, H. L., <u>Mencken Chrestomathy</u>, Vintage Books, 1982

Mencken , H. L., <u>Vintage Mencken</u>, Vintage Books, 1956

Morris, Edmund, <u>Dutch: A Memoir of Ronald Reagan</u>, Random House, 1999

O'Rourke, P. J., <u>Parliament of Whores</u>, Vintage Books, 1992

Podhoretz, Norman, <u>Ex-Friends: Falling Out with Allen Ginsberg, Lionel &
    Diana Trilling, Lillian Hellman, Hannah Arendt & Norman Mailer,</u> Free
    Press, 1999
Stevenson, Adlai, <u>Major Campaign Speeches of Adlai E. Stevenson,</u> Random
    House, 1953
Talbott, Strobe, <u>Endgame,</u> Harper & Row, 1979
Thomas, Benjamin P., <u>Abraham Lincoln,</u> Knopf, 1952
Toobin, Jeffrey, <u>A Vast Conspiracy,</u> Random House, 1999
Trillin, Calvin, <u>Too Soon to Tell,</u> Warner Books, 1995
Vonnegut, Kurt, <u>Palm Sunday,</u> Dell Publishing Co., Inc., 1981
Walker, Martin, <u>The President We Deserve,</u> Crown Publishers, 1996
Wouk, Herman, <u>The Winds of War,</u> Pocket Books, 1973

Index

273

Port-au-Prince, 50
Porter, Eleanor, 204
Posner, Gerald, 181
Potemkin, Gregori, 206
Povich, Elaine S., 51, 75, 198, 200
Powell, Colin, 175
Powell, Jody, 175
Powers, Thomas, 48
Presley, Elvis, 35
Preston, Jennifer, 190
Primary Colors, 44
Princess Di, 138
pro-choice, 95, 116, 158
Puls, Edward, 55
Purdum, Todd S., 35, 81, 87, 164, 188, 206, 210, 221, 226, 253, 263
purveyor of half-truths, 135. *See* Reagan, Ronald

Q

Quayle, Dan, 28, 30, 56, 57, 62, 67, 81, 85, 98, 100, 115, 117, 124, 135, 146, 155, 162, 180, 193, 205, 213, 217, 221, 224, 225, 226, 239, 244, 245, 252, 253, 268
Quayle, Marilyn, 58
Quindlen, Anna, 29, 36, 39, 79, 82, 95, 106, 116, 162, 182, 199, 209, 219, 222, 242, 266
Quintanilla, Ray, 251

R

Radcliffe, Donnie, 198
Rainie, Harrison, 175
Rangel, Rep. Charles, 64
Rasky, Susan, 84
Raspberry, William, 79, 87, 243
Rather, Dan, 107, 138, 139
Rauch, Jonathan, 159
Reagan, Maureen, 97
Reagan, Michael, 97
Reagan, Nancy, 28, 49, 76, 90, 94, 97, 230, 245
Reagan, Patti, 127

Reagan, Ronald, 30, 34, 36, 39, 42, 57, 60, 67, 69, 76, 84, 86, 87, 93, 94, 95, 106, 109, 110, 112, 121, 129, 133, 134, 135, 151, 154, 155, 161, 163, 167, 176, 177, 178, 189, 211, 212, 213, 221, 224, 227, 228, 230, 231, 240, 243, 252, 254, 257, 265
Reaganomics, 231
Rebozo, Bebe, 261
Red Sage, 44
Reed, Ralph, 144, 150
Reed, Scott, 102
Reform Party, 36, 85, 223, 235, 236, 264
Regan, Donald, 76, 144
registered Republican. *See* God
Reich, Robert B., 206
Renaissance Weekend, 58
Reno, Janet, 107
Republicans, poor, silly, old, 107
Restaurant Nora, 44
Reykjavik, 88
Ricardo, Ricky, 266
Rice, Donna, 110, 256
Rich, Frank, 35, 37, 49, 50, 56, 58, 63, 64, 68, 73, 78, 85, 89, 95, 99, 114, 118, 127, 128, 134, 144, 150, 156, 164, 169, 172, 179, 181, 186, 189, 193, 212, 218, 220, 223, 224, 225, 237, 242, 248, 253, 255, 261, 266, 268
Richards, Horace, 55
Right To Life, 95
Rimer, Sara, 136
Rivers, Caryl, 84, 90
Robb, Sen. Charles S., 231
Roberts, Steven V., 96
Robertson, Pat, 95, 101, 112, 144, 150, 235, 251
Robertson, U.S. District Judge James, 108
Rockefeller, Nelson, 51, 109, 111, 201

ABOUT THE AUTHOR

John E. Clay was born in Kansas City, Missouri. He received his B.A. degree from Carleton College and his J.D. degree from Harvard Law School. After practicing law for 40 years he retired in 1988 as a senior partner of Mayer, Brown & Platt in Chicago. From 1988 until 1998, Mr. Clay was the Executive Director of the Public Interest Law Initiative at DePaul University College of Law, administering an internship program in public interest law for law students and recent law graduates.

Mr. Clay has been a logophile for many years, combining his passion for words with a strong interest in politics. In the 1976 presidential campaign, he was Eugene J. McCarthy's vice-presidential running mate in Illinois. He was also active in the presidential campaigns of Adlai E. Stevenson in 1952, 1956 and 1960, of John Anderson in 1980, and of Eugene J. McCarthy in 1968.

Mr. Clay is an enthusiastic skier, mountain climber, log cabin builder and tree farmer. He is married to Mary Dailey and has two sons, Peter and Scott, and a daughter, Anna Novikova.